Older and Wiser
Wit, Wisdom, and Spirited Advice
from the Older Generation

Older and Wiser
Wit, Wisdom, and Spirited Advice from the Older Generation

Eric W. Johnson

Walker and Company

New York

First published in the United States of America in 1986 by the Walker Publishing Company, Inc.

Published simultaneously in Canada by John Wiley & Sons Canada, Limited, Rexdale, Ontario.

Library of Congress Cataloging-in-Publication Data

Johnson, Eric W.
  Older and wiser.

    Bibliography: p.
    Includes index.
    1. Aged--United States--Attitudes. 2. Aged--United States--Social conditions. 3. American wit and humor. I. Title.
HQ1064.U5J65 1986   305.2'6'0973   86-5630
ISBN 0-8027-0903-6

Printed in the United States of America

10 9 8 7 6 5 4 3 2 1

Contents

To the 136 elders, aged 65 to 97, whose free sharing of 10,488 years of experience provided much of the substance of this book.

Introduction

Many people think that "oldsters" are crotchety, unhappy, and moderately to extremely pitiful. But they aren't. Most of them enjoy life, and have lots of humor, wit, perception, and wisdom to share with each other and everyone else. Read, for example, the following dozen brief utterances, almost randomly selected from the approximately twelve thousand I collected from 136 elders, men and women 65 and over, as I prepared to write this book:

68/W:* Old age is honorable, beautiful, natural, still full of possibilities.

70/W: I do not feel old inside—I feel no great change. I'm simply appalled at how old my children are.

72/M: The bird of time is on the wing. I'm enjoying all the questions and delights I never had time for when I worked.

74/M: I take an obstinate delight in being obsolete. It seems to be fun for everybody.

77/W: Here is my message to the world: Dear Friends, When you greet us, look into our eyes. See the marvelous things we elders have experienced—joy and sorrow, success and frustration, ecstasy and desolation. Ask us how it was. Share your life's journey. Together we will bless each other with new appreciation of the oneness of life.

81/W: I've about decided that the only way I can change the world or my grandchildren is to change me. I am finding that rigidity uses up more energy than I can spare. I feel impelled to relax and let live! Easy often does it.

82/M: Don't strike your colors while the iron is hot.

*****68/W** means 68-year-old woman; **69/M** means 69-year-old man.

1

83/W: The biggest surprise about being my age is that I am succeeding, so far, in not being a nuisance.

84/W: Old age is a time to drop guilt and learn to love yourself, for yourself and your uniqueness. Then from you will flow love and concern and help for others.

85/M: Danged if I can think of what in my life makes me feel hopeless. Life is a bowl of cherries, and if you have to pick out a few ants along the way, that's the way it is.

86/M: I'm waiting with bated breath. When will I feel old?

96/W: I'm glad to be alive; thank God for the blessings I have, for the memories of a full life and the ability to see things in perspective.

Getting Old Enough to Write This Book

For years I've thought that it would be fun and useful to write a book about elders. It seemed to me that their wit and wisdom ought to be gathered and available to read. It would make the world better, wiser, and more enjoyable. But for a long time I couldn't get a contract to write the book. Why? First, because I'm not an M.D.,* and too many people see old age as a disease. Second, because I wasn't "old" yet; I was barely 60. Well, I'm still not an M.D., but according to the law I am now certifiably "old." As I write these words, I'm 67; I have a contract to write the book; I'm genuine! However, an 88-year-old woman wrote to me, "We place too much emphasis on age 65. At that age, we're still in our prime. I suggest you use 80 or 85 as the

---

*Even though I'm not an M.D., I do recognize that a book which deals with elders is bound to deal with medical questions and state some medical facts. Therefore, I am most grateful to geriatrician David Galinsky, M.D., clinical assistant professor of internal medicine at the Medical College of Pennsylvania; attending physician at the Philadelphia Geriatric Center; and author of a number of scholarly papers on matters geriatric. Dr. Galinsky has checked the medical facts set forth in this book and corrected a number of mistakes I had made. He does not necessarily agree with all the judgments and opinions expressed by my elder respondents or by me, even though his reactions to some of them were most useful in keeping me on the right track.

I am grateful, too, to M. Powell Lawton, president of the Gerontological Society of America. Dr. Lawton did not read this book before publication and is in no way responsible for its contents, except that he steered me onto the road to truth in several valuable ways, and gave me some excellent suggestions, including the one that I ask Dr. Galinsky to review my manuscript.

beginning of 'old.' " An 81-year-old woman wrote, "What you do not seem to realize is that old people are not different from what they were; they're just older." And author Elizabeth Gray Vining, at 82, stated, "There's as big a gap between 65 and 95 as between 40 and 65, maybe bigger. So don't lump us, Eric!" We must keep in mind the important points these elders make.

The Term "Elders"

"Elders?" you may ask. "Why do you use that term?" I use it because I think it best describes those of us who are over 65. "Old people" ("old woman"; "old man") won't do; "older people" is only slightly better; "senior citizen" is perhaps accurate, but too hackneyed (except when followed by "discount"); and "golden ager" nauseates me and a lot of my fellow elders. "Geezer" is O.K., if used with a smile, but never "hag." "Ancient" can be a compliment if you're over 80 and feel proud of it. But "elder" is moderately complimentary and accurate, and so the subject of this book is people called elders.

My Main Source of Material

The main source of original information and material for the book is the replies of 136 respondents to an in-depth written interview I mailed out to elders whose names and addresses I found in various ways. A few of them are my friends; quite a few were suggested by people I knew who thought that so-and-so would do a "wonderful job" with the interview; another group I found through nursing homes and life-care communities; still others came through gerontological organizations. Thus, you must understand that my sample is quite select—selected from among people who like to read and write . . . and who were willing to undertake a fairly large task, for the questionnaire, as I called it, is twenty-eight legal-size pages long and contains 133 free-response questions (very few multiple-choice questions or checklists). That's why about 100 elders of the 240 I mailed to either returned their questionnaires unanswered or didn't return them at all. One, Burt Garnet, replied from Key West, Florida, "I'm now 97; I'm writing a book called *Century Bound*. So how can I answer your questionnaire?!" (But he did send me some wonderful bits from his book.) Here are some other reactions:

70W/: Filling out this thing was the biggest ego trip of the week.

71/M: I'm exhausted. I have aged considerably in filling out this questionnaire, Mr. Johnson!

75/M: This is the first time in over a year I have attempted to write. I can only write with great difficulty. My right hand has to be guided by my left hand. But I answered your questions!

80/W: This has provided me a wonderful chance to look into myself and my life. Almost as good as a psychiatrist (I've never been to one) and, I gather, a lot cheaper. Thanks!

81/W: I seldom answer questionnaires, but I shall certainly answer this one, though it will probably take me most of the summer to do it.

On the questionnaire, I wrote that the title of this book might be *We Elders Speak for Ourselves: Some Wit and Wisdom*. My impression is that about a third of those who replied said something like this: "I'm afraid you won't find much wit and wisdom in what I've said." But almost all were wrong: I did find wit and wisdom in large amounts and varied styles. You shall see!

My Particular Sample of Elders

I said that I make no claim to be reporting on a national cross section of elders. I have read a lot, though: several major studies of the cross section, including trade books and textbooks on health, sex, social problems, retirement, law, geriatrics (a branch of medicine), and gerontology (a branch of knowledge).* I've read books of eloquent, genuine, well-founded, constructive outrage, like Dieter Hessel's *Maggie Kuhn on Aging*. I've read careful, comprehensive, deeply affecting books like Robert Butler's near-classic *Why Survive? Being Old in America*. I've also read some practical books, like B. F. Skinner's *Enjoy Old Age* and Alex Comfort's excellent, well-informed, and practical *A Good Age*. I even made it through some wittier-than-wise funny books, like George Burns's *How to Live to Be 100 or More*.

The two most useful books I've referred to are both published by The National Council on the Aging, Inc. (NCOA).† They are titled

---

*Both words based on *geron*, Greek for "old man" and *geras*, "old age."
†The National Council on the Aging, Inc. 600 Maryland Avenue, SW, West Wing 100, Washington, D.C. 20024.

Myth and Reality of Aging in America, published in 1974, and its update, *Aging in the Eighties: America in Transition,* published in 1981. These studies were conducted for NCOA by Louis Harris and Associates and are based on a carefully constructed cross section of the American public 18 years of age and over, randomly selected, with correct proportion of people from various economic levels; races; educational levels; rural, urban, and surburban areas; and geographical regions. In 1974, the Harris staff conducted personal in-household interviews with 4,254 people (1,457 under 65, 2,797 over 65). The 1981 sample involved 3,427 people. If you're interested in the statistical details, get the NCOA reports. Throughout this book, I sometimes refer to the two Harris studies as *NCOA, 1974* and *NCOA, 1981.* Even though 1981 may seem rather long ago, there are no later, equally comprehensive studies available. Also, it is interesting to note how similar the 1974 and 1981 reported opinions are, and there is no reason to believe that major changes in the data have occurred between 1981 and 1986. Where later special reports are available, I have used those as well.

The two best textbooks on aging are Douglas Kimmel's *Adulthood and Aging* and Robert C. Atchley's *Social Forces and Aging.*

There are two other books that have provided rich sources of material. One is *Growing Older, Getting Better: A Handbook for Women in the Second Half of Life,* by Jane Porcino, who is the mother of seven children, has a Ph.D. and a masters in social work, and is director of the Gerontology Project at the State University of New York at Stony Brook, as well as editor of *Hot Flash,* a newsletter for women in midlife and older. The other book I found quite by chance on the shelves of a local library. It is titled *On Growing Old Gracefully,* by Charles Courtenay, and it was published in 1936, long before the statistical and scientific data I have used were gathered. Courtenay, who wrote his book at age 87, had been vicar of St. Peter's Church in Tunbridge Wells, England, and his book is so full of wisdom and wonderfully turned sentences that I have found myself quoting him frequently. In fact, I have considered him "honorary respondent" but of course have not included him in my statistics. Nor have I been able to ask his permission since there's no return mail from heaven, where I'm sure he must be living, if there is such a place. (A more-or-less complete bibliography appears at the end of this book.)

As I wrote this book, I kept in mind what I have learned from all this reading. But my major sources of fresh data and wit and wisdom are the responses to the 136 twenty-eight-page questionnaires. The average age of my respondents is 76; the range of ages is 65 to 97. I calculate that the answers arise from 10,488 years of experience.

Here is some information about my "sampling": 57 percent are female, 43 percent male. 9 percent single, 31 percent widows or widowers, 53 percent married (including the remarried), and 7 percent divorced and not remarried. Eighty percent live in their own homes, 16 percent in retirement or life-care communities (higher than the national percentage), 2 percent in nursing homes (lower than the national percentage).

My sample, comparatively speaking, may be somewhat privileged economically. When asked to "describe your financial situation," 15 percent checked "well off"; 75 percent "comfortable"; 8 percent "it's a bit of a struggle"; and 4 percent "it's a big struggle." I say my sample is privileged in comparison with the national cross section, but not extremely so. According to *NCOA, 1981*, only 17 percent of elders (compared to my 12 percent) say that not having enough money to live on is a problem; 83 percent say it's *not* a problem. However, 68 percent of the general public *thinks* that most elders are impoverished. Of course, there are tens of thousands of elders in America who are desperately poor and miserable, and that our nation allows it to be so is a disgrace, but there are economically desperate people in all age-groups, and that's a disgrace, too.

About religion: My group of 136 includes people from just about every stripe of belief and nonbelief from enthusiastic heathen to born-again Christian. The questionnaire didn't ask about membership in religious organizations, but it did ask a lot of questions about religion (see Chapter 11, "Religion and Life").

Between the time I sent out the questionnaires and the time I'd gotten well started on the first draft of this book, word got around about what I was up to, and scores of people, in conversation and by mail, kept sharing with me materials they thought would be useful for the book, especially stories and apt quotations about elders, as well as accounts of their own experiences. I have not counted these people in my statistics, but I have very often included their words in the direct quotes that I give from elders. The most common way I quote a response from a respondent is thus: **81/W:** *We're glad to be* *wise but we hate to be wobbly.* This means that an 81-year-old woman wrote the comment. However, if I quote someone who had something useful to say but who was not a respondent to the questionnaire, I give the name if the person is or was a public figure: **82/M** *(General Douglas MacArthur, 1880–1964): When your heart is covered with the snows of pessimism and the ice of cynicism, then and only then are you grown old.* Rarely have I given the names of my 136 respondents, except in a few cases where they are well known and did not object.

The Arranging and Editing of Responses

As you read, you will notice that very often there are a number of reactions to a given question or statement about the life and experiences of elders. Usually, there were many, many more than I had space for, and one of the most difficult things was to decide what *not* to use. I also had to decide how to arrange the responses, and decided to order them by age, youngest to oldest. A wide variety of opinions are mixed together, however, giving the impression of a sort of conversation.

In every case, I have been careful to retain the exact sense of what each elder wrote, but sometimes a bit of editing was needed for the sake of clarity. Quite often, I have also shortened responses to give the essence, but always kept to the words of the respondent, and tried never to omit important nuances. When people's names were used in a response, I have almost always changed them to avoid any possibility of embarrassment.

What to Do About Funny Stories and Bits of Verse?

One of the problems I've had in selecting materials has to do with giving proper credit for jokes, poems, and apt bits of wit that respondents have sent me. Quite often the very same item was sent by two or more people, sometimes as if it were their own. Occasionally, I'd even recognize an item that I'd read a while ago in *The Reader's Digest,* perhaps one of their wonderful "submitted by" items used as fillers at the ends of articles. So what to do? Give credit to *The Reader's Digest* (or wherever)? Well, that I would do if my submission were verbatim in *The Reader's Digest,* but, to the best of my knowledge, I've used no verbatim items. So very often it's impossible to identify the exact source of a story, joke, or piece of doggerel . . . harder even than to know whether Shakespeare wrote all of Shakespeare.

Thus, I have taken what my respondents sent me and used it, giving credit, of course, where they give credit.

My Own Aging

It's an interesting exercise to trace one's feelings about one's own age. I can remember that once I felt old in kindergarten—I was at school! Age 21 was "old"; 45 was older. I began to defend myself against feeling old (and tried to avoid feeling a bit miffed) when at mere age 57 or 58 I was offered senior citizen discounts on the basis of my appearance. Another landmark: In my early fifties, my doctor told me I had "degenerative arthritis." The next day he went off on a vacation and I was shaken—"degenerative"! My God, I'm degenerating! I agree with the 82-year-old woman who wrote: "Doctors should be forbidden to use the word *degenerative*. It's enough to *make* you degenerate, and it sounds like a crime." Only later did I learn that vast numbers of people have degenerative arthritis; and, despite it, I still jog happily three miles a day and can beat a lot of people up mountains.

Then, when I was 59 or 60, I grew a wen—a benign sebacious cyst—on the top of my head. Schoolchildren (so honest!) would ask me, "How did you bump your head?" or "What's that on your head?" And when I spoke from a stage or platform, the wen looked a bit ugly with the overhead lights shining on it. So I asked my doctor whether it could removed. He poked at it a bit and said, "No, I wouldn't do it. It's harmless, and you have old skin." Old skin?! At 60?! Yikes! Two years later another doctor said it would be easy to remove, and he did it right in his office, leaving no scar, no wen. "That stuff about old skin is nonsense," he said. I now know that in most cases it is.

Then, sometime around 60, I found myself forgetting names more often than I had done before. Some members of my family, well educated medically, said with a laugh, "Oh, it's just presenile dementia." I laughed, too, and then got some good laughs when I told teachers that their kindergartners, when forgetful, were just showing presenile dementia. But the term seems an evil one to me now.

"Senile." I'm about there. "Dementia." I'm demented, crazy, or almost. A command to doctors would be: Don't use *senile, senility, dementia,* or *demented* in the presence of any patient. Even be careful how you use these words among yourselves, even though *dementia* does have a bona-fide medical meaning for you.

When I was 63, my wife and I drove into Grand Teton National Park and the guard at the gate looked at me and asked, "Would you like a special free pass?" Ten minutes later I had a cheerful, colorful Golden Age Pass. I was glad to save the money, but the government had now told me that as of age 62 I was a Golden Ager. Ugh!

While visiting a good Florida retirement community as part of my preparation for writing this book (I was 66 at the time), I decided to sit and chat with some elders who were grouped near the entrance. I explained to a very cheerful, bright 87-year-old woman in a wheelchair that I was writing a book about old age. She looked surprised. "How old are you?" she asked. "Sixty-six," I answered. "Well!" she exclaimed with certainty and a slight smile. "What do *you* know about old age?"

What indeed? One of the major effects on me of writing this book has been to convince me that 67 is young. I'm a mere squirt compared to 75- and 85-year-olds. But even most of them say they don't "feel old." And despite all sorts of diseases and handicaps, 90 percent of my respondents checked *yes* to the question "Would you say you enjoy generally good health?" It makes me realize that in these modern times—in America, anyway—old age is not longer than it used to be; it just starts later.

"The best is yet to be. . . ."

I don't *feel* old! Neither do two thirds of the people whom I surveyed for this book, including some over 90, some elders who are bedridden, and those many elders who are managing to be active and creative and joyous even while fighting a galaxy of diseases. Perhaps the line most frequently quoted to me by elders was "You're only as old as you feel." Another oft-quoted saying was "Old age is great, especially when you consider the alternative." And a dozen of my respondents wrote out the bit from Robert Browning's (1812–1889) "Rabbi ben Ezra":

Grow old along with me!
The best is yet to be,
The last of life, for which the first was made. . . .

As you'll see, it is the best time of life for many, many people. You don't believe it? Wait! We individual elders feel much better about being 65 than the public, including other elders, thinks we do. According to the facts in the NCOA 1981 report, here's the public perception of elders compared with how elders feel about themselves:

The problem that a person might have	Percentage of the general public which thinks that elders suffer from the problem	Percentage of elders who say they actually do suffer from the problem
loneliness	65%	13%
not feeling needed*	54%	7%
poor health	47%	21%
not enough jobs	51%	6%
not enough medical care	45%	9%
not enough to do*	37%	6%
poor housing	43%	5%
not enough friends*	28%	5%
Average percentage	45%	9%

It's interesting, though, that we elders generally see *other* elders pretty much as the public sees them: having a lot of bad problems. We adopt the bias of society and turn it against our own kind. However, the individual elder who is being asked doesn't feel that she or he (more are she's than he's) has the problem. As a 73-year-old woman said, "Among us elders, everybody's an exception."

I was surprised that most of my 136 respondents feel that they are not a burden on people. They feel that they are more, not less, intelligent than they were when younger, except when it comes to recalling names and recent facts. But in judgment, wisdom, and figuring things out soundly, they figure they are much better than young people. They report that they get more joy and satisfaction out

*These items are from NCOA, 1974. The questions were not asked in NCOA, 1981.

of each day of life than they used to. In short, they feel good about themselves and about their time of life.

Many of us elders recognize that we are becoming a rapidly increasing percentage of the population of the United States. In 1900, only 4 percent of Americans were 65 and older; in 1950, it was 8 percent; today it's about 12 percent; and by the year 2020 it'll be about 20 percent (5 percent of Americans will be 85 or older!). A 77-year-old woman wrote to me, "They call it 'the graying of America.' What a put-down! I think it ought to be called the *wising* of America. If America is wise, it will use our wisdom, which might even save the world. Remember, we're in a little more of a hurry to save the world, because we haven't got as long to live in it. So wise up with us and we'll *all* be better off!"

The Main Purposes of this Book

My main reason, then, for writing this book is to share the delightful bits and larger pieces of wit and wisdom of elders on what "old" means; on intelligence, health, doctors, nurses, families, friends, and neighbors; on where to live, how to work and retire; on sexuality, religion, dying, death—and, mainly, life. I think that what's in the book—the ideas, the humorous stories, a sprinkling of practical suggestions, occasional verses, the gemlike bits, will amuse and enlighten anyone of any age. But it will especially help strengthen us elders and make life even more enjoyable. To the younger generations, it will provide some boons, a few warnings, and some advice, tactful and not so tactful. In that sense, this is a practical book.

Chapter 1

WHAT DOES "OLD" MEAN?

Generally, people resent having the word *old* applied to them. "Don't call *me* old!" an 80-year-old friend shouted at me when I threatened him with my questionnaire. And his feeling is understandable. The classic descriptions of old age are not pleasant, and they persist. Shakespeare in *As You Like It* describes the sixth and seventh ages of man: "With spectacles on nose . . . shrunk shank . . . big manly voice turning again toward childish treble, [and] . . . last scene of all, is second childishness and mere oblivion, sans teeth, sans eyes, sans taste, sans everything." Old women in their later life were frequently called hags, usually toothless hags. They didn't laugh; they cackled.

So no wonder most people dislike being called old. Most of us would rather go with Confucius: "Age is not a problem; it's a blessing. . . . At 20 you're hardly on your feet, at 40 you know what you're doing, at 60 you're mentally mature, at 80 you're a perfect man [or woman]"—even though we know we're not perfect.

Up until less than a century ago, only a few people lived into their sixties or beyond. In the U.S.A. our life expectancy at birth is now about 72 years for men, 78 for women. And what of our life expectancy if we make it to 65 and are still healthy? It's 14 more years for men, 19 more for women. On the average, we'll make it to 82. Beyond 65, the figures are:

Age	Life expectancy	Expected age at death
70	13.6	83.6
75	11	86
80	8	88
85	6	91

Gerontologists say that if we didn't die of some disease or combination of diseases, our organisms would simply wear out and we'd die at about age 115. All of this puts into perspective the story told by the ground crew for a small plane. It had landed, and the only exit was down a long ramp so narrow that each passenger had to make it on his or her own. The crew felt relieved when a 70-year-old woman negotiated the exit satisfactorily. But then she turned back toward the door of the plane and shouted, "O.K., Mom, it's all right to get off now."

So, What Does "Old" Mean?

One item on my questionnaire was: *What does "old" mean to you? How do you feel about the word being applied to you? Do you ever refer to yourself as old?* Here's a cross section of the replies I got (arranged in order of age):

69/M: "Old" means someone else . . . not me! "Old," to me, is a stage of frailty and degeneration. I don't like the word being applied to me, because I don't feel old, to the best of my knowledge don't act old. I refer to myself as old only in a kidding manner.

69/M: "Old" means being shriveled up, dried out, stale. I resent it's being applied to me, and I *never* think of myself as old. Old has nothing to do with chronology. I've known people who were old at 40, others who were young at 100.

70/W: I *am* old, so why mind being called old—but (and here's the crazy part) I *feel* vivid! Like a tree in its most glorious, autumnal colors with *all* its leaves on. I know they'll fall off soon, but that makes this stage of life even more precious. I am living life to the fullest.

71/M: "Old" means to me inactive, creaky, querulous, baggy, weak, and rather incompetent.

71/M: Old age is that time in life when, as a result of experience, education, adjustments, etc., you have a great deal of knowledge— *but no one asks you any questions!*

72/M: "Old" to me means rigid, reactionary, resistant to change, to any new idea or point of view. Very sad condition.

73/M: "Old" means maturity; old means wisdom because one has lived long enough and experienced enough to become wise.

77/W: Of course, I sometimes refer to myself as "old" but usually with a twinkle in the eye. I feel like a 16-year-old (in spirit) caught (trapped) in a 77-year-old body. I don't mind if people call me old, if that is what they see—a slowed-down, halting-in-gait, white-haired, learnèd woman; but if they talk with me, they usually leave with a different feeling about calling me old.

83/W: To me, being old means being decrepit, untidy, stooped, self-centered, confused. If the word is applied to me, I feel hurt; if it is applied to others, it is probably richly deserved.

87/M: Recently, I heard there are two new categories: old and old-old. This gave me an unpleasant start, for, according to that, I'm old-old.

96/W: An expression I have been using is that I am *getting old*.

What's It Like Being This Age?

The responses I got on my questionnaire illustrate the need for caution in generalizing about elders. At the same time, the responses amazed me with their predominantly upbeat attitude toward being an elder. Item 16 of my questionnaire read: *Complete this statement with three words or phrases: I think being (your age) is: ____ .* Here are the replies of elders ages 65 to 96:

65/W: Fantastic. I'm here and I have my dear ones! No different than being any other age, because I am me; the *shell* is all that changed.

66/W: I don't like being tired after three sets of tennis or having my back hurt after weeding the garden. Would like new joints and muscles. But life is great.

66/W: The cat's pajamas; a piece of cake; a bowl of cherries.

66/W: Great, in the freedom it brings for projects of one's choice; depressing, as I see the time ahead lessening, leading me to value in a heightened way the friends I cherish; bothersome, when I wake up stiff and creaky in the morning, and when I can't hear what is said in meetings.

67/M: *Old age is a lovely time,*
              My sisters and my brothers.
              Old age is a lovely time,
              And so are all the others.

69/M: The best age I've experienced so far!

69/M: A stage of appreciation, reflection, and very enjoyable.

70/W: A challenge, a delight, an adventure.

70/M: There are no advantages to getting older. I'm not happy because I'm 70—I'm just grateful it's no worse than it is.

74/W: Very frustrating because of less physical dexterity and speed.

76/M: Like being in a game of living, and so far I am winning!

81/W: Challenging; fulfilling; humbling.

82/M: Better than advertised (with luck); no time to abandon self-reliance; time to increase, not curtail your interests.

83/W: I'm enjoying it to the hilt.

86/M: Somewhat lonely—my peers are dead.

87/W: Like walking a tightrope. Exciting when you "make it," but a fall is imminent; and when you're ill, you don't have a very large mental or emotional margin of error.

88/W: Hell—it's no fun to grow old. My interest in government still remains strong, but my colostomy—and my knee—make it impossible to be active.

Do We Feel Old?

I asked this question: *Do you feel "old"? Yes __No __* . Even though all of my 136 respondents are, like me, certifiably old, candidates for any survey being done on "old people" or "the aging," 52 percent checked *No*, while 29 percent checked *Yes*. About 19 percent gave "yes-and-no" answers or didn't answer the question. (It's interesting that my sample agrees very closely with the large, scientifically selected NCOA 1981 national cross section, of whom 51 percent answered *No* to the question "Do you feel old and somewhat tired?" However, 45 percent of the NCOA sample answered *Yes*, and only 3 percent were "not sure."

Of all those who replied one way or the other to my question, almost two thirds said *No;* they don't feel "old." Here's a breakdown of the answers by age-group, including only those who checked *Yes* or *No:*

65–74:	27% yes;	73% no
75–84:	41% yes;	59% no
85 up:	53% yes;	47% no

Think about that: Almost half of those over 85 say they don't feel old!

Do We Feel Hopeful or Hopeless?

Dr. Robert Butler, gerontologist at Mount Sinai Hospital in New York City and author of the near-classic *Why Survive? Being Old in America,* describes how younger people stereotype elders. The older person, he writes, is seen as "irritable and cantankerous, yet shallow and enfeebled . . . aimless and wandering of mind . . . a study in decline. . . . Feeble, uninteresting, he awaits his death, a burden to his society, to his family and to himself." Knowing of this stereotype, I decided to ask these two questions: *What in your life now makes you feel most hopeless and least confident?* and *What in your life now makes you feel most, or somewhat, hopeful and confident?*

Let's start with the hopeless side. The elders feel most hopeless, according to their replies (and with many exceptions, of course) about two things: the state of the world and the attitudes and behavior of youth. They generally don't feel hopeless about themselves, although, obviously, they know that they are nearer the end of their lives than they were. But, as you will see in Chapter 12, even the prospect of death does not make many of them feel hopeless.

Here are some typical replies about the state of the world:

68/M: I feel hopeless because I've lost confidence in the integrity and competence of U.S. government leadership. I used to disagree with many policies but *assumed* an underlying sincerity, competence, and integrity lay behind them. Nixon destroyed that. I am now cynical, and have just deep and distressing contempt.

68/W: Seemingly more ubiquitous trashiness, ugliness and mediocrity and violence.

75/M: The future of the human race and of this beautiful world, which we are now capable of destroying: nuclear holocaust, overpopulation, ecological pollution, and so on and so on. I have no desire to see what may be here in the coming century, but looking out as I do at this moment upon the peaceful fog and enshrouded waters of the bay gives me great spiritual happiness.

79/M: The lack of respect, indifference, and arrogance of youth toward the old I accept—it's part of the process of growing up. But I deplore the lowering of our moral values in this world of today. Crime, divorce, single-parenting, legal cheating, unethical business leaders and politicians, union chiefs who are more mobsters than leaders—and so on. With overpopulation and overcrowding in our cities, we are not rising up to a better future—we are grinding down to the low values of the slums.

83/W: I am often amazed at the youth of people in top government positions and in various executive capacities elsewhere. A university degree is not enough when judgment and experience are lacking. The brashness and self-assurance of such young people in high places often conceal shallowness and lack of humaneness.

96/W: It seems to me that there is less respect to elders now than ever before. Teenagers, especially, rush into buildings, call out insults to older people and disregard suggestions made. When I was a child and growing up, the standards of politeness were very different. We were taught polite gestures of respect. Young folks today are not.

And here are some comments about the sense of hopelessness about self, although there were surprisingly few of them among my respondents:

67/W: Not having someone close who cares, to call on if I run into physical problems.

71/W: I feel 90 or 100 when I look at my skin and sagging flesh, and am surprised that I am now "old" after years of looking on and caring for those who were aging. I am trying to take calmly the failure of my mind to come up with the right name at the right moment. Anything that begins with a capital letter seems to escape me. *Making decisions,* I hate, even little ones. I'm wishy-washy and getting worse. Everything bad about me is getting worse and everything good is getting less.

78/M: I know you've got to keep adjusting to things all your life, but when you get old, you have more to adjust *to* and less to adjust *with.* You've got to adjust faster and oftener when your adjustability is slower and less. Adjustability—the more you need of it, the less you've got of it. It's not fair, but it's so.

On the brighter, more confident side, even those who felt hopeless about the world usually did not feel hopeless about themselves. Here are some replies, chosen to give a cross section of feelings behind a hopeful outlook:

68/W: Friendships get better and better, except sometimes I feel overwhelmed by the large number of people I want to keep in touch with.

69/W: Having overcome or learned to live with my own restrictive weaknesses of personality and some hard knocks along the way, I feel I can deal with whatever is dished out in my remaining years.

78/W: Ability to change, to be flexible, to be caring and helpful with enthusiasm. Attitude of determination to keep going in positive and meaningful experiences.

82/W: Acceptance of things as they are, personally and universally. I accept, and I *do,* and it makes me feel hopeful.

83/W: Beauty of nature. Friendship and the fact that there are *so many* good people in the world. It seems *impossible* to believe that life on earth will cease as a result of man's stupidity and wipe out *man's precious cultural heritage,* such as art, music, and literature.

83/W: As I am no longer trying to prove anything to anyone or to myself, I am free to sit back and do only those things that I enjoy doing, feeling delightfully serene while I am doing them.

84/W: I've found out who, what, and why I am. I feel content, vibrant, and curious. Finally, in old age, I've accepted myself fully.

Being an Elder: The Pleasure and the Anger

Here are some more comments about what it means to be "old." These are in answer to my question *What pleases you most about being (your age) years old?:*

75/W: I greatly enjoy being cherished by someone I love on a *daily basis.* My husband and I have great fun just being together, each sharing our different interests. It's much better than being young!

79/M: My spouse; my family; opening my eyes every morning and trying to do "good" for my own.

80/W: The pleasure of meaning so much to the people who mean so much to me!

80/W: My experience of life has made me able to feel closer to people in their sorrows and joys than when I was younger.

81/W: Maybe, now that I hike less and go to museums, etc., less easily, my greatest real satisfaction comes in having the leisure to read what I want and to listen as long as I want to, to the glorious music of stereo, and just sitting and communing with nature, out-of-doors.

82/M: I can still make people laugh, with me or at me.

84/W: An incredible freedom. Also, it's fun to change habits.

84/W: That I've lived through so many "ages"—the horse and buggy age, the electrical carriage age, the gasoline age, the flapper age, the flight age, the Pill age, the dope age, the pants age (when women started to wear the pants)—and now the space age.

84/W: I enjoy seeing the world from the perspective of age. I remember so many crises which no longer exist. I find comfort in anticipating solutions to many present problems. I *know* human beings will solve their problems.

96/W: That I can remember. That I can reason. That I can adapt. That I can love life. That I can let the "good things" overshadow the "bad things."

But there's the other side. I asked, *What makes you most angry about being your present age?* Well, very few respondents said they feel angry. For example: A 74-year-old man wrote, "I don't feel 'angry' about anything or anyone—except in a passing way when I read or hear of some act of Human Folly." But there are the angry few:

66/W: Being at the mercy of my bones and muscles and digestion.

70/W: The combination of poor vision and poor balance produces a bad scene. It is frustrating and often angers me in a way that I'm not proud of. I would like to be in better control of mood and disposition as I grow older. Instead, at times, I seem to go backward.

71/W: That I haven't done more to make this world a better place for my children and grandchildren; I think of all the things that they're going to have to put up with. But being 71 doesn't really make me angry. Perhaps "scared" and "disappointed" would be better adjectives.

73/M: The fact that politicians could so easily vote away our rights, such as the taxing of social-security income. I have never been the reformer type, but I could become one in the interests of the elderly.

80/W: Sorry, but though I know I need a lot of help (on stairs, etc., and lifting or carrying things), it makes me angry to have to accept it.

84/W: Other people's assumption of my physical or mental incompetence, of which I am unaware or with which I disagree! But I'm annoyed, amused, rather than angry.

88/W: I think the hardest thing I've experienced in old age was having to give up my car. I had driven my own car for over fifty years, but this spring decided to give it to my 19-year-old grandson, and now I feel that all my independence is gone.

90/W: It makes me angry to be patronized—called Girlie or Grandma or Dearie.

Are Elders Misunderstood?

When I asked about any major misunderstandings elders had met regarding old age, the principal one, by far, was people's assumption that an old person is incompetent and miserable.

Several elders also remarked on the unfortunate stereotypes in children's books. For example:

71/W: Small children often equate old age with dying in the near future. (Many old stories say, "So-and-so grew old and died.") And the pictures! What a bunch of shrunkens! Several 3- to 5-year-olds have asked if I'm "very, very old." When I assent, the next question can be "Will you die soon?" And then, "Are you glad?" I try to reassure them that I like being old and am not dying at the moment.

A couple of people suggested that parents screen their children's stories for such damaging biases in both text and illustrations.

A woman who described herself only as "well into the 80's" sent me the following account of a recent experience. She'd taken on a volunteer job supervising children at a local nursery school during the late afternoon, when they were waiting for their parents to come and pick them up. She wrote:

A 4-year-old boy and I were looking out the window waiting for his mother to come for him. I didn't know the child at all, but he was one of those ponderers who work things out in their own fashion, if given a chance. He said to me, "You are very old, aren't you?"

I answered, "Yes."

"You are going to die soon, aren't you?"

I gasped a little and answered, "Yes."

Much thought on his part. Then—"A police car will come and take you to the cemetery." I made no comment. Then still more introspection. "No, not a police car. An ambulance will come and take you to the cemetery."

I still said nothing as he went on pondering. "No, not an ambulance. God will come and take you to the cemetery, and He will get you out too."

Is it any wonder that we who have worked with little children feel so privileged!

What an upbeat, enjoy-the-moment elder! I'd say. But three of my male respondents take a less positive attitude toward youth:

69/M: Yes, there *are* misunderstandings! The most important is the demeaning attitude of younger persons toward many if not most "oldsters." As a consequence, I have erected a barrier of mild distrust of the youngsters, and tell them nothing about my forgetfulness or aches and pains or other infirmities. (Never trust anyone under 30.)

75/M: Lots of people think that when you become old, you've never experienced being young.

77/M: When I'm with the younger generation, I feel that what I say does not count anymore.

Surprises—Mostly Pleasant

What has surprised you most about life since 65?

69/M: I am often surprised when I realize I am the oldest person at a meeting, or in any group of people.

70/W: Time goes faster than ever, and I feel as if I have so little time to do all that I want to do, so it becomes more precious than ever.

71/M: That the scenery of the world gets better as you have more time to enjoy it; that our children are so kind, entertaining, and pleasant; and that machinery and gadgets get more fascinating and cheaper!

74/M: That I am as alert as I am, that I still have ambitions to fulfill—travel, job completions, sexual desires, etc.

74/W: After having always lived under the umbrella of someone's loving solicitous care (my parents' and then my wonderful husband's), I have been amazed to discover that I can handle life on my own.

75/W: All of life is full of surprises—especially as one nears the end of it—some happy ones and some cruelly unhappy. The most surprising is the way we learn to face and overcome difficulties as they arise.

78/M: The ability to enjoy and give enjoyment in sex. The brotherhood of the old; as the drawing together of old classmates without regard to accomplishment or money.

80/W: Wearing so well!

81/W: I am like C. S. Lewis, *Surprised by Joy*. The beauty of the world in which I live, my recent trip to the British Isles, the friends who mean so much to me, the Meeting for Worship that we have here. I did not expect to enjoy all this in such a young way—as if it were happening for the first time.

83/W: The biggest surprise is that I am succeeding, so far, in not being a nuisance.

86/M: That I am basically so little different than I was in early maturity.

87/W: The second day after the orthopedic surgeon placed a plate and five screws in my leg and ran a rod to top of the femur, they took me to P.T. With one physical therapist on one side and another on the other, I was to walk. You can understand my apprehension. I was standing between bars. I glanced over and saw a funny-looking old woman with her face screwed up like a dried apple. *Then* I saw the mirror at the end of the walkway. The old woman was me! Even then, I had to laugh—in surprise!

GEM COLLECTION

My respondents frequently made some comments, both light and profound, and beyond the scope of specific questions that especially delighted, enlightened, or moved me. I have collected these in what I call Gem Collections, which appear at the end of several chapters. I hope you will find them good for browsing. As you will see, they include a few items you may have heard before and occasional bits of old-fashioned rhyming verse that sophisticates may dismiss as doggerel.

70/W: Enjoy the astonishing, unexpected joys of old age, and don't hesitate to love anyone. With age, the big news is that one can be free of many inhibitions. Who *cares* how foolish you are now? If being "old" is an excuse, then just go ahead and be eccentric and have fun doing it.

70/W: Old age reminds me of city streets in the spring—one learns to drive *around* the terrible holes, but one is aware that they are always there and that there is the dread of more to come.

72/M: I like this story about Somerset Maugham (1874–1965). Throughout his life he was bothered by a hesitation in his speech. He was invited to address one of the most prestigious groups in England on his eightieth birthday. After the dinner, he rose, thanked his hosts, took a sip from his glass of water, and began, "Old age has many benefits . . ." There followed a long and painful pause, while he turned to the head table for help, sipped more water, shuffled his notes, and several times started to speak. At last, holding the audience firmly in his grasp, he said, "I'm trying to think of some," and sat down.

74/M: An advantage of being an elder is that you can make an ass of yourself and get away with it.

75/M: Once I shuffled, sort of liked it. Then I saw someone else shuffle, and boy did I stop! I learned to stride—in moderation.

75/M: We were on a bus. Someone gave my wife a seat. I was standing and holding on as best I could. A young attractive woman was seated beside me where I stood. My id was working her over when suddenly she stood up and offered me her seat. A shock wave hit me after I had accepted her offer. Yes, my pride was gone as well as my id. I had to admit it—"Yes, I am an old man."

76/W (Maggie Kuhn, born 1905, national convenor of the Gray Panthers): I'm glad I've reached seniority. I feel free to speak out and act in ways I wasn't able to when I was younger. I've outlived a great deal of my opposition. I don't dye my hair, can't afford a face-lift, and regard my wrinkles as badges of distinction—I've worked hard for them. It's really wonderful to be able to tap into the incredible energy of the young while making use of the knowledge and experience that comes after living a long, full life.

78/M (General Douglas MacArthur, 1880–1964): I promise to keep on living as though I expected to live forever. Nobody grows old by merely living a number of years. People grow old only by deserting their ideals. Years may wrinkle the skin, but to give up interest wrinkles the soul.

78/M: It now takes half a day to do errands formerly accomplished during lunch hour, so I learn to enjoy it and observe the scene as I mosey along.

78/W: Elders are more diverse than people of any other age. They are peculiarized by more experience.

79/M: *Since my illness, I feel "old";*
              That's why I did retire,
              But as long as I have a finger,
              I'll keep it in the fire.

80+/W (Rose Fitzgerald Kennedy, born 1890): Now I am in my eighties and I have known the joys and sorrows of a full life. I can neither regret nor ever reconcile myself to the tragedies. Age, however, has its privileges. One is to reminisce and another is to reminisce selectively. I prefer to remember the good times.

81/W: My friend (98) and I played anagrams every Friday. If I used a word which wasn't in her 1867 dictionary, which she always had handy, she ruled it out.

81/W: My life has experienced (and still does experience!) the pain, satisfaction, and challenge of *continuing* growth—growing pains. Though I believe that seeking security may still be an evanescent pursuit, I think I still want to pursue greater awareness, greater understanding, greater compassion in my daily life. My spirit wants to *stay alive!*

81/W: I guess I think more, feel more, and empathize more as I get older, but I still get impatient and sometimes put my tongue in gear before I engage my brain.

82/M: An older personality is like a stew cooked over a low flame for a long time, well flavored, well balanced.

84/W: Elders have some good and needed things that the younger people don't have. They have knowledge, freedom, leisure, time, perspective, and more freedom from guilt and conventions. They are able to be as much of a "character" as they wish.

86/W (Gabrielle "Coco" Chanel, 1883–1970, French fashion designer, to a reporter): I will tell you that my age varies according to the day and the people I happen to be with. When I'm bored, I feel very old, and since I'm extremely bored with you, I'm going to be one thousand years old in five minutes if you don't get the hell out of here at once.

90/W: *What have I known in my ninety years?*
Many anomalous things, my dears.
Seventeen presidents, several wars,
Horses and buggies and motor cars,
Oil and gas and electric lights,
Ladylike manners and women's rights,
Stoves electric and coal and wood,
Fanny Farmer and instant food,
Long white woollies and undershirts,
Bustles and hobbles and miniskirts,
Music boxes that played a tune,
Television and men on the moon,
Extra papers at dead of night
And news from Asia by satellite.
Age is hard, but it's rather fun
*To have these things to look back upon.**

*This verse was sent to me by three respondents. Each labeled the author as anonymous.

Chapter 2
MIND AND MEMORY

In our society, most people think that when you grow older you become less intelligent. Passively, quite a few elders accept this idea. Whenever they forget a name, lose something, or can't figure out a new gadget, they think, "Well, I'm getting older. My mind is starting to go." A 75-year-old man wrote: "I lose my keys. Or I have a great thought, and while having it forget where my glasses are. Well, when I tell a younger person about these things, I'm amazed. They almost always reply, 'I do the same thing myself!' and I don't think they're just being kind. It's me who's being unkind to *me*."

Or take me, Eric Johnson, 67/M. For years, I've written my books in a little study in the woods 220 feet behind our house. In winter, I want to be able to turn the heat on before I go out there so that it will be warm and ready. This means that when I leave the study to go back to the house, I leave the heat on and turn it off by means of a switch in the cellar. But often, while I'm walking back to the house, a great idea will invade my head, or the beauty of nature will hit me, and when I get to the house I've forgotten all about the heat, and it stays on all night—expensive! So I thought up a simple device: When I leave the study, I hang an unbent paperclip over an earpiece of my glasses. It dangles benignly there and reminds me, no matter what, "Turn off the heat!" Well, in the past couple of years, since age 65, I've unconsciously felt that it's "because my memory is going" that I need the paperclip. Then, just the other day, I realized that I've been using the paperclip device for about twenty years—since I was in my late forties. Only when I unconsciously applied the old-age label to myself did a bright idea become a sign of deterioration—a false sign.

As Dr. Samuel Johnson (1709–1784) wrote, "There is a wicked inclination in most people to suppose an old man decayed in his intellect. If a young or middle-aged man, when leaving a company, does not recollect where he laid his hat, it is nothing; but if the same inattention is discovered in an old man, people will shrug their shoulders and say, 'His memory is going!' "

Human Intelligence Is Complex

Too many people think that intelligence is a simple score on an IQ test, or a reading, math, or vocabulary score, or the ability to talk cleverly, or invent things, or whatever. But intelligence is not simple; it's very complex, and people's intelligences vary even more than their faces do. Perhaps half in fun, the inventor, philosopher, anthropologist, engineer, and architect Buckminster Fuller (1895–1982) described how complex a human being is. He handed a copy of the description to me a few years ago while my wife and I were driving him to a lecture he was giving near Philadelphia. It read: "A person is self-balancing, twenty-eight jointed, adapter base biped; an electro-chemical reduction plant, integrated with segregated stowages and thousands of hydraulic and pneumatic pumps with motors attached, 62,000 miles of capillaries, millions of warning signals . . . guided with exquisite precision from a turret in which are located telescopic and microscopic self-registering and recording range-finders. . . ."

Well, perhaps with older bipeds the range-fingers may become less efficient and the pumps and motors a bit worn, but think of how much information and experience our "stowages" have stowed! Unless we're weakened by diseases or discouraged by "agist" attitudes in others and ourselves, we have so much more than younger people have to apply to problems that may need solving or judgments that must be made.

Garson Kanin, in his book *It Takes a Long Time to Become Young,* written when he was 68, tells a story about a town that had lost its electrical power and blacked out.

Efforts to repair the system failed until someone remembered the elderly, retired engineer who had worked on the original installation. He was sent for, arrived, examined the equipment, took a tiny mallet from his pocket, and tapped a switch. The crisis was over. Later, the town clerk received his itemized bill.

Services:	$1,000.02
Tapping:	$ .02
Knowing where to tap:	$1,000.00

Of course, we must be careful not to generalize too freely about the relative intelligence of young people and their elders. When Samuel Johnson was asked whether men or women were more intelligent, he replied, "Which man? Which woman?" So we must ask, "Which youth? Which elder?"

Following are two statements by elderly men that illustrate the dangers of generalizing. Both men were extraordinarily intelligent and experienced, yet they react in different ways to the effects of being old. One is governor, statesman and diplomat Averell Harriman (born 1891), who wrote at age 80: "It is true that our culture discriminates against age. . . . The most important computer is the human brain. Good judgment comes from years and years of that brain's storing up millions and millions of important impressions. A wise decision comes when a man who has lived a long time is able to dig deep into that brain. To throw away people who have developed such magnificent mental computers is a great waste."

The other statement is from pianist Arthur Rubinstein (1887–1982). He was told, at age 80, that he was playing better than ever. He said, "I think so. . . . I am 80. Isn't that so? So now I take chances I never took before. You see, the stakes are not so high. I can afford it. I used to be so much more careful. No wrong notes. Not too bold ideas. Watch tempi. But now I let go and enjoy myself and to hell with everything except the music!"

According to careful research done over the past decade, the intelligence of elders does not decline, except in relatively minor ways. Even those who are suffering from serious physical diseases are much more intelligent in their minds than their "pumps, motors, capillaries, and range-finders" allow them to reveal.

Psychologist John Horn of the University of Denver, a researcher in the field of intelligence, uses special terms for two main kinds of intelligence.* One is *crystallized intelligence:* a person's ability to use an accumulated body of information and experience to solve problems and make judgments. According to Horn, crystallized intelligence increases steadily throughout life. In old age the rate of increase

*Good accounts of Horn's work are found in "Introduction of Structural and Developmental Concept of the Theory of Fluid and Crystallized Intelligence," pp. 162–81, in R. B. Cattell (ed.), *Handbook of Multivariate Experimental Psychology,* Rand-McNally, Chicago, 1966; and (with Gary Donaldson and Robert Engstrom), "Apprehension, Memory, and Fluid Intelligence Decline in Adulthood," pp. 33–84, Vol. 3, *Research on Aging,* 1981.

is slower than in earlier years, but the crystallized intelligence goes on growing as long as the person enjoys generally good health. We elders go on getting brighter; we just get brighter slower.

However, there is in many elders a loss in certain relatively minor areas of intelligence, called *fluid intelligence*. Fluid intelligence involves the ability to recall names or phone numbers or the exact day on which a recent event happened. This decline in fluid intelligence (a leakage, maybe, of the fluid of today's and yesterday's facts) I myself often experience, and I'm sure the same is true for elder readers of this book. There are a number of effective techniques to deal with it, some of which I offer at the end of this chapter.

By the way, the common belief that human beings lose intelligence because of the billions of neurons lost from our brains over the years is incorrect. We do lose neurons, but we have so many billions more than we'll ever need that the loss has no effect on our intelligence. (This is not to say, of course, that strokes, or brain damage caused by excessive use of alcohol or drugs, do not lower intelligence. They do, but the ability to recover even from such damage, and even at advanced age, is extraordinary.)

How We Respondents Describe Our Intelligence

On my questionnaire, I asked three questions about intelligence. The replies, written and collated before I had read the materials John Horn sent me about crystallized and fluid intelligence, certainly confirmed his research. The questions I asked were:

In what ways, if any, would you say you are more *intelligent than you were at, say, age 45–50?*

In what ways, if any, are you less intelligent?

Do you ever find yourself apologizing for lack of intelligence in ways you didn't used to do? Yes __ No __.

The answers to the first two questions are so varied that I can't tabulate them. Instead, I give a sampling—first of ways in which we consider ourselves less intelligent over the years (only a quarter of my respondents answered this question at all):

67/W: I don't know if it means I'm less intelligent, but I have no interest in or desire to learn about computers. When I cash a check or make a deposit, I go to a teller, not a machine. [*Note:* Many respondents gave replies like this one.]

71/M: I am surprised by the fact that memory, especially of names and places, is much poorer. Also, it applies to recent events, while memory of childhood events is, if anything, more vivid than ever. [*Note:* The inability to remember names, places, and numbers was *very* commonly mentioned, including the majority who feel they are more intelligent than they were at an earlier age.]

71/M: Learning new codes, understanding computer instructions or new mathematical-navigational procedures involves too many facts for me to remember. Even after four or five practice runs, I need to go back to the instruction outline, often several times. It didn't used to be like that. Then, I got it the first time through.

74/M: I recognize, particularly with my children and grandchildren, that there is just an awful lot that they know that I don't.

74/W: I don't think I'm more or less *intelligent,* just a little lazier about doing things my intelligence suggests I do!

78/W: I'm less intelligent when it comes to remembering names, historical data, authors, fictional characters in the classic works of songs and poetry, and I have to use the dictionary more, and I *was* an excellent speller. [*Note:* I didn't, however, have to correct any spelling in this comment.]

80/W: I don't think I'm more intelligent at 80 than I was at 45–50. I'm definitely less quick and less sharp. In fact, I'm pretty dull and slow. My memory is very poor. Perhaps somewhere tucked away there is some wisdom.

81/W: One doesn't change her intelligence but hopefully does improve her understanding and wisdom with life's experiences. I do honestly believe that I am more understanding (and need to improve, too!!) and perhaps somewhat wiser than I was at 45–50–65. But I don't feel any brainier.

And then there was one elder who reported about the intelligence of a friend: "She has hardening of the categories."

Now in what ways do we find ourselves *more* intelligent?

66/M: In town government I find it much easier to recognize problems and accidents about to happen. I can anticipate with ease what people are likely to do when given various choices. Then I can forestall actions by them which would be detrimental to the town. I could not have done that twenty years ago. Whether this is intelligence or experience, I don't know. I like to think I'm wiser.

70/W: I'm not so ashamed of knowing so little as I used to be. This is a form of intelligence? Or is it bravery? Not to mind being stupid helps *me* to ask questions. Sometimes I understand the answers, and that is exciting.

71/M: I distinguish intelligence from learning rate. I feel equally—or more—intelligent than in earlier years. However, I don't think that my learning rate is what it was twenty-five years ago.

71/W: I'm not any more intelligent, but I think I've become more *thorough* and more able to advise gently and with empathy.

75/M: Perhaps I don't remember things as well as before, but if so, they are the things I am not greatly interested in remembering. What, to me, is important, I do remember. [*Note:* I know an elder who has developed a definite policy of emptying his head of things he doesn't need to know—"to leave," as he says, "space for what I need to know." He's a terrible Trivia player but a vastly creative person. He's like the Scot who, when told of a complex problem he knew nothing about, said, "I'll not charge me mind wi' that." It's said that Sherlock Holmes and Einstein, one in fiction, one in real life, practiced the same head-emptying process.]

77/W: Since 70, a creative center has been opened. I don't know whether you call it intelligence or not, but I seem to be able to connect bits of knowledge that had been hanging loose. I use words that I used to be afraid to use (for fear I wouldn't pronounce them right). I seem to have more confidence in expressing a point of view.

83/W: The functioning of your brain cells does decline, but accumulated knowledge from past experience gives you greater wisdom. You lose "smartness" but gain "intelligence."

84/W: I'm more intelligent: have 84 years of perspective. Can relate everything new to the old. Can see the "whys." Am quick to try new things. The "I can't," or "I'm too old," has changed to a challenge: "I bet I can figure that out."

86/M: I'm less likely to jump to conclusions—more reflective. More likely to *understand* different points of view, and open to acceptance of change in my own judgments. I have more understanding, less intolerance. At the same time, I am more secure in conviction of fundamental values.

96/W: My idea of intelligence is more a matter of reasoning than memory. I do not think age itself affects reasoning, at least not in my case.

Do you ever find yourself apologizing for lack of intelligence? Of the 94 percent who answered this question, 71 percent checked *No,* and 29 percent checked *Yes,* and almost all of the 29 percent said they apologized for forgetting people's names. A common technique elders use is not to apologize but to say to a person, "Don't take it personally. I don't remember *anybody's* name, so tell me yours. Thanks." Then they can go on to have an interesting conversation on an interesting subject. For, among elders, interest is a main factor for the exercise of intelligence. Many of us use our intelligence only when we are interested. Thus, for quite a few, word puzzles, contrived logic problems, and the silly games that are considered to be therapy in some senior-citizen communities and nursing homes don't turn us on. However, just give us opportunities to figure out something useful and we apply our brains and our store of experience, methods, and wisdom. New challenges can lead to new sources of delight.

One 74-year-old woman, Anna S. Morris, reported to me that she has found new delight in writing haiku. "Two years ago," she wrote, "I heard a Taoist priest, Khigh Dhign, say that if one wrote a haiku every day for a month, one would become more relaxed and discover deeper beauty in life, and thus would improve the health of the psyche. This challenge was irresistible, and I began to experiment with this age-old form of spiritual expression."

A haiku is a strictly patterned three-line minipoem: five syllables/seven syllables/five syllables. Here's one I made up to illustrate:

> *Elders, write haikus!*
> *Enjoy their stimulation.*
> *They rejuvenate.*

While visiting some of her grandchildren, Anna Morris wrote:

Annie coos and laughs.
Dave, Odin, and Gennie smile.
Love entwines them all.

On the joys and problems of aging, she wrote:

Aging can be fun.
Joy flows through me with power.
I am one with God.

My world is shattered.
I cling to bits of ideals.
God-Trust makes me whole.

Death comes to us all.
Transformation looms ahead.
Life renews itself.

And a friend of Anna Morris wrote some good haiku-advice on getting along with others by really hearing what they say:

Listening well means
Discarding expectations
Of what I will hear.

Intelligence and Caring

Certainly an aspect of intelligence, broadly defined, is caring. I asked my respondents this question: *It is said that elders don't become mellow and tolerant; they merely care and feel less. Is this true of your own experience? Yes __ No __.* Twenty-six percent of my respondents checked *Yes* (they cared or felt less); 64 percent checked *No* (they felt and cared more); 10 percent gave a mixed answer.

69/M: Caring is as important in life as knowing—maybe more so. I haven't cared enough about an issue since I was 65 to go to jail for it; I hope I won't have to say that when I'm 80. It's intelligent to care.

70/M: Most of my friends seem to care and feel *more*. I grant they are often frustrated about life, as the body may not allow them to do what the heart wants to.

71/M: I still weep over books. When I pass a bad road accident, I'm really sad and upset and watery for an hour. The physical world seems to me to be growing in beauty, as do small children, young women, and athletes.

75/W: I believe my feelings are deeper and stronger, but experience in handling them gives me seeming control.

80/W: I've seen a lot of people become less raspy as they grow older.

83/W: Since 65, I know I have become more understanding and sympathetic to other people's feelings. For example, I had no idea how very hard and very lonely it is to be left alone when your husband dies, especially after sixty-five years of married life, as was my case. So I sincerely try to be more sympathetic and helpful to the newly widowed now. I care. I feel with them.

85/W: *Acceptance* to me is the greatest goal of Old Age—taking things as they *are* and not as I wanted them to be. Acceptance gives peace—and energy and the ability to care. So mellowness and tolerance mean we care *more!* That's why I'm learning to hug people. I'm not used to it, it doesn't take a high IQ, but it's intelligent, good-producing, and satisfying.

Lack of Stimulation or Sudden Disorientation

A number of respondents reported that women who were mainly housewives all their adult lives have come to depend on their dominant, beloved, stimulation-bringing husbands for much of the richness and interest of their lives. In other words, marriage has in a way restricted their lives. Then, maybe suddenly, or maybe after a period of intensive, wearing caregiving, comes widowhood. Stimulation has gone; their lives are restricted, partly by society, partly by their own inability to strike out on their own. They don't use their intelligence, and allow themselves to deteriorate. (As the saying goes, "Use it or lose it.")

People often assume that such deterioration is the beginning of the end, and do little to help. Dr. Jerry Avorn of the Harvard Medical School's Division on Aging reports on a similar problem that happens when elders who are institutionalized become suddenly disoriented and seem to have suffered an abrupt decline in intelligence:

> What can happen is that an older person who is admitted to a hospital for something like a broken hip or heart attack can become confused as a side effect of drugs or simply from the strangeness of the hospital routine. The condition is reversible, but the family, or even the physician, doesn't recognize that fact. They assume this is the beginning of senile dementia, and pack the person off to a nursing home. No one knows what exact proportion of people in nursing homes needn't be there, but we have ample clinical evidence that the numbers are large.

Later on, I say more about nursing homes and life-care communities, but here is a word from one of my respondents, 70-year-old Allen White, who was the first executive director of Foulkeways, a pioneering community for older people in Gwynedd, Pennsylvania. He served in this capacity for twelve years. He writes:

> As part of training staff members to work with the elderly and in an effort to create more understanding generally of the elderly, I often said, "They are the wisest group of people in the world. They have lived longer, have learned more, have had more experience. We must treat them as such and not as children." At Foulkeways, I told the staff members that when they had ideas about erecting a sign which started with the word "No," they must have my written permission. Life being a growing process, our wisdom and intelligence grow with age.

Another inhibitor of intelligence, perhaps more certain than widowhood, sudden institutionalization, or staff nay-saying, follows a loss of hearing acuity or sharpness of vision. These conditions mean that the mind has less to work with, not that it is less able. Hearing poorly or seeing poorly makes people seem dull and unintelligent, but they're not. As they move about and try to relate to people, their intelligence is simply less obvious.

75/W: My friend has a sister, older than me, who neither sees nor hears well. In conversation with people, she doesn't hear things correctly and answers out of context and is thought to be senile. She's *not!* She can outwit me any time she has the evidence!

81/W: An old friend said to me once, "Deaf people talk all the time. It's the only way they know what is being said."

87/W: My hearing loss cuts off part the spoken word. Result? I seem "dense."

Tips and Techniques

While answering a question, respondents frequently suggested specific tips and techniques for dealing with the daily challenges of life. I've put some of these tips in the text of the chapters, but others, I felt, would be more helpful if presented in a group. Following, then, are some techniques to help memory and sharpen intelligence:

• Be sensible: *Never* put your wallet or your spectacles down at all!

• When you are about to leave a store, or someone's house, or anywhere other than your home, specifically (and aloud, if necessary) ask, "Have I left anything?" Then deliberately and slowly look around, 360 degrees, to make a thorough check.

• When you're talking and a very interesting thought occurs to you in midsentence, *don't digress.* Just plow on ahead and finish the main idea. Otherwise you get caught on a conversational sidetrack and may never find your way back to the main road. This requires great self-control, because the digressions may be more interesting than the main idea. (By the way, forgetting what you were going to say is a behavior not unique to elders. Hundreds of times during my schoolteaching career, a pupil who has raised his hand in a discussion and waited patiently and eagerly to be called on was confused when finally recognized, looked at his raised hand as if it were a foreign object, and had no recollection of what he was going to say.)

• If you are talking and someone interrupts you, listen to the interruption and don't then remark, "As I was in the middle of saying . . ." If nobody asks you to continue after the interruption, chances are that what you were saying wasn't very interesting.

• If you can, get a computer (or, cheaper, a good notebook) in which to store items of information you're likely to need.

• If you have something you must remember to take with you when you go out—like a package or envelope—put it smack in the middle of the doorway, or lean it up against the door so that it will yell at you as you leave.

- Keep an erasable message board or a small blackboard on a wall you often pass, and list on it what you must not forget that day. Make a law for yourself to look at it a couple of specific times each day.

- Leave messages for your spouse or housemates—and have them leave notes for you—on a sheet of paper in the middle of a floor that you frequently walk across. When the message is attended to, throw it away. (Scrap paper is cheap.)

- Never go off to do a set of errands without writing a list of what you want to do. When each item is done, cross it off. (Keep a tray in the car with pencils in it.)

- Remember: "A place for everything and everything in its place." Don't improvise! If you do decide to change the place for something, tell your housemates. (If you are a briefcase type or a purse type, *always* leave them in a certain place or you'll get frequent cases of the briefcase wanders, usually accompanied by moans of distress.)

- When you're carrying a glass or some small item, you might let your fingers relax while your mind is suddenly taken up by a great thought. To avoid breakage, *always* slip your little finger under the bottom of what you're carrying.

GEM COLLECTION

Plato at unknown age (he died at about 80): The eyes of the spirit begin to grow sharp only when those of the body begin to fail.

69/W: A certain amount of neatness (in moderation) allows your brain to go on to other, more important business.

70/W (Elizabeth Gray Vining in *On Being 70: The Measure of a Year*): I do not see birds as well as I used to. So I think I shall take to trees. They are eminently visible and stand still to be examined. They have leaves, blossoms, and fruit that can be carried home to compare with pictures in a book. In winter their leafless shapes and varied bark offer points for identification as well as enjoyment.

74/M: Habits can save the mind and free the intelligence. Four that save me are:

Temperance in food and drink.
A daily walk of some length.
The joy of reading.
Sunday and church attendance.

76/W: Admit frankly that you have a problem, like deafness or cyberphobia (fear of computers) and you'll suddenly find a lot of people who have the same problem. That gives *me* courage and comfort.

76/M: I feel more intelligent in *the things that really matter* (and that doesn't include lost names and glasses) than I have ever been, so hear me, and make me hear you, and we can have a noble argument that will work us nearer to truth.

77/W: A story I like: There were three women having tea together and one of them said, "You know, the funniest things are happening to me. I sometimes find myself at the bottom of the stairs and wonder whether I was going up to get something or was coming down to get something."
The second woman replied, "You know, I sometimes find myself in front of the refrigerator. I can't remember whether I just put something in or I have come to take something out."
The third woman said, "Well, I don't have anything like that happening to me, but perhaps I had better knock on wood"—which she did, three times. Then she looked, startled, at her guests and said, "I guess that was somebody at the door. Excuse me!"

79/W: I think that there are widowed women who now on their own might become more radical than they dared to be in the shadow of a conservative spouse.

80/W (Pearl Buck, 1892–1973): I have learned so much since I was 70, more within the last ten years than in any other decade. Why should I quit? What would I sit and wait for?

80/W: When I seem stupid or distracted, it's *not* that I'm stupid. I just get so *attracted* by a joyous or stimulating great idea that it takes over my mind. It flows in, and I'm brilliant—only to you I seem distracted and absent.

80/W: My minister told me a couple of years ago that at my age I should be giving some thought to what he called "the hereafter." I was pleased to report that I think about it many times a day. "Oh, really?" he said. "That's very wise." I explained that it's not a matter of wisdom. It's when I open a drawer or a closet and ask myself, "What am I here after?"

A geriatric social worker: I went out to the home of an 81-year-old lady today to do an assessment. I found a very frail, tiny, white-haired woman who very slowly came with her walker to let me in the door. I was delighted with her perky optimistic attitude. She faced her future of continued fractures of those porous bones with resignation and valor. But when she said to me, "The only problem I have in managing is when Mother acts up," I was crushed. How could I have missed all the signs of hallucinating? In my career, I have dealt with the phantom-spouse situation time and again, but this lady had seemed so well oriented and realistic. And she was, because just then in walked Mother, age 105!

84/M: We get to be pretty good at knowing the way to go. It's like the old Maine fisherman. When he was asked, "Do you know where the channel is?" he replied, "Oh, I certainly do. I've been on all the rocks and sandbars."

96/W: In many minds the fact that a person is old in years means that he is old and feeble in mind, judgment, reason, and even in feelings—while in reality he may be superior in all of those things. Because his body is weaker and he needs help physically, it is very hard for an old person to be deprived of his right to judge and decide for himself what he wants.

Chapter 3

ABOUT OUR HEALTH

Remember as you read this chapter that my respondents were healthy enough to answer my long, demanding questionnaire—even though some said they felt a bit worn out or noticeably older after they'd finished. Therefore, you are reading the views, experience, and wisdom of a group who've managed to keep going—who, on the whole, are growing old successfully.

The first question I asked was *Would you say that you generally enjoy good health at (your age)? Yes __ No __*. Eighty-nine percent checked *Yes*, 8 percent *No*, and 3 percent didn't answer or answered a mixture of yes and no. Over half of those not checking were 86 or older. In the national cross section of elders interviewed in the 1981 NCOA study, 79 percent said poor health was not a problem, as compared to my 89 percent. About half the general public, on the other hand, thought that poor health *is* a serious problem for elders.

Good Health, Despite . . .

Something that amazed me was the number of ailments and diseases that an elder can have and still check *Yes* to "Do you enjoy good health?" Here are some examples:

75/W: Yes, I consider myself healthy except for certain disabilities—such as failing eyesight and hearing; stiffened joints, early tiring, worn-out parts (such as heart, lungs).

75/M: I went to a doctor because of a pain in my left knee. He told me, after examining my knee, that it was due to old age. I asked him why my right knee didn't hurt; it was the same age.

75/M: My trouble is: I can't keep this leg from resenting it when I walk on it!

43

75/W: When you're sick, the responsibility to get well is yours. After the M.D.'s and nurses call the shots, don't be a professional patient. Don't be sick. Get out and enjoy! Be a *temporary* patient.

75/W: This business of getting older physically when inside you feel young and ambitious is the most frustrating part of the whole business. I get so angry when my hands, my fingers, or my feet refuse to do what I expect them to do. I hope I shall learn to *accept* my physical limitations soon, because I waste energy being *angry* about them. So, elders, don't panic; adjust!

75/M: What do old folks talk about? The number one subject is the state of their health or lack of it. On greeting one another, the first question is, "How are you?" The normal answer is "Pretty good," which doesn't mean good at all. If one feels good, the answer should be "Great." Sometimes I answer, "Pretty good—or do you really want me to tell you the truth?"

77/M: I seem to be in good health, though getting out of bed in the mornings makes the raising of Lazarus look like a cheap trick by comparison.

79/M: A slightly older doctor friend says, "When you get to be around 70 or so, if there is nothing wrong with you there is something wrong with you." In other words, after 70 most people must expect to have more and more medical and/or physical problems. As you look around, you can always find many poor souls who are much worse off than you are.

79/W: Old age and misery don't go together well any more than any other age goes well with misery. Down with misery! Get it fixed.

80/W: This year I had knee-joint replacements and am exercising my way back to security. It is a long, slow process, but I'm hoping for total recovery within a year. I have high blood pressure controlled by medication—no real problem.

80/W: Yes, I'm healthy now. In September 1978, I suffered a stroke, which has left me with very poor coordination and balance and a weak left side. I stagger like a drunken sailor and have an increasing tremor, but can still live alone and care for myself. Also, I have had bilateral cataract operations with loss of peripheral vision and depth perception. But my driver's license was renewed!

89/W: I have had a mastectomy and bladder polyps but have completely recovered, eat what I want three meals a day. In good weather I take a twenty-minute brisk walk and do not need a cane. Where I live, people here are divided between the canes and the ables.

93/M (Eubie Blake, pianist and composer, 1883–1983): If I'd known I was going to live to be this old, I'd've taken better care of myself.

Such answers make it quite clear that enjoying good health is frequently a matter of having a positive attitude toward life, including a sense of humor. Bruce Bliven, at age 79, wrote in *Modern Maturity* (December–January, 1976–77), "I have calculated that the diseases I don't have outnumber those I have by 20 to one, so I am only five percent ill."

People Don't Die of Old Age

Because most Americans these days die when they are old, there's a common idea that we die of old age. But we don't; we die of a disease or a combination of diseases. Aging, which we've all been doing since birth, is not a disease, but being an elder, especially one who is 75 or older, increases the likelihood of getting diseases. (Except colds: I've noticed that many elders seem to float coldless through the colds season, as they never did when they were younger. "I don't get colds anymore," I've heard many elder friends say. I don't know of any studies that support this observation, but I wager there will be some. Meanwhile, we should remember that we are more susceptible to the complications of influenza and be sure to get flu shots every year.) We tend to have what some doctors call, rather formidably, "multiple chronic" medical problems: arthritis, weak bones, enlarged prostates, cancer, diabetes, cataracts, hardening of the arteries, dizziness, loss of hearing, weak vision. So we shouldn't deny our diseases. We should have annual checkups and accept the news they bring. The checkups should include blood-pressure measurement, rectal exam, a test for blood in the stools, a glaucoma test, and a mammogram for women, a prostate exam for men.

We shouldn't allow ourselves or our doctor—doctors, more often— to blame our troubles on old age. Instead, we should recognize that each trouble may be curable, or that we can learn ways to live with it and alleviate the suffering and disability it causes. A sensible view was that of Benjamin Franklin, who not long before his death (at age 84) wrote: "People who live long, who will drink the cup of life to the very bottom, must expect to meet some of the dregs."

Should There Be a Medical Specialty Called Geriatrics?

What's the best way to deal with the health problems of elders? There are those who argue that these problems are so special that we need geriatricians ("old folks' docs") to deal with them. However, there are others who argue that a kidney is a kidney, a lung is a lung, and we don't need old-kidney and old-lung specialists. Listen to two respondents:

69/M: Organized medicine tends to emphasize "acute care" and "procedures." What we elders often need is maintenance, gentling along, understanding as total people, not discrete bits of disease. We could use a lot more helpful, non-M.D. support services, not acute care. We're not a bunch of crises, but whole people with lots of continuing body troubles. We need people who'll care for all of us, not bits of us. If that's geriatrics, I'm in favor of geriatrics, not body-department specialties.

71/W: Let's not have another medical specialty—but let the special knowledge of geriatrics infiltrate the other specialties (except pediatrics), so that a kidney doc or a VD doc or a heart doc will have some geriatric discipline and have a human knowledge of us elders and our special needs.

Those of my respondents who wrote about this matter were nearly unanimous that what elders want (and some pointed out that it's what people of *any* age should want) is a doctor who will look at the whole person, listen to what he or she says, and help the patient to manage sensibly and comfortably, with referral to specialists only when necessary. We want an understanding *person* who knows when to refer us to a specialist—and not a specialist on "old age."

There's no question that for most physicians geriatrics seems a comparatively unrewarding field of medicine. The "cures" effected don't last as long and usually aren't as dramatic as those of younger patients. The investment per year of life expectancy is much higher—although that's rapidly changing as we elders live longer. And many doctors, being human, tend to look upon elders with some distaste (usually professionally masked), or at least not with the enthusiasm generated by an attractive youthful patient. This attitude has a name, gerontophobia (fear of old people), and doctors are not immune to it. It's interesting that in 1984 elders comprised about 35 percent of the average internist's "patient load," 25 percent of the surgeon's; and yet less than 4 percent of medical students took any elective course in geriatrics.

But maybe this will change. An 80-year-old physician recently wrote to me, "Medical care for elders used to seem quite dull, but now it has become quite exciting. Why? Because what used to be considered aging is now recognized as disease, and disease is curable."

I have observed, along with many others, that in some cases when a person begins to act old—perhaps because of the effects of a serious illness or the confusing environment of a hospital—family, friends, and professionals begin to treat him or her as old and incurable. This devastating attitude is catching, especially for elders themselves. Thus, instead of being encouraged to work themselves out of their temporarily low spirits and physical weakness, too often they are tranquilized, pitied, and allowed to deteriorate into nonentity. Read what four respondents wrote:

74/M: Beware the label "senile"! Don't ever apologize! And don't let it build up against you, bit by bit—one day you forget a word (he's senile); another day you can't button your shirt (he's senile); the next day they start saying, "Let me do it for you," and *they* push you into a second childhood. So assert and demonstrate your capacities—nicely but convincingly.

81/W: "Senility" is a wastebasket category—for any old person who shows confusion. I've noticed that in nursing homes people "act senile" because it's easier—and, damn it, I think it's encouraged. You're less trouble if you just fold up fetuslike and don't bother anybody.

82/W: There's a great big mental trashbin around here and they throw a lot of us into it. It's got one word painted on it and the word is SENILITY. A lot of us would like to climb out, but I feel as if they are sitting on the lid.

84/M: We've got a lot to work against to keep from being discarded as old. Even the Bible works against us, I'm afraid. Take Psalm 31, verses 10–13:

> For my life is worn out with sorrow,
> My years with sighs;
> My strength yields under misery,
> My bones are wasting away.
> To every one of my oppressors
> I am contemptible,
> Loathsome to my neighbors,
> To my friends a thing of fear.
> Those who see me in the street
> Hurry past me.
> I am forgotten, as good as dead in their hearts,
> Something to be discarded.

From my own observation, I know that it's very easy for residents of nursing homes, and those who are related to the residents, to blame "homes" and hospitals for encouraging senility. In Chapter 9, I'll say more about how many institutions are working bravely and skillfully and lovingly to keep people out of the "wastebasket."

One of my respondents, Allen White, the already-quoted former director of the life-care community Foulkeways, a man with vast experience, wrote, "All too often doctors are diagnosing senility simply because a person is old. By doing so, they often overlook the real problem, which may be treatable. This is one of the most serious ways the old are being treated unfairly—in fact, undergoing discrimination."

Alex Comfort, M.D., author of *A Good Age*, says, "Senility is to the geriatrician what 'failure to thrive' is to the pediatrician—evidence of something wrong that calls for active investigation."

What elders need is for their doctors to discern how much of their condition is old and how much is sick—and vigorously treat the sick part. A 72-year-old woman wrote, "Don't blame your troubles on 'growing old' and resign yourself to them. Get going. What you've got is probably curable."

Our Attitude Toward Medicines

One of the biggest health concerns of elders is medicines. Many of us—and younger people as well—tend to become dependent on various medications to maintain our well-being. For instance, I myself am very grateful for drugs that keep my blood pressure under control. On the other hand, I'd hate to be subject to the sedative effects of certain substances to which some of us become habituated. To find out what my fellow elders think, I asked this question: *There are some strong views pro and con on medicines for elders, both for diseases and for moods. What are your views?* All those who commented on the question—a quarter of my respondents—were against medicines for moods, except for a brief, carefully monitored treatment with tranquilizers or antidepressants in times of crisis. There's no question that such medications can be a great help to many people. Be that as it may, the most frequently expressed view was the one expressed by a 78-year-old man: "Solve your problem. Get help. Don't get medicated out of people's way and into peaceful nonentity." My impression is that, contrary to what most doctors actually do, some of my respondents would agree with Voltaire (1694–1778), who wrote, "Doctors pour drugs of which they know little, to cure diseases of which they know less, into patients of whom they know nothing." Of course, reverence for authority was not one of Voltaire's virtues.

As you will see in the next chapter, the vast majority of respondents are deeply grateful for doctors and their arsenal of weapons against disease. But there remains a strong bias against medicines:

65/W: Doctors find the writing of prescriptions an easy way to terminate a medical visit with an elderly patient. Emphasis should be on preventive medicine and the building of positive ways of living.

71/M: Laughter is the best medicine, particularly if you laugh at yourself.

73/M: What makes me mad as hell are "child-proof" bottles of pills. What they are is *me*-proof. Be sure to tell your druggist you don't want child-proof bottles, and then keep the pills and grandchildren distant from each other. [*Note:* A helpful device for pill-taking elders can be bought at almost any drugstore or from your local AARP (American Association of Retired Persons) pharmacy. It is a seven-day pill dispenser. It has seven compartments with lids marked S M T W T F S (and in braille) for the days of the week. They're a great aid to the memory. Just load up the dispenser after your last dose on Saturday.]

77/M: Medicines often get old people into trouble. I would use only what seems specifically indicated. For most old people it seems better to lie awake than to take sleeping pills.

78/W: Information about vitamins instead of strong medicines needs to be taught in medical schools so that physicians have a thorough knowledge of nutrition and need for prescribing vitamins. [*Note:* This was common criticism of doctors—ignorance of, or inattention to, good nutrition.]

80/M: I deplore the "pill for every ill" attitude of many M.D.'s. I realize that this may be the result of the way they were trained and also because it is so lucrative for that pharmaceutical industry. Too many doctors have been brainwashed, it seems to me.

This skepticism toward pills is reinforced by a study done at the University of Kentucky which found that:

> "Sixty-seven people aged 60 to 90 had been prescribed 221 different drugs for 125 different medical conditions. In a local hospital an 84-year-old woman was recently admitted for depression. A geriatrician asked her husband to bring in all her medications so that he could determine her medical history. Eighty-two prescription medicines were found in her medicine closet, purchased over ten years, prescribed by the twenty or so physicians she had visited in her search for good health."*

So we elders should keep track of whatever medicines we are taking, prescription and over-the-counter (including tobacco and alcohol) and be certain that any doctor we see gets a thorough list of them. Dr. Galinsky says, "I encourage my patients to bring all their medications with them. This not only prevents misunderstanding but

*Jane Porcino, *Growing Older, Getting Better,* p. 331.

enables me to throw away the outdated ones. Some people come in with shopping bags full of medications."

However, a few of my respondents felt that there is something to be said for the "pill for every ill" approach:

76/M: Thank God for pills and powders! They make us *know* we'll get better. And if you believe in charms and spells and magic dances, so do witch doctors. What else do you think keeps them in business? . . . Witchery and science together. That's for an oldster like me.

87/W: I've long believed that the main thing that gets you better is yourself—your body's self-recovery powers and *especially* your mind's power to get your body's powers working. That's one reason why doctors have been so successful for centuries. They make us *believe* we'll get well, so we get well. If they say, with authority and charm, "Take two of these pills twice a day for a week; they'll do the trick," we believe it (and maybe the doctors do too), and the charm works. Some pills work by chemistry, some by faith; most by both, I suppose.

But we elders must be careful not to fall for the commercial exploitation of simplistic "cures" for inevitable conditions that are just a part of aging. This warning is well expressed by Marian Sandmaier in *Gray Panther Network* (Summer 1985). In a piece called "Holding Back the Sands of Time," she writes:

> A recent hearing by the House Select Committee on Aging reported that older Americans spend $2 billion every year on products promising a . . . reversal of the aging process. The items reviewed by the Committee included a staggering array of ersatz rejuvenation creams, memory-aid tablets, cellulite-arresting lotions, hair-restoration shampoos, energy tonics, anti-senility herbs, male-potency formulas, even a special herb tea to repair the prostate. "Heal the prostate at home for pennies," glows the ad in dozens of magazines.
>
> The Congressional committee found that these quick-fix "youth elixirs" represented the fastest-growing segment of the medical quackery market, suggesting the pervasiveness—and enormous profitability—of our culture's anxiety about the natural aging process. Such products simultaneously exploit and magnify our fears about growing older, and particularly about *appearing* older in a society that rewards

the most superficial markings of youth. The Committee's terse conclusion about these so-called age cures: "They are a rip-off, pure and simple."

Just Getting Tired

A number of elders are concerned that people don't recognize that often a part of getting older is simply—or not so simply—tiring more easily. In a way, *fatigue* should be recognized, if not as a disease, at least as a problem. Otto Pollak, a sociologist at the University of Pennsylvania, at age 76, writes to me: "One gets slower. I have never been busier in my life, but that produces also an element of fatigue. I am always shocked when I read the gerontological literature how little attention is being paid to being tired. Being tired is a daily recurring element in an older person's life as far as my and my wife's and also my friends' experience goes. I think that part of life's management, if you want to continue to be active, is to space, judiciously, your periods of rest so that you can go on."

Dr. Pollak said that some years ago he made it a habit to look at the index of books on aging. He found that hardly anybody wrote about fatigue. My own recent reading verifies and updates his observation.

Here are three other comments from respondents:

70/M: *I used to burn but now I smoulder*
          That's how I know I'm getting older.

Elders have an honorable right to get tired!

78/W: Sometimes if I'm at a party (even at my own house), after dinner, if things are going well, I sneak upstairs, find a bed, and zonk out for fifteen minutes. I carry a wrist alarm to wake me up.

81/W: Listen to your body! It tells you when you need a rest.

Several of my respondents also had strong things to say about the insensitive omission of certain vital treatments from their typical health plans, related in particular to four parts of the body:

68/M: You ask about health. Eyes are to see with; teeth are to chew with; ears are to hear with; feet are to get about on. Well, would you feel healthy if you couldn't see, chew, hear, and get about? So why aren't EYES, EARS, TEETH, FEET included in health plans? I asked my dentist and he said, "Because they aren't part of death-dealing diseases." So *I* say: "Ophthalmologists, otologists, dentists, and podiatrists of the world, unite! We elders have nothing to lose but our joy in living."

84/W: What special device would I like to have? I'll tell you: a monthly podiatrist. It's hard to reach my toes, and I can't see the nails.

Exercise

A great number of my respondents came out vigorously in favor of moderate exercise, not just of the brain but also of the body. Only one maverick, a 74-year-old man, told me, "Eric, if you feel the urge to exercise coming on, walk around the dining-room table once and then sit down and sip some sherry." Perhaps he's what one respondent called a "senior sitizen." However, among the well-informed, there is little question that one of the main causes for deterioration of our bodies is disuse. One might say that the most easily available anti-aging pill is exercise, and it's free.

68/M: To hold back from exercise that is pleasurable because of a cold or malaise or ache is asking to go downhill.

74/W: People are always telling me to exercise more. I have an exerciser where I can lie on my back and pedal for forty-five minutes while I read a book!

84/W: Despite having my right eye removed and being legally blind, an accident resulting in weakened circulation in one leg so that I can't stand long, and two back operations, I refuse to be an invalid. So I jog very gently and dance free to music. Also, I do a few special exercises.

85/W: The house doctor asked if I got enough exercise. I replied, "Instead of using the elevator, I walk down stairs (two flights) every day, feeling very virtuous, to all three of my meals." His reply was "How about walking *up*, too!" So now I do, and I know it's a good habit.

97/M: When I was about 75, I found myself being very tired and worn out after a round of golf. I told my good doctor about it.

"Why do you play golf, then?" he asked.

"Well, it is supposed to be good exercise, isn't it?"

"Not if it wears you out," he said. "Does it amuse you? Are you having fun?"

"Not as much as I used to," I admitted. "Ever since I found that I could no longer get 200-yard drives. That makes me mad, and I feel like throwing away my driver."

"If I were you, I'd just quit playing golf," he said.

So I quit. I began to feel better right away. I found that walking to the post office and back was about as much walking as I liked. I'm still off the course and on to the P.O. and a happy guy.

I also wave at people—exercises the wrists. I'm also good at shaking and nodding my head—with vigor. Great for the neck, *and* the opinions. Viva exercise! Viva me!

Of course, no one, young or old, should leap into strenuous exercise without consulting a doctor to be sure it's O.K. An especially risky heavy exercise is snow-shoveling. It can harm your heart and back unless, as one geriatrician said, your usual leisure activity is ditch-digging. The main thing, though, is: Don't lapse into lethargy.

Pain

Several respondents brought up the subject of relieving pain during serious illnesses. Unfortunately, they said, too many doctors, in situations where there is long-lasting, severe pain from a major operation, accident, or inoperable condition, still prescribe pain relief on an "as-needed" basis. That means, in effect, a cycle of agony, drug-out, agony, drug-out—since the patient must request the dose *after* pain begins. It may take the nurse a while to free herself to give the dose—usually by shot, not by mouth—and then many minutes of suffering pass before the medication takes effect and the patient is zonked out.

Dr. James Cox-Chapman, a young physician at Hartford Hospital in Connecticut, who has a special interest in pain relief, wrote to me:

> The pain associated with terminal cancer is the cruelest pain of all. Relentless and pervasive, it saps the remaining strength of people

already debilitated by spreading cancer. It affects all aspects of a remaining life, interfering with sleep, movement, and rewarding relationships with other people. Unfortunately, most physicians, because of fear of addicting patients to narcotics, write prescriptions thus: "One to two pills every four hours *as needed* for pain." This system virtually requires that one be suffering from pain in order to legitimately take the medication.

Actually, the most important thing should be that the pain cycle *never be allowed to begin.* This is accomplished by around-the-clock mandatory doses of medication, at regular intervals *before* the pain begins. If patients receive adequate amounts of medication and are never allowed to experience pain, their total intake of pain medications is less than with the as-needed regimens. It means less medicine, no pain. The alternative is pain and anguish, then medication, then a doped-up feeling of relief—until pain begins again, a terrible, life-ruining cycle.

My view is that we elders should make a special point of talking with our doctors about pain relief—if possible, well in advance of the urgent need for it. Talk about it with spouse and family. Let them know what your desires are. If your doctor won't agree in principle to the regimen you feel you need, consult another doctor.

Sleep

My respondents had several common-sense suggestions about sleep: First, it's perfectly normal to undergo a change of sleep habits as you get older; and it's just as normal to worry about it. Many people who were brought up on the "eight hours or else" philosophy get anxious when they wake up constantly after only six hours. Others who've done well on six and now need eight or nine hours worry about that. It's O.K.; take eight or nine if you can.

Further, if you stop worrying, you can *enjoy* lying awake. Just get comfortable, let your mind float, don't itemize sheep, and relish whatever goes through your head, including conscious vacuum.

If you're tired because you don't sleep enough at night, enjoy a nap—ended by an alarm clock, unless you are an expert self-waking brief-napper.

Here's another idea a physician respondent gave me. Research shows that the first three hours of sleep are the most beneficial—

deeper, more total. Therefore, get *two* first three hours. Go to bed, say, at 10:30; get up by alarm at 1:30; work or read—refreshed and brilliant—till 4:30; go to bed again for another first three hours of sleep. Then get up at 7:30.

My respondents were virtually unanimous in deploring sleeping pills. They lead, many said, to grogginess, depression, dependence, impairment of mental capabilities, and loss of interest in life.

69/M: I went to a sleep clinic once. It was so boring, I went to sleep. However, I remember five practical suggestions: (1) Cut down on tea or coffee, even alcohol. (2) Don't eat a big meal late in the evening. It may make you drowse off right afterward, but it will prevent a good night's sleep. (3) Take a relaxing walk outdoors just before going to bed. (4) Take a warm bath, not a jazzy shower, before bed. (5) Have a warm drink (milk, herb tea; *not* regular tea, chocolate, or coffee) just before going to bed.

75/W: Beware! Never take sleeping pills because you're upset. They may mess up your reactions and make you act senile, and the first thing you know they'll send you to a nursing home, where you'll get angry and have to be medicated into lethargy, or you'll just withdraw and become a vegetable. So learn to endure sleeplessness. It's better than nonentity.

83/W: Deep breathing helps me when I cannot sleep, or when I am tired, or when I am nervous. I just breathe and breathe and, kerplunk, I'm asleep.

Arthritis

Here is a plague that creeps up on most of us with advancing years. Arthritis is a general term for inflammation of the joints, and we've got lots of joints. There are also many kinds of arthritis—osteoarthritis, rheumatoid arthritis, gout, bursitis, tendonitis, and others. The treatment for each is different, so don't accept a diagnosis of just plain arthritis.

A friend of one of my respondents said, "The first sign of old age is when you hear 'snap, crackle, pop' in the morning and it isn't your cereal."

There are no magic, easy cures for arthritis, even though thousands of dollars are spent each year on useless nostrums promoted by quacks. Again, respondents had several useful thoughts:

67/M: I am an arthritic of twelve years' standing, but without suffering or major inconvenience, thanks to a nearby YMCA, where I swim five days of the week early in the morning.

70/M: I know a pediatrician who was a passionate birder. But he got arthritis of the neck so badly he couldn't look up anymore. So, at 70, he adjusted. Now he's a passionate studier of algae, fungi, ferns, and mushrooms. He looks down, not up; it's O.K. with his neck. And now and then he finds something edible!

75/W: About arthritis, my advice is: Be a patient coper. Sure, things that used to fit, used to be openable, used to be tie-able, used to be take-apartable and put-togetherable, now aren't. So—cope! A little slower, a little weaker, yes, but patiently cope. Arthritis will never reach your head. There are no joints there.

80/M: I am very arthritic and find it difficult to get up again after I have been working in my garden on my hands and knees. I hoist myself up with the aid of a small metal step-stool and a spade firmly embedded in the soil. [*Note:* Another way for arthritics to enjoy gardening is "raised gardening" in containers on platforms or shelves.]

80/W: (Maggie Kuhn): My arthritis is getting worse. My right hand is a nuisance. I have difficulty cleaning my teeth. Isn't that ridiculous? I have to clean my teeth with my left hand, which is hard to get used to after eighty years with the right hand! But these fingers all go right instead of left. I'd be happier about them if they'd go left instead of right.

85/M: Get one of these "Comfortably Yours" catalogs. They've got knob-grabbers, high-shelf-reachers, joint-heaters, and arm-lengtheners, etc., etc. All you need is money, and not that much! Address: 52 W. Hunter Ave., Maywood, NJ 07607.

High Blood Pressure

High blood pressure—hypertension—is a "silent killer," usually without symptoms. But hypertension is certainly one disease that doctors have learned to control. It is a major health problem for many elders, and several respondents commented on the importance of its treatment.

67/M: Thank God for these pills! Without them, I might be dead or stroked out.

67/M: When I started taking pressure pills, I noticed that when I stood up suddenly I felt so dizzy that I almost blacked out and fell. I learned that this is quite common and a minor condition. All you have to do is to hold onto something, bend over to lower your head, and wait a few seconds. Then you're ready to go—normal. However, if you are troubled a lot by this situation, have your doctor review your medications.

68/M: Have your blood pressure checked at least four times a year. Take your medicine! If your medicine has bad side effects, keep working with your doctor till you get the problem fixed. [Good advice!]

78/M: I know that loving my dog keeps my blood pressure down.

85/W: Doctors disagree on whether I have high blood pressure. When my own doctor gives me the time to relax and talk for a while, my pressure is normal. A rushed doctor *causes* my pressure to go up.

Surgery

Too many doctors, I gather from my respondents, just don't believe in surgery for elders. But geriatricians and surgeons are coming to recognize that elders' ability to undergo and recover from surgery is much greater than had been thought a few years ago. And, of course, great improvements in procedures have helped. A 75-year-old M.D. respondent wrote, "Don't let a scalpel-and-clamp enthusiast go after your insides or your joints just for the adventure and the money, but keep your doctor's mind open to the possibilities that surgery may fix you up, no matter what your age. *However,* before you decide, get a couple of opinions, or more, until you are absolutely clear."

Incontinence

Incontinence means the inability to contain something; in the case of us elders, usually urine. Its opposite, a state devoutly to be desired, is "voluntary voiding," to use the medical jargon. Here's a story, from an 81-year-old woman, that is instructive about both incontinence and surgery:

> All my life I was an activist. My husband and I were Quakers, worked for peace and against racism, sexism, and agism. At age 78, after a minor operation, I returned home incontinent—an enormous embarrassment. I wouldn't wear those diapers, so I stopped going anywhere—even to Sunday meetings. This depression and withdrawal lasted two years. I went to three doctors and the first two said, "What do you expect at 78—incontinence is a part of growing old." The third doctor whisked me into the hospital for minor surgery, which ended the incontinence; I was free again to resume my old activism. When will doctors learn that we're treatable until we die?*

If you show signs of incontinence—and only your best friend will tell you, since leaking urine does smell—go to a urologist and see what can be done. Meanwhile, consider these words:

70/W: I can foresee that I may outlive my bladder valves, which will be a major inconvenience.

88/W: We just have to learn to excuse some people for their urinacious smell. There's more to a person than absence of smell. Get used to it. Tolerate it! And then, talk and enjoy each other. If simple odor drives you away, you're a bigot—with a very narrow, negative definition of what's really important: odorlessness.

There is a self-cure for incontinence that sometimes works, and it's worth a try. The muscles that hold urine in the bladder are called sphincter muscles. With age, they may weaken, but you can do an exercise that may restrengthen them. Simply contract the muscles that you use to stop the flow of urine; then relax the muscles again; then contract them again, and so forth. Squeeze hard about twenty times. Do this routine about three times a day. The exercise also helps strengthen the anal sphincter muscles that stop your bowel movements, since both sets of muscles contract at the same time.

Another tip: Urinate quite often so that there is less pressure on your sphincter muscles.

*Jane Porcino, *Growing Older, Getting Better*, p. 289.

Prostate Disorders

The prostate is a fine gland: It helps make semen, the muscles around it provide the power that ejaculates the semen, and it makes hormones. But with age it grows larger. This hypertrophy gradually slows down urination, may even block it. Some cases of prostate enlargement are benign; others involve cancer. Periodic prostate examination is important as a part of your annual physical checkup (or more often if your doctor so advises).

Surgery on prostates is now quite common: Twelve percent of men in their sixties have had it; 24 percent of those in their seventies; and 42 percent of those in their eighties. After surgery, about 80 percent of patients report that they still experience "high enjoyment of sex."*

In the old days, when necessary, the prostate was removed surgically through the abdominal wall. Modern surgeons now perform the operation through the urethra, so that it is not quite so serious. Often, it is only a matter of reducing the size of the gland so that urination can occur easily. If your doctor recommends surgery, here's a point to consider:

72/M: Doctors, I'm afraid, can be prissyish about sex. So be sure, if you need surgery, that your surgeon doesn't assume, because you're old, that you're nonsexual. Make him talk plainly about the probable sexual effects of the method he proposes to use. If the answer isn't satisfactory or he says, "What do you expect at your age?" go elsewhere. Surgery may very well not have to be radical.

Bones, Tissues, Women, and Estrogen

A number of women respondents complained about weak bones that break easily and cause them or their friends to fall and break more bones. This condition, osteoporosis, seems to affect women more severely than men. Bones become soft, weak, and breakable because the body is losing bone tissue faster than it is making new tissue.

One way to help prevent osteoporosis is to maintain a diet with plenty of calcium in it: foods like milk, cottage cheese, yogurt, and dark leafy greens. Another, even more important way to prevent both osteoporosis and tissue troubles is to take supplements of estrogen (a

*These figures from Edward M. Brecher et al., *Love, Sex, and Aging.*

hormone whose production declines at menopause). For many years, estrogen drugs were considered a sort of "cancer food," but this idea has now been found erroneous. Recently, a panel of experts at the National Institute of Health, and also the American College of Obstetricians and Gynecologists, have endorsed estrogen replacement therapy. It should not be undertaken without a careful medical examination and consultation, of course, but the arguments for it are compelling. They are stated well by Mary S. Calderone, M.D., one of my respondents, who, at age 81, wrote:

> Every health condition carries its own risk level. At present there is increasing medical recognition that the risk factor for taking estrogen is very significantly less than that for developing osteoporosis. Osteoporosis is a condition having a risk not only as regards pain due to loss of bone structure, but even more as regards general health, because of the twisting of the spine, distortion of the neck and shoulders with resulting compression of the chest cavity because of stooping posture ["widow's hump"], which means trouble with heart and/or lungs and/or circulation. There is also the risk factor associated with bone fractures from falls. When older women break hips or legs, they are bedridden for a long time. Some of them never get out of bed again at all. A considerable percentage of them die within six months from conditions associated with confinement to bed—pneumonia, blood pooling and clotting due to immobilization, local infections— whereas the risk of estrogen-associated cancer is much, much less. If a physician resists prescribing estrogen, a woman should seek a second and perhaps third opinion, preferably from gynecologists on the staff of a teaching hospital.

Another condition that can be alleviated with estrogen replacement is vaginal atrophy, in which the vagina feels "weak and dry," as one respondent put it. This condition may cause chronic discomfort and itching; treatment can be a blessed relief!

Alcohol

A great deal has been written about elders and alcohol, most of it negative. I think the negative side has been overemphasized. Of course, one must acknowledge that excessive drinking is bad for people of any age. Also, there's no doubt that when people are lonely and depressed, or in pain, they sometimes turn to alcohol for solace and become addicted. But it's interesting that, according to the latest statistics I can find, the instance of alcoholism in men between ages 21 and 39 is *twice* that in men 60 and older. And alcoholism among elderly women is not common at all.

67/M: I've been enjoying a drink before dinner for years. If I don't have one, no big problem. It's just a pleasant part of my daily routine, and my wife joins me. (We now share the cooking!) If I have to go to a hospital for some reason, I'm going to ask my doctor to prescribe some *spiritus frumenti*, or, just plain, "an ounce or two of gin or vodka" or "a glass of wine." He's ready, even though I know more Latin than he does. Why not go on enjoying a drink unless there's evidence it's doing some harm?

75/W: A nice drink before dinner I like. It enhances my day—it even relaxes my blood vessels.

76/W: I enjoy a drink. I think it's good for me. My doctor says it's O.K. But my advice to elders (or anybody) would be: If you can't do without it, drop it!—and get help from Alcoholics Anonymous if necessary.

86/M: If I hadn't enjoyed a glass of wine at dinner pretty regularly, my guess is I'd be dead by now. It's just a pleasant, restoring moderate habit.

When I visited some nursing homes before writing this book, I usually asked, "What is your policy about alcohol?" The answer was, with one rather moralistic exception, that it's the doctor's responsibility to decide, and that doctors generally recognize the wholesome social effects of a presupper "happy hour," with the amount of alcoholic beverage carefully prescribed. A glass or two of wine, a beer, or a shot of whiskey, gin, or vodka, fosters congenial conversation and relaxation. It reduces arguments, isolation, and miserable withdrawal.

However, there is one necessary warning. If, because of some disease or condition, you are prescribed a medicine, be sure that the medicine does not have adverse effects when combined in your system with alcohol. Specifically ask your doctor about this, because some doctors neglect to advise about it.

Another Drink: Water

One of the main problems some elders suffer from is dehydration—not enough water in their bodies. So, for your health, drink six to eight glasses of water and/or juice every day. If you need calcium, make some of it skim milk. A 68-year-old woman who follows this advice wrote, "Yes, eight glasses of water drive me to the bathroom quite often. So I've made the bathroom nice, and I like life there. Any fool can learn to enjoy a bathroom. And what a cheap way to keep healthy!"

A good way to close this chapter on health is with a bit of humor and practicality. One of these quotes is from a 96-year-old respondent, the other two from men who never answered my questionnaire but whose wise words are well worth borrowing:

80/M (John Quincy Adams, 1767–1845, sixth president of the United States, in answer to the question, "How are you?"): John Q. Adams is well. But the house in which he lives is becoming dilapidated. It is tottering upon its foundation. Time and the seasons have nearly destroyed it. Its roof is pretty well worn out. Its walls are much shattered and it trembles with every wind. I think John Q. Adams will have to move out of it soon. But he himself is well, quite well.

87/M (Charles Courtenay again): A secret of a long life is to be found in a *good disposition and character.* Nothing shakes the constitution of a man so destructively as a bad, morose and violent temper. It knocks a man to pieces as an earthquake brings the houses tumbling down. One bad fit of temper may inject poison in us which will shorten our days . . . while a placid, sweet and lovely temper acts as a wonderful preservative to the whole of our being.

96/W: Here's some advice:

1. As you get older you need more rest, not in a long stretch but frequently throughout the day when you tire. So rest.

2. Do not overeat.

3. Relax in mind and body.

4. Prayer helps people, so pray.

5. If you get upset, think of something pleasant.

6. Do something nice for someone.

7. Call up a friend if possible.

8. Get a mirror and smile. Making your mouth smile helps your mouth—and your expression.

Tips and Techniques

• (This from Charles A. Lewis, horticulturalist at Morton Arboretum, Lisle, Ill.): Grow things. Plants are nonthreatening and nondiscriminating. They respond not to the race, intellect, wealth, or physical capacity of the gardener, but to the care given them. Plants ease anxiety and tension, give a sense of tranquillity.

• While you're still healthy and can express yourself, work out a finger or toe code (yes, no, maybe, I love you, good-bye, and perhaps the alphabet) so that if you have a stroke and look gone and blank on the surface, you may still be able to communicate.

• Take long baths—to think, to refresh, to solve problems, to make transitions, and to be clean.

• Listen to your body. If it tells you that you are very tired, go to bed instead of pushing yourself to accomplish a given piece of work.

• Do fifty strong shoulder shrugs forward, then fifty backward; that is, rotate your shoulders so as to stretch the muscles. A 66-year-old woman reported, "It cured my arthritic neck. It's called shrugging away, not shrugging off!"

• If you have a disease or a problem, *name* it and don't be afraid to mention it to people. When you do, you'll find that other people will say, "Oh *I* have that, and . . ." or "My uncle would love to talk with you about *his* [whatever it is] . . ." This makes you less embarrassed and less ashamed of a sign of aging, and it does the same for others. It's a service; people are relieved to hear they're not alone in their troubles. A 67-year-old man wrote: "I've found this so with my hearing aid. I almost enjoy it, because of a new fellowship!"

• In serious medical matters, get a second opinion. You're the one who's in charge of your body.

- In driving long distances, if there are two drivers, be sure to change drivers every hour or 1¼ hours at most. If you have to drive by yourself, pull off to a rest area every 1½ hours and relax for half an hour. Before resuming, get out, and run or walk around the car five times.

- How to get out of the tub more easily: Turn over in the water, get on your knees, and *then* get up with aid of the handrail.

- If you have to use a walker after an operation, you may feel ashamed and belittled and helpless. Try saying right out, "Look how this thing works! I've got six legs." It changes embarrassment or pity or awkward silence into a good subject for talk. Don't block yourself in by silence or humiliation. Show off your new device.

- If you suffer from unusually severe pain, you want relief, and yet you may also wish to stay at home, not in the hospital. If other methods don't work, ask your doctor about a painkilling pump, an apparatus that injects painkiller into the bloodstream in regular doses programed by the doctor. It gives steady relief and uses almost a third less medication than "as-needed" shots. There is no anguish. You can live life with some equanimity.

Chapter 4
GETTING ALONG WITH DOCTORS AND NURSES

Though most of us say that we generally enjoy good health, we elders have more diseases and spend considerably more time with doctors and nurses and in hospitals and recovery places than younger people do. Considering how many ways there are for the complex business of medical treatment and care to go wrong, I was impressed by the admiring, positive, and grateful feelings that most elders have toward health-care professionals. But, as you will read, there is still plenty of room for improvement.

How We Are Treated

I asked: *What do you think of the way you have been treated by doctors?* Most respondents had high praise, not just for doctors but for nurses in particular. Here's a full and expressive statement written by one of my respondents, Emil Weiss, 85 years old. It is titled, "From a Hospital Bed":*

"Be right back," said the nurse, which usually means a good deal later. But who can blame her? The nurse, God bless her, has many charges under her care, and her patients' needs are constant and demanding. So she flits from one to the other. Flits is not quite the right word, because her work must be performed in an orderly, methodical manner.

They say that the physician is God's helper, and how should the nurse be characterized? I think the proper term should be, "The doctor's right hand." I would say the medical doctor is one of the world's noblest professions. God provides life, the doctor preserves it and, in many cases, restores it. The nurse, while she functions in the

*From *Voice*, publication of the Philadelphia Geriatric Center.

same field, in addition has the instinct and the urge to bestow a sort of mother's love upon her charges. And this emotion furnishes the sick with the comfort, the compassion, the solicitude that in many cases are more remedial than medicine.

When the nurse's bright, smiling face comes into view, your spirit soars, your confidence in your eventual recovery is improved, your belief in the goodness of Man, of humanity, is reinforced. All respect, all admiration, all gratitude due the doctor should be given him. But the nurse deserves all these accolades, with the addition of your deep felt love!

79/W: Thank God for doctors and experts. They are why most of us are alive and well.

87/M: Bless physicians and nurses. They have saved my life on many occasions. Besides being efficient in their professions, they are compassionate and humane.

If there was one major complaint, perhaps an inevitable one given the demands made on doctors and nurses, it was that they are in too much of a hurry. And there were several respondents who felt that doctors tend to regard themselves as infallible. Two individuals told me the joke about a man at the gate to heaven who notices a small fellow riding around madly on a bicycle, carrying a black bag.

"Who's that on the bicycle?" the man asked St. Peter.

"Oh," replied St. Peter, "that's God. He thinks he's a doctor."

So there were some criticisms, as one would expect:

72/M: A lot of the younger doctors are more interested in big bucks than in treating and curing people. But you still find real honest-to-God medical men. The trick is to spot the frauds, the big-buck boys, and move. A lot of people "don't want to hurt the doctor's feelings" by getting another diagnosis or another doctor. Very foolish.

73/M: I received the most arbitrary and insensitive treatment at the hands of the ophthalmologist who removed my eye. He was cold-blooded and uncaring—postponed for twenty-four hours the removal of a particularly uncomfortable bandage so that he could go to a football game.

75/W: I've been treated decently by doctors, considering that they often give me the creeps. I guess my trouble is that I don't approve of the doctor's technique (taught in medical schools?) of being mentally armed with a list of questions to which patients are supposed to conform in their answers. I'd prefer doctors to have training in the art of listening to subjective description and then in translating this into their own vocabulary if necessary.

80/W: I have seen elders, especially in nursing homes, treated like children when there was no need for it.

84/W: On my first visit to a fancy, top ophthalmologist—with sonar, fluorescence, etc., tests—he said, about my torn and displaced retina, "At your age it's too difficult and uncomfortable an operation. As you go out, make an appointment at the desk for a year from now." I passed the desk, got home, telephoned his office and said, "Schedule the operation." It worked. My retina is now O.K. I advise people to take initiative and get their troubles fixed.

Actions and Words That Elders Appreciate

I think it is useful to doctors and nurses to know the sorts of things that please patients and make them feel good. Thus, I asked these two questions: *What are two or three very nice things a doctor, nurse, or other professional did for or to you? What remarks addressed to you by doctors, etc., did you most appreciate?* Here's a representative group of replies:

68/M: I like a doctor who I know will tell me the truth and what the truth means for my future, and help me to know which part he'll help me to struggle with and cure and which part he'll help me to accept and live with. I want no false optimism or pessimism.

70/W: When one young medical attendant I know talks with a patient in a wheelchair, he always squats down to the physical level of his patient so they look directly *at* each other. The patient doesn't have to look up and feel inferior. (The attendant's wife says the knees of his pants wear out fast this way, but it's worth it!)

70/W: Our old country doctor is a humble yet capable, *listening* man. He is humorous and respectful—absolutely no "airs." He tells you immediately what is on his mind—no "mysterious secrets." He is quick to refer you to an expert if he judges it wise. He does not appear to regard you as "a case"—or a piece of meat.

70/W (a geriatric nurse): As I was about to be anesthetized prior to surgery, my surgeon, already gowned and masked, realized that I was scared and nervous. So he engaged me in conversation. He said, "I know you are a geriatric nurse-practitioner but I've never understood what they really did. Tell me a little about it." I felt good and began to explain, not even aware of the needle. Perhaps I got one or two sentences out. The next thing I knew, I awoke in the recovery room.

83/W: When I spent six weeks in a hospital with hyperparathyroidism and was not expected to live, my morning nurse nagged me back to life. She insisted that I eat when food tasted dreadful. She insisted that I get out of bed and walk. I have told her that she helped to save my life, but I still do not know how to thank her properly.

86/W: What I love is an *old* doctor. He doesn't go so mechanically by the book all the time.

87/W: When my sister Edith died, I felt the loss deeply and for a long time. Still do. Our excellent director of health service, a nurse-practitioner, was examining me about five or more years after Edith's death. She asked me how I was getting along. I burst into tears. She embraced me. It comforted me.

Personal remarks from doctors also mean a great deal to these patients—and can make all the difference to one's recovery. Doctors can give compliments . . . or simply words of inspiring encouragement:

69/M: A young doctor to whom I had recently been referred told me that in addition to looking younger than my years, I had a "young voice."

71/W: Introducing me to a young assistant, my doctor said, "Mrs. Cromley is a very young 68. You won't see her often."

74/W: My doctor said, "You help take away my fear of growing old because you seem to enjoy life."

78/W: "Keep on doing what you are doing—you couldn't be in better health for your age"—truly a morale builder.

79/M: "Keep fighting," she said. "All will end up well."

· **80/M:** When one time I recently stumbled and fell flat on my face on a concrete walk, getting pretty much banged up, a nurse said, "He is a *very* tough guy."

Objectionable Actions and Words

And then I asked: *What actions and words by professionals were objectionable?* Well over half of respondents had nothing to report. However, those who did report objectionable actions and words were quite specific and, I think, instructive.

65/W: The nurse said, "You've shrunk!" That really shocked me back, or pushed me forward, into age. Even though I am no longer 5'1¾" but 5', I resented this and didn't believe her! Later, I learned that my daughter is suddenly taller than me by more than she had previously been. And she hadn't grown!! Ye gads! I'm still bright enough to know that I've "shortened" (*not* shrunk) only 2.8 percent!

66/M: Nurses use the falsetto voice associated with infant care, indicating that they feel they are caring for a child.

70/W (Maggie Kuhn, a few years ago): The ultimate indignity is to be given a bedpan by a perfect stranger who calls you by your first name.

70/W: I very much dislike being called by my given name on first meeting, because I think it rude. Now I know it is the custom. I solve the problem for myself by calling the doctor by *his* first name. That usually gives him quite a shock.

71/W: I can't take care of my husband properly at home since his eye operation. But there's no reason why we cannot make love. Yet when I come to visit him, we must meet only in "public" areas. Even if we *could* be alone in his room, there's only a narrow hospital bed there. When I suggested to the home's director that he put at least a three-quarter bed in my husband's room, the man looked at me as if I were some sort of sexual monster. [*Note:* I'll deal with the insensitivity of some hospitals and nursing homes, and separation among elders, more completely in Chapters 8 and 9.]

71/W: I was told, "At your age we expect it to be malignant."

71/W: Several times I've been required to arrive at a doctor's or X-ray office at 8:00 A.M. without breakfast. Then I've been kept waiting an hour or more while young executives who arrived after me are taken "because they must get to their jobs." By the time I'm taken, I'm trembling and feel faint.

72/M: When I complained to a nurse once about the hideous cost of the room and my surgery, she said, with no sign of humor or a smile, "It's cheaper to die, Mr. Converse." I was tempted to.

72/M: I was horrified to hear a neurologist say in the presence of a stricken and speechless 80-year-old whose *hearing* was unimpaired, "The brain damage is extensive and irreparable . . . no chance for recovery." It was not intentional malice, just bone-headed. [*Note:* When something like this happens, I think it's best to work up the courage to speak to the doctor about the mistake. This should help teach the doctor to be more sensitive.]

73/W: What I hear mostly is, "Turn over!" "Get up!" "Sit down, dearie," "Wait a minute!" "This won't hurt," and "You can do it," when I can't. Now is that entertaining?

78/M: A nurse once left me on a bedpan and went to a Christmas party.

83/W: A young doctor was trying to remove water from my knee with a huge needle. Nothing happened, so he wiggled the needle. I screamed with pain. He scolded me for screaming.

83/W: The night nurse kept all the lights on, walked in and out, talked to people in the hall, and rustled papers all night long. [*Note:* She should have been told how disturbing her behavior was. She was probably unaware of it.]

84/W: When I say to someone who greets me, "Come close so I can *see* who you are," some yell as if I were deaf, too. Also, if I visit a new doctor and have one of my family sit in on the consultation, some surgeons talk, not to me, but to the one with me, as if the old were automatically witless. I prefer to visit M.D.'s alone (with my tape recorder). [*Note:* A tape recorder and/or notebook should be standard patient equipment.]

How Should We Elders Treat Professionals?

I've reported a considerable number of words and actions of doctors and nurses that we elders object to. But of course we must remember that these professionals are human. They're under stress; they have dozens of people to see, and each of us is only one. They work under enormous time pressure; often there are several crises that demand their attention at once; their jobs and the decisions they make are complex. Therefore, we must do our best to see things from their side of the fence. Often that is not easy, especially when we're sick, uncomfortable, and almost inevitably self-centered.

I asked, *What advice would you give elders about how they should treat health-care people?* The most frequent answer was essentially "Say thanks. Show appreciation. Remember that they're very busy, so be grateful."

65/W: Think of them as trained individuals, many of whom are overworked. They love praise and patients showing confidence in them. Patients should not be rude or scoff because the professional is younger.

68/W: Be ready to capitalize on the doctor's visit; be appreciative. Remember: You're bored, they're rushed; they have long hours, little reward, much pressure, competing urgencies, complex tasks that you cannot see the whole of, and they need outlets for *their* angers and frustrations.

70/W: Learn and use the names of professionals. Show pleasure in being given the care. A very old man whose care was difficult used to say each morning to his attendant, "Are *you* going to take care of me today? That's lovely!" And the care he got, though very difficult, was the best I ever saw given. Extend yourself to people.

74/M: Don't be a complainer, but try to elicit the medical facts in understandable form.

75/W: Don't talk too much. Just tell them what they need to know. Keep in mind that you are not their only patient.

76/M: Treat them with a sense of humor and a grain of salt.

78/W: Don't treat them as if they were gods. Ask questions and get answers. Tell the truth about your condition. Write everything down. Be courteous. Talk about costs and financial arrangements.

80/W: If you want to talk about death, let them know. You should be encouraged to do so. They may be scared of it, because of *you*. So you open the subject.

85/W: Before going to visit a doctor, outline the things you need to discuss. Otherwise you forget and feel annoyed. Make a copy for the doctor and one for yourself.

87/W: Treat them with courtesy and forbearance. Keep in mind that they, too, bleed. Many have family worries, get tired and irritable just as we do. Choose a good time to report a grievance or make a request.

87/M: Just remember—they are people too. Most of them respond to your interest in them as persons. My physician, three of whose children are M.D.'s, responded to my expression of humorous sympathy that *only three* were doctors with "Oh, but the fourth one learned to read and write!"

Words Medical People Should Be Cautious About

In the introduction to this book, I mentioned the shock to my feelings when my doctor told me, quite casually, that I had "degenerative arthritis" and then left for a vacation. My doctor knew perfectly well what it meant, and to him the term did not signify what it did to me: that I was on the brink of a descent into ruin. Reading the comments of my respondents has made me realize that there are some disturbing words doctors and nurses use—not disturbing to *them*, because they know the medical jargon and the exact medical meanings, but disturbing to those of us who hear the words as ordinary users of English and know only their common meaning. Following is a list of such words. After each one I've stated the meaning to the common citizen and then the meaning to doctors. If you hear doctors or nurses use these words when addressing you or an elder you know, stop them with a smile and say what the given word means to you.

Senile—*ordinary meaning:* old, infirm, weak, helpless, worn out, incompetent; *medical meaning:* associated with old age, usually applied to a specific condition, as in "senile macular degeneration," a condition of the retina of the eyes.

Degenerative—*ordinary meaning:* causing degeneration, a breaking-down into great weakness or ruin; associated with "degenerate," as in "She is a degenerate person," meaning inferior, debased, degraded, immoral; *medical meaning:* breaking down, getting worse, or weakening.

Dementia—*ordinary meaning:* insanity, inability to reason; associated with "demented"; *medical meaning:* loss or reduction in power of coherent thought.

Insidious—*ordinary meaning:* cunning, treacherous, evilly inevitable; *medical meaning:* steadily, gradually getting worse and probably unstoppable.

Terminal—*ordinary meaning:* inevitably ending in death, probably pretty soon, and nothing can be done about it (said of an illness like cancer); *medical meaning:* about the same as the ordinary meaning but without the overtones of utter, immediate hopelessness.

Hypochondriac—*ordinary meaning:* a person who is unreasonably concerned about illnesses that are only imaginary—an insulting term; *medical meaning:* a person who is persistently anxious about his or her health.

Chronic—*ordinary meaning* (related to disease): you've got it forever and nothing can be done about it; *medical meaning:* lingering, continuing over a long period (as opposed to "acute"), but, of course, chronic diseases can often be treated even if not cured.

Deteriorate—*ordinary meaning:* to fall to pieces, rot away; *medical meaning:* to get worse, to break down. [*Note:* Watch out for *deteriorative,* too.]

Incurable—*ordinary meaning:* impossible to cure; you're going to have it forever; *medical meaning:* having no known cure or remedy. [*Note:* Doctors, you can be truthful, but say it less baldly; for instance, "We don't know any cure for this, but we're working on it. Meanwhile, there are some things we can do. . . ."]

Other words to avoid whenever possible are *permanent* (except when followed by *wave*), *inevitable,* and *hopeless.* Also, there are a few innocent-, pleasant-sounding terms that most of us elders don't like; they may be well meant but come across as condescending or even insulting. Never address an elder as *dearie, good boy* (as in "Now be a good boy and . . ."), *young lady,* or *young man* (obviously insincere, and implies that oldness should be denied).

Examples of Kindness and Cruelty Toward Patients

I asked this question: *Have you seen any examples of unusual kindness on the part of professionals? Yes __ No __*. A little over half of my respondents didn't reply to this question (which shouldn't be taken to mean that nobody had treated them kindly). Of those who replied, only 14 percent specifically checked *No,* 86 percent checked *Yes,* and most gave examples. Here are a few:

66/W: I heard my doctor say to a colleague about another patient, "Just because she is 79, let's not give up on her. She is a vital, active lady, and shouldn't accept becoming an invalid." The colleague, who was a specialist in the problem under discussion, agreed to take her.

70/W: I have seen retired physicians/surgeons who keep track of former patients and friends in the hospital, calling upon them daily and resolving annoyances with an appropriate word here or there.

72/M: The exercise-therapy nurses who cared for my father-in-law were marvelous, dynamic young women who showed their concern and confidence and hope in every cheery way as they worked those wasted limbs tirelessly, joking, jollying and flirting with the hopelessly paralyzed man, giving everything they could to do the impossible.

74/M: A doctor or nurse just visiting and comforting people in terminal conditions, out of a spirit of love rather than as a professional.

78/W: Doctors and nurses taking time to explain, teach, and help confused and scared patients.

87/W: I was waiting in a New York hospital rehabilitation and physical med department to see the chief about my troublesome back. A young man in obvious pain was being wheeled in. The chief instantly knelt before the patient, took his hand, and asked him a question. The doctor's action was so immediate as to appear instinctive.

87/M: A nurse who cared for chronic patients used to take one of them each Sunday to her home, for a Sunday dinner and recreation. She used to call the sick under her care her "children," though she treated them like adults.

Then, on the other side of the fence, I asked, *Have you seen any examples of cruelty done by professionals to people over 65? Yes ___ No ___.* Twelve percent didn't reply or said something like "It depends on what you mean by cruelty." But 75 percent specifically checked *No;* only 13 percent checked *Yes.* However, a few examples of reported cruelty may be instructive:

71/W: A nurse didn't supervise an old lady trying to feed herself from a bed table. The soup and tea spilled into her lap. The nurse scolded the woman and punished her by removing the entire meal.

72/M: Leaving my mother-in-law on a litter in the corridor of the hospital and forgetting her.

75/M: I was left in the hall on a stretcher with nothing on but my number bracelet and a sheet. I called for my glasses. No response. A real dehumanizer!

75/W: At the hospital I visited a woman I'd been regularly visiting before she was committed. She was about 85, blind, and almost totally deaf. She had been a weaver—a charming, sassy old lady. I found her tied to her chair and with no stockings on because she was incontinent and the nurses were tired of changing her. She was bitterly cold. The nurses (whenever I visited) were all congregated in a glassed-in office where they could forget the sights, sounds, and smells in the ward.

78/W: Saying, "Nothing more can be done for you," and not letting you die with dignity but instead prolonging the pain and misery of an obviously terminal condition.

82/M: My father was having difficulty taking pills one time when in the hospital, and the nurse stuffed them in his mouth. I regret I didn't hit her.

84/W: A doctor very cruelly and very deliberately told a 90-year-old friend of mine he would have to amputate his leg. It turned out that amputation was not necessary.

86/W: I've had an aide kick my feet—I don't like to discuss these things.

87/W: A student nurse gave an elderly man the routine morning bath and change of linen but with no word or touch to show she felt for him. I think she could not do so. He was sweaty and smelly and she derived no satisfaction from making him clean and maybe a little more comfortable. This is given as an example of what I think of as cruelty, but by one apparently *unable* to behave otherwise. The faculty and the student later decided she would do better in another kind of work.

A Wise Doctor Speaks

One of my respondents, Dr. Herman Weisberg, age 70 when he wrote, exemplifies to me the kind of doctor who knows just how elders should be treated. Perhaps you might help your own doctors by showing them this statement with a comment like "What do you think of this? I think there are some good ideas here."

> As a physician, I deal with problems of the elderly every day. A few simple devices provide immeasurable comfort and peace of mind to many of the older patients I see.
>
> 1. Treat older people as physical and mental equals.
> 2. Pay attention to their complaints. You may not be able to solve their problems, but they get the feeling of belonging, not being abandoned.
> 3. Use physical touching, hand holding—a gentle pat on the cheek. Such gestures serve as a sign of affection and are appreciated. Many doctors treat elderly people as lepers and are reluctant even to shake hands.
> 4. Remember that all older people were once young and appreciate being reminded of their younger days. Listen to what they say and show interest, no matter how boring or repetitious it may be.
> 5. Jokingly discussing the marital lives of elderly people frequently brings bright lights to their eyes. A line I sometimes use is "I hear you were quite a gal in younger days. Let's get married!"—and it causes giggles, some pleasant embarrassment, but recalls pleasant memories for some.

Dr. Weisberg also criticizes the attitude of many health-care professionals about sexuality among elders. "Some nurses are prudes!"

he says, remembering when he was called at home by a distraught, alarmed nurse who said, "Mr. X and Mrs. Y are in bed together in her room fooling around. What shall I do?" Dr. Weisberg replied, "Shut the door."

Some Specific Suggestions for Professionals

I asked, *If you could give some advice to health-care people about dealing with elders, what would it be?* Here are some useful items. I quote them without age labels:

- Speak louder and more slowly to the hearing-impaired, or at normal levels but close to the ear. If possible, keep your face directly in front of the person while talking; they can get additional clues from watching your lips, even if they have not formally learned lip-reading.

- Offer more choices: "Would you like to put on your blue or pink sweater?" "Which chair would you rather sit in?"

- Remind low-vision patients of who you are when seeing them for the first time that day.

- Remind confused patients of the next step in their care before proceeding.

- Elders need careful, thorough explanations of what is going on—as does everyone—but perhaps their understanding is a bit slowed down. Directions may need to be repeated patiently several times when day-to-day memory is confused (even though intelligence is there).

- Do not discuss an older patient's problems with another worker in the patient's presence unless you make sure to include the patient in the conversation.

- Respect elders' opinions; encourage independence.

- Take a lead in showing warmth and concern. Seek out what is good. The elder yearns for affection.

- Most people are happier if they can relate to a physician whom they have known for some time, even if he is not the specialist calling the shots. If one can have a nurse whom one knows and likes, it is a very great help.

- Docs, don't believe everything our children say about us! They sickify us (probably out of love and concern)! Examine us objectively.

- Wear a uniform or a doctor badge. That way we know we're dealing with a trained expert.

- Too many doctors keep us well-informed in the hospital and then wave good-bye to us as we go out into the world. Give clear instructions to us or our family about post-hospital care.

- Patients should have a right to refuse treatment. So tell the patients their options; tell them your recommendation and explain it, more than once if need be; never deny them the truth—but be careful when and how you say it; and, whatever the patient chooses, give compassionate care.

Chapter 5

GETTING ALONG WITH SPOUSES, FAMILIES, AND FRIENDS

One of the myths about us elders is that we don't know many people, have difficulty getting along with those we do know, and are therefore lonely. Of course, some of us are terribly lonely, but so are some people in every age-group. According to what many of my respondents say, loneliness is indeed an especially severe problem when a tragedy hits us, like the disabling illness or death of a spouse, close family member, or intimate friend, but most of us recover, forge new links with people, and learn to enjoy life all over again, sometimes in new ways. Also, occasionally we experience the temporary loneliness caused by retirement, but most of us deal pretty well with that, as you shall read in Chapter 7. Nationwide, according to the 1981 NCOA study only 13 percent of people over 65 find loneliness to be a serious problem, even though 65 percent of those under 65 think we are lonely.

Losing and Finding Friends

A number of questions I asked gave elders a chance to state some convictions and suggestions about how we elders can get along with family and friends—perhaps even spouses—and some problems that get in the way.

66/W: We lose old friends. Making new friends in a new community is difficult in some ways. There are no common experiences like those the old friendships were built on. Therefore, to get along, we elders must reach out—not sit on our asses and expect the young to make all the moves.

68/W: I do think elders—especially those who live alone—tend to run on at the mouth sometimes. I have to watch myself in this regard. [*Note:* Two other elders put it more strongly: **73/W:** "The first screw that gets loose in a person's head is usually the one that holds the tongue"; and **75/W:** "Pause before going off half-cocked."]

70/M: With age, our really good friends move or die and we have to substitute many who were never more than good acquaintances, but we cultivate them so they become friends.

71/M: A small child helped me learn how to get along with people in a very specific way. I was playing a game with a grandson, and suddenly he said to me, "Grandad, you smell!" It was hard to take, but I thanked him, and now I make a greater effort to wash more and use powder. We should value children's candor and try not to be hurt.

71/W: I am torn between two needs: to be independent and self-reliant, and to be cared for and cherished. I try to balance my needs and the needs of others. It's not always easy, but then it never was.

71/W: Defer to, don't fight, your grown children's ideas about child-raising. Then share with amusement!

71/M: Be an *evoker*, not a *provoker*.

74/M: Other people wanted to talk about *their* problems and I wanted to talk about *my* problems, so it was a sort of contest, until I decided one day to listen. That way I even learn more about *my* problems.

75/W: The old saw about reaching one's anecdotage comes to mind. It *is* a temptation to tell anecdotes rather than to converse.

73/W: I yearn many times for someone physically and mentally attuned to me with whom I can talk freely and who will be nonjudgmental. So I have begun by taking cautious, considerate initiative. I physically touch a person, if it seems welcome. *I* am nonjudgmental. I try to tune in. I talk freely, but not at length. I listen. And I think I may find a comrade spirit. It's not exactly love. It's nonthreat congeniality.

76/W: I recognize that I have less to lose and so have more to give, and to give evenly and joyously and acceptably. People like that!

78/M: As I work on getting rid of my own biases and prejudices, I find everyone else more tolerant and agreeable.

82/M: I boast about my family and they about me; mutual admiration.

87/M (Charles Courtenay): Some [old people] appear to . . . make a habit of a spirit of ungraciousness. . . . [They] rather pride themselves on speaking their minds forcefully. But such are not among the world's favorites; nor can they expect to be. We all know many old people who wear their thorns outside and keep the points uncommonly sharp. Can we wonder that these ungracious rude old things live loveless lives, and die uncherished?

92/M: I'm so used to giving it's hard for me to learn to accept, but I've been amazed when I manage to accept with joy how much joy I seem to give!

And finally, the challenging words of a 78-year-old man. Not all of us elders will agree with him, but I think it would be good if we could manage to. He says: "Barring accidents, we shall all become old, and age often connotes sickness, psychic dependence, bother, and hurt feelings. To change these into serenity, freedom, and love, one simple, but often very difficult change of attitude is required: that we elders be convinced that we owe children and friends more than they owe us."

Tips for the Younger Generation

My respondents had a good deal to say about how they like to be treated. I report on much of this opinion later in the chapter, but here are five suggestions and statements for a start:

67/M: I admit I may be too talkative and dominating. My family, mainly my daughter, told me so. But my defense is that my children never let me know that they are listening. I like to be sure my message is received. So, children, at least say, "I understand" or "I hear you," even if you can't honestly say, "Thanks, I agree."

77/M: To have one's good points appreciated improves living relationships, but criticisms seldom do. Therefore, family and friends, if adjustments in living relationships must be urged, urge them in private with a relaxed time to receive the elder's point of view.

87/M (Charles Courtenay): We have most of us noticed how old people tend to presume on their old age, make a weapon of it, and use it as a battering-ram to force the door. My advice is to stop all this presumption. Old age has no right to set itself on any pedestal.

Our best opportunities are when we are "called in for consultation," like a doctor; or in some other voluntary way we are given a right of entry and a chance to do the good turn we are thirsting for. But that is not interference at all. Interference begins when we "poke our noses" into other people's concerns.

After all, you will not have us old people long on your hands. Every day we slip a little nearer to the end. A little attention now will save tons of regret by and by. Gorgeous tombstones and glowing inscriptions will not be of any earthly benefit to us. A few rays of kindly sunshine now will avail much more. [*Note:* So, youngers, *do* call us elders in when you think we might help. The least it can do is make us feel good. And it might actually be useful to you.]

87/M: Do what my daughter and her husband frequently do: Come and bring lunch.

94/W: Being dealt with as "a problem" by a younger person is inherently threatening to the inner security of an elderly person.

One of the greatest problems of getting along is how to relate to elders who have lost their ability to speak. A 46-year-old doctor told me about such a situation with his 71-year-old mother. She had had a brain hemorrhage and seemed completely "out of it." She could not utter a word. But when her son visited her, he would lean over her bed and give her a hug and a grunt of pleasure, and his mother would grunt back, grunt to grunt, pleasure to pleasure. It meant a lot to both of them. (By the way, later she had surgery, and when her son came to see her just after the operation, she looked at him from her bed, smiled joyously, and clearly exclaimed, "I'm speechless!")

The fact is that very often there is life *looking out* from beneath the lifeless surface of elders who appear to be total nonentities. This state was movingly expressed by the artist Vincent Van Gogh (1853–1890), who was an epileptic and often lived in loneliness and despair. In one of his letters he wrote, "One may have a blazing hearth in one's soul, and yet no one ever comes to sit by it. Passers-by see only a wisp of smoke rising from the chimney and continue on their way." Keep in mind that the blazing hearth, the feeling heart, the living mind and feelings may be there, invisible, inaudible. Say a word, tell a story, express love, sit awhile and touch.

Some Gains and Losses

It will help us elders get along better with each other and other people if we all understand what we see as the gains and losses of growing older. I asked, *What would you say have been the gains for you since you became an elder? What have been the losses?*

First, some gains. The most frequently cited gain was *grandchildren:*

69/M: Grandchildren are the finest invention since the wheel. Playing hide-and-seek with a 3-year-old who tells you where to hide, and "hides" by lying on the floor with eyes covered is more fun than a Phillies game.

70/W: The freedom to be with grandchildren as much, or as little, as one has the energy for—not steadily forever. A great thing about grandchildren is that they go home!

70/W and 73/M (joint answer): Seeing the world again through the eyes of our grandchildren in activities such as: planting of beans with a 2-year-old; playing games; watching grandchildren play with the same toys you built for your daughter—dollhouse, cradle; building toys for them—stove and sink, doll beds; exploring nature; devising ways to encourage small grandchildren to complete the climb up a mountain; having our 8-year-old demonstrate how to fry pancakes with initials on them.

The second most frequently cited gain was, in the words of an 86-year-old man, "knowing your children in new ways."

67/M: We used to enjoy our children, of course, but it's wonderful to have them on their own and free enough to say they enjoy *us*. One of my daughters even calls me "CSOE"—which means "constant source of entertainment," and another daughter's husband calls me "RMJ"—Renaissance Man Jenkins. It's fun, also, to be called up and asked a question about grammar or punctuation and have it nothing to do with homework. They come to dinner and joyously wash the dishes while they talk more stimulating talk than the dishes in childhood ever provoked.

68/W: I liked my four children as babies. I liked them as teenagers. But I must say I like them much better since they're older and have left home. Now I like them as people—as "old" friends with whom I've shared many years of experiences. We can, and do, choose to do things together which we enjoy. We have contact and companionship without daily responsibilities.

71/W: If no one needed my accumulated insights into children's feelings and needs, I'd feel rather cast up on the beach. I'm delighted and flattered that I'm still occasionally sought as a source of "wise old owl" perspective.

I had thought that there would be frequent mention of the effects of growing older on marriage, but there were few. Several elders quoted the Bess Truman truism, "I married Harry for better and for worse, but not for lunch," but most said they really didn't find it true of themselves. Here are a few opinions:

68/W: At last, we have *time* to be married and to enjoy each other!

75/M: Retirement hasn't put any strains on our marriage. My wife and I are so busy that there are long periods of time we don't see each other. When we get together, it feels as if we're courting.

77/W: Intimacy is fine, but so is arm's-lengthness, I think. If you let your hair down all the time together, things get kind of tangly (my husband's bald, but that doesn't stop the tangles). So he can fish (carpenter, mow, etc.), and I can cook, play bridge, etc. I say moderation in all things, including togetherness. Let there be some solitude and some different friends.

Another aspect of gain, a surprising one to me, was the feeling of emerging into a new independent identity, this reported only by women. Here's an example:

77/W: A few months after Elsworth [husband] died, I decided that I was Joanna Fiske Morton—no longer Mrs. Elsworth P. Morton. The fact that I decided to stop using his name in no way undercut all the years that I had used it, nor the loving partnership it implied. It meant that now I was ready to explore the world of Joanna, to experience a new freedom. I changed my name on all of the charge plates, the magazine subscriptions, the organizations to which we belonged or contributed. I find that I can get along very well with my own name and that I am now free from the need to lean on him and his family's reputation in the community. I have a new sense of my own worth.

And now, what about losses? By far the most frequently mentioned and deeply felt loss is that of the elder's spouse.

Age not revealed/W: For the first time in thirty-nine years, I awoke on July 31st and Beck wasn't here. No quiet voice said, "You had better get up, it's six-thirty." I didn't hear the hum of his electric razor, nor smell the manly scent of his aftershave. I drank my coffee alone at a table that now seemed large enough for a banquet. The morning news was on as usual—but there were no comments on the events thrown back and forth across the table. Our dog watched me pretend that things were the same, as she searched every room for Beckett. It was a long day, made to seem even longer as I realized that the rest of my life will be spent like this.

68/W: My husband of forty-two years died quite unexpectedly last year. Since then I have been living the life of a lonely recluse. It's not that our friends don't invite me, but I feel awkward, and even more alone with them. My children continue to ask me to dinner or the movies, but I feel it's out of a sense of duty and I don't want to be a burden to them. Who wants an old person around all the time? It was different when Philip was alive.

74/W (Jane McPhedran):

You Are Not Near

You are not near. I listen for your call,
But hope is drowned in silence. You have gone
Beyond my need. There's no one to forestall
My errors; or to hear them and absolve.
Now I am oldest, and account to none.

Your wet feet cannot track across the porch
In early darkness, or your key revolve
To open on the warmth and smell of baking.
No children to crowd about, no dog to fawn,
No thrill of greeting lets the supper scorch.
No need to be on time; I serve myself.
Independent, now, and on the shelf.

78/W: Since his death at the end of 1982, I am not only amputated but devoid of any joy in life. [*Note:* But I know from other answers this woman wrote that she has reached out and begun to live again.]

84/W: My husband's death was unexpected, sudden, and apparently painless to him. I rejoiced that he did not suffer a debilitating illness, which he would have hated. My marriage vastly enlarged the world in which I lived and that gave me strength to deal with his loss.

86/M: I have lost my companion of the past half century and more. The loss came relatively suddenly. Initially the effect was devastating. Subsequently, there is adjustment. Physical things remain. And in a strict sense we communicate again. It is a relationship that seems more realistic than I could have believed.

Many respondents, as one would expect, mentioned the loss of friends and the old neighbors they were used to and enjoyed:

71/W: I miss my original neighbors on Washington Lane, when we did a lot more visiting back and forth.

73/W: When my husband and I had to move from our large house, we left a wonderful tangle of friends. We like living where we do now, but that wonderful, security-giving, pleasure-giving (sometimes annoyance-giving) bunch of folks can never be replaced. [*Note:* And yet elder after elder reports that old friends are replaced by new people with new ways of life. So we should keep ourselves open, reach out, not mope or hide.]

73/M: There's an old saying, "All my friends have died or moved to Miami." Well, ours—some of them—have died. None of the others are in Miami, but they're not here. We're impoverished.

82/W: The obituary page gets read before the comics. *Then* the news!

These losses result in the need for affection and appreciation, and touching. Said a 77-year-old woman, "Whether married or not, we have a deep need for the touch of a hand, a hug, a special gleam in the eyes of recognition and acceptance." An 82-year-old woman put it differently: "I call it 'A Shoulder to Cry On,' and I believe that everybody, regardless of age, should have one. A shoulder to laugh on is also a pleasant convenience!"

We need to have such people, with such shoulders, "just available anytime" but not pushy. Wrote a 72-year-old woman: "I don't need advice; I need a listening ear—not about what I should *do*, but about how to deal with my *feelings.*"

Nice Things Our Families Do and Say

How do we elders like to be treated by our families? What kinds of things do we object to? We consider ourselves to be individual people, and we don't like it when we're considered a lower form of life. Several elders recognized an interesting problem, stated thus by a 70-year-old man: "The old can understand the young, for they have been young themselves, but how can the young understand the old? They have never been there." And a 65-year-old woman suggested a solution: "The young and middle-aged must try to put themselves in the position of older people; they must use their imaginations and think what it's like. That's the basis for consideration." How true! We must all remember that the young will become old, so when we talk about old age, we're talking about all of us. It's not just "the other guy"; it's everybody!

Another point made by some respondents concerns a major difficulty some families have that is really hard to get used to. It's a sort of *role reversal.* Children are used to being taken care of by their parents. Then, little by little, or even suddenly (like after an accident or illness), the children have to care for the parents. It's tough on the habits and egos of both. I think one of the most important things is to talk it over, and not just once. Says a 75-year-old woman: "Kids, be sure you're giving what's wanted, not infantilizing your parents." I must add: Elder parents, lovingly turn down what you don't need, and express gratitude as you accept what you do need. No matter what, role reversal is a hard adjustment to make. I'll say more about this in Chapter 8.

Now, let's get quite specific. I asked these two questions: *What are the nicest things members of your immediate family have done for you or to you since you turned 65? What remarks have been addressed to you (by family) in the past six months or so that you most appreciated?*

65/M: The children and their children came here a couple of weeks ago and cut our winter supply of firewood.

66/M: My brothers and sisters have made the effort to keep in touch more often. They use Ma Bell freely and also write more letters. We even make the effort to visit each other. It's better to get together in life than at funerals! I don't think I'll get much pleasure from my funeral.

66/W: My children show that they care—by actions and words. It makes me regret that I never told my own father what a wonderful sense of humor he had, or that I admired his accomplishments or that I loved that he cared.

69/M: Encouraging me to do things I might otherwise wonder if I could. My wife pushed me to undertake a grueling four-day trek with full pack over the Inca trail to Machu Picchu in Peru—over two passes of 14,000 and 12,500 feet—at age 68 because she knew I could do it and would love it. I could and I did.

69/M: Our children threw a party in honor of my sixty-fifth birthday, and, thereafter, the nicest thing they have done has been to continue to leave my wife and me to lead our own lives and not try to run them for us.

70/M: The nicest thing that my friends, family, relatives, acquaintances, associates in my profession have done is *not* to treat me as an old man. I've been able to continue to be reasonably active in my profession and social life and will continue to do so as long as I can.

70/M: Our son Mark and wife Jane gave us a Christmas present of dinner for four (the two of them and us) at the most expensive French restaurant in town—which on their meager income they could not afford. But they wanted a lavish treat, which was not a dinner but a memory. What a memory! A meal can be a spiritual experience!

70/W: When I turned 65, my daughter-in-law hosted a surprise luncheon. What touched me most were the gifts from the 7-year-old and the 11-year-old grandchildren. The 7-year-old had designed, cut, sewed, and filled a beanbag! The 11-year-old had written a very personal poem and had labored to write it in his best handwriting!

71/W: My children cooperated in giving me a seventieth-birthday party at the home of the youngest child. Cards made by grandchildren, a banner on the front porch, a toast "to a great lady" all combined to make me feel special.

72/M: Our son-in-law who lives in New York City has several times pushed me in my wheelchair several blocks to take me to the Metropolitan Opera.

73/M: It is especially pleasing when a grown son with his own family says, "Pop, I need your advice."

75/W: There are things I have a hard time getting done around the house. Well, one day my son called me and said, "Mom, I've got an idea. Let me be your 'hired boy' for a day—tomorrow? Give me a list, and I'll do all I can. For wages, I get the privilege of taking us out to dinner." It was great—and so useful.

86/M: A niece of my wife provided her with a scooter when her legs became about immobilized through arthritis of the knees.

Another gesture that some elders reported they appreciate is when families can arrange for them to spend specific periods of time at daycare centers for elders right in the community. It relieves the family of excessive responsibility, and it gives the elders a sense of independence and pleasure, and a change of scene. If the program is good, the centers are far from the "glorified playpens" that Maggie Kuhn has inveighed against, often with good cause. A couple of comments:

79/W: My days would be dull, very dull, if I didn't come to the center. My husband is dead and my friends are dead, or those that are left have moved out of the city. This center keeps me going. I've met a lot of fine people here.

86/W: My son and husband died last year. The loss was just too much to take. I became depressed. Then, through my daughter's initiative, I got this call inviting me to a luncheon a year ago, and here I am now, established three days a week at the Senior Citizens Center. I don't like the name, but I like what it's helped me to do for myself—and I'm bright and alive again. It rehabilitated me. It made me come out of myself.

Perhaps an added word about community centers will be useful. They can be small. One near my home is organized by a Presbyterian church. It's open from nine to five, Monday through Friday, and can take fifteen people at a cost of fifteen dollars a day (as of this writing), less for those who cannot afford the full fee. They provide a good midday meal, blood-pressure checks, an exercise program, the assistance of a nurse for health matters, plus a gamut of activities from bingo and balloon toss to current-events discussions, poetry sharing, arts and crafts. Transportation is provided for those whose families cannot bring the elders to the center. The center does not pretend to provide full nursing care. Its qualifications for membership are that the person be (1) over 60, (2) able to socialize, (3) noncombative, and (4) willing to try the program. Throughout the United States, there are thousands of such small family-relieving, elder-strengthening centers, organized by neighbors, community centers, the American Legion, and most often churches and synagogues. They may do their work in modest premises—church basements, converted corners of warehouses, and so forth.

So much for the sorts of actions that we elders appreciate. Now what about remarks we like? I regret to say that the most frequently reported comments were ones like the following. Of a 75-year-old man: "Mr. Castleberry, you don't look your age"; of an 80-year-old woman: "I can't believe you're 80. You don't look it or act it!" The implication here is, of course, that old is bad and young is good.

Here are some other appreciated remarks:

70/M (an M.D.): "You look great, Doc. You never seem to change. Don't quit!"

70/W: "You're terrific!"

71/W: Being greeted by my Presbyterian pastor: "Hello, beautiful person." Having family and friends who often say, "I love you." Having my granddaughter-in-law say, "Please teach me."

71/M: A letter from a daughter with unsolicited appreciation of how much she loves her parents and is grateful for what they have done for her. People may know they feel this way about each other, but it is gratifying to hear them *say* it.

71/M: My granddaughter was sitting quietly at the breakfast table Sunday morning while visiting us, and when asked why she did not start her breakfast, said, "I'm waiting for Granddad to read from the Bible the way he always does Sunday morning."

74/M: My daughter saying, "Dad, I appreciate you now more than ever," and another daughter saying, "I wish I had listened to you when I was a teenager."

75/W: I guess the sweetest music I've listened to and been flattered by has been when my young nieces or my sons or my friends have said, "I don't know *why* I'm telling you this—I never told anyone else. . . ." That is the supreme ego-booster.

78/M: A granddaughter, age 6, when asked what she wanted most for her birthday, said, "To go to the zoo with Granddaddy."

80/M: "You are a one-in-a-million person, and having you for a father will always be my rainbow."

84/W: Grandchild: "When I grow up, I want to be just like you." College sophomore: "I don't know what I'd do without your letters. They are so inspiring and they helped keep me from being a college dropout."

89/W: My grandson and his bride wrote, "Your kindness, generosity, humor, and intelligence are an inspiration to us. You set a very high standard for people of any age."

96/W: About a month ago, while I was visiting at my son's house, where his mother-in-law was staying, she was depressed. I talked to her and kissed her good night and told her to go to sleep and think of something nice. She said, "I'll think of you." I feel foolish to recount this, but I feel so happy.

Some Annoying Things Our Families Do and Say

Of course, there's the negative side of family life, although my respondents reported far fewer annoyances than nice words and deeds. I asked, *What are the worst and most annoying things members of your family have done for or to you since you turned 65?*

67/M: My children have a very strong wish that I should *never* grow old, and they refuse to accept the fact that I *might* not be as competent forever as they believe me to be.

67/W: The children shut me out of the problems in their lives. I suppose this is because they think that I wouldn't understand, or how could I possibly know how they feel since "things" were different when I was young.

70/W: My children cut me out of their lives when they were having hard times—*very* sad!! It felt like rejection.

71/M: Children who think primarily of grandparents as convenient baby-sitters.

75/W: They call my complaints imaginary instead of helping me deal with them. Don't deny my complaints. Help me get independent!

78/W: When my children and grandchildren *ignore* the obligation and courtesy of acknowledging gifts. They are so thoughtless, or so it seems to me.

83/W: When I came out of the hospital in 1983, my daughter became bossy and tried to tell me what to do about almost everything. But after I refused to be treated "like a senile old woman in a nursing home" (she is director of volunteers at a nursing home), she stopped completely. We are now good friends.

84/W: They come, have drinks and, after we talk our heads off, dinner. Then they leave without saying, "Any little thing I can do for you, Mother, before I go?" But I've taught them now. Children can take you for granted if you don't let them know, clearly, of your limitations and what you need.

86/M: Some younger members assume you'll *always* take the initiative in family occasions as in the past, when *they* should begin to lift the load, even return some entertainment and hospitality!

89/W: When I visit them, I can't hear their table conversation. They talk too low and fast. And they eat so fast, or I so slowly. I'm embarrassed to be still eating when they are all finished.

And then I asked this question: *What remarks addressed to you in the past six months did you least appreciate?*

65/W: "Oh, Mother, you don't remember." Of course my memory is bad, but I don't like being told about it. Why not just refresh my memory and let it go at that?

71/W: Don't tell me, "You can do it!" when I damned well can't. Instead, help me figure out what I need so that maybe I can learn to do it.

71/M: "You always . . . !"

72/M: Telling me, "Wake up!" during a meeting. This from my wife and others. I suppose I really in the long run appreciate this admonition, but I feel, "I'm old, but why rub it in?"

82/M: I don't like kowtowing remarks to me because of age.

One 73-year-old woman gave some sound advice on a common objectionable remark: "*Never* ask people to guess your age. It can force the person who is asked to give an insult or to tell a loving lie. If *you* are asked to guess, just say, 'I'm no good at guessing ages. How old *are* you?' That may get the conversation back on a more sound track."

About Family Relationships in General

It's impossible to divide a subject like family and intergenerational relationships into neat categories. Here are some words about these relationships that may help both generations please each other more, annoy each other less.

68/M: If we feel lonely, if we feel the need for tenderness, we could try sharing our feelings with our family, even our spouse, maybe especially our children. Remember, the chances are you don't *look* as if you needed tenderness. I remember once feeling tender and loving toward the world as I was leaving a restaurant. As I went around a corner and toward a hallway to pay the bill, I met a cold-looking, severe, rather repelling man who kept walking right toward me. I didn't like him; I resented his grim coldness. Then suddenly I realized I was walking toward the image of myself in a full-wall mirror. How different our outside looks from what our inside feels! So sometimes tell your family how your inside feels.

69/M: When I was young, my father, who seemed old to me, often preached to us about the lack of real values in the younger generation, referring to our "having fun" rather than concentrating on more serious matters. I thought of my father, then, as "ultraconservative." Now, my own children place me in somewhat the same category as I placed my father. I try to keep it in mind!

70/W: As my mother waited to die of cancer at 90½, and lay in her hospital bed, a mere skeleton, she said, "You shouldn't have spent all that money coming out to see me. But now that you're here, I want you to know what worries me greatly! I fear that the family might disintegrate once I'm gone. Don't think I haven't been aware that some of you don't call each other very often, let alone see each other." Perhaps her concern was the impetus. Now we all do keep in touch and do get together, just as though our mother were still alive.

70/M: While I was walking with my 6-year-old grandson Ben through the woods, he said, "Granddaddy, you're getting old. You're going to die. So let's make the most of it." (He also told me, when he saw I knew my way around, "You've been in the woods for seventy years.")

75/W: *Tell* what you need if you really need it and can't provide it. *Offer* what you can give, but don't shove it on anybody.

97/W: I try to let the love I feel for my family—and by now the whole world seems to be my family—show, by smile, by word, by touch. So, elders, push through your agedness and your pains and your weaknesses, and shout forth love.

Grandparenting

You have already read about how much grandchildren mean to grandparents. (It works the other way around, too.) In response to my questionnaire, Nancy Reagan sent me something she had written about the Foster Grandparent Program: "On the other side, you have the elderly, who are at a point in their lives where their children are grown and have left home. They have so much to give somebody, a great deal of love and a great deal of experience. Plus, they have those special traits that only come as one gets older. They are more patient, more tolerant, more aware of little changes in their grandchild. Children always sense this warmth and immediately respond to it."

Recently I came across a small book, *Grandparenting*, written by some eighth-graders at the Pembroke Hill School in Kansas City. They wrote some 147 "Dos and Don'ts of Grandparenting." Perhaps it will be useful to us elders, even those who have no grandchildren of our own but who like to be with young children, if I quote twenty-four of these commandments:*

- Be light-hearted. Leave all the bad or important things to the parents.

- Don't defend your grandchildren when they have done something wrong and parents are going to punish them.

- Don't give your grandchildren presents all the time so they just want to see you for the presents.

- Love your grandchild, and I'm sure he or she will love you back.

- Never ever show your grandchildren off to your friends. Children hate this.

- Don't interfere with parents' ideas of rearing the children.

- If you live *too* close to your grandkids, don't act like glue. If you live far away, visit only once or twice a year. [*Note:* I agree with the glue part of this, but I must report that most grandchildren I

* The entire set of commandments is available from Pembroke Hill School, 5121 St. Line Road, Kansas City, MO 64112. Send a check for $2.50.

know would love to have more than two visits a year from faraway grandparents, with a couple of cranky exceptions!]

- When your grandchildren are young and spend the night at your house, tell them stories. Never tell them horror stories, but they enjoy stories that are a little scary.

- Ask the parents of your grandchild if he would like what you're buying him.

- Don't make funny faces at a little kid; he may cry!!!

- If you're good at something, ask your grandchildren if they'd like to do that.

- Joke, relax, and have fun with them, as opposed to trying to make everything perfect.

- Take your grandchild to the zoo often when he or she is young, but not past the age of eleven.

- Do a lot of things the child suggests, but don't do too much or else he will feel superior.

- Grandparents should not try to organize their grandkid's life.

- Don't volunteer him or her for anything.

- Don't be strict and give orders or commands.

- Don't let your grandchildren tell you what to do; be nice, but be firm and don't get suckered in. Children are a lot smarter than you might think.

- Do tell stories about past experiences, but don't compare your experiences as a child with those of a child today.

- Don't make a big deal about his hair or about how tall he's gotten. Say it once, but don't drag it on. He may get embarrassed and a little mad.

- If you try to remember all the things that weren't supposed to be done when you were young but that were fun to do anyway, you can better understand your grandchild's actions.

- Let them lead the discussions.

- Help them out, especially when they are teenagers and quarrel with their parents a lot. [*Note:* But beware of meddling and taking sides. Perhaps the best approach is objective listening.]

• Don't ask your grandchildren broad questions like "How's school?" or "What's going on?"

Pets as Family

One of my respondents replied thus to my question *With whom do you live?*: "With a charming golden retriever bitch." This vividly makes the point that for many elders, pets are a major part of their satisfaction at home, for some almost their only satisfaction. Nursing homes and life-care communities should try to make arrangements for elders to have their own pets, even if it has to be in special quarters outside the main residence. Better, though, for residents who really want them, is live-in, live-with pets, with careful regulations to keep the pets from annoying others by noise or smell.

Here's a gamut of responses to the question *What do you have to say about pets and elders? Any advice?* You'll notice that there is no unanimous opinion on the subject.

65/W: Don't expect me to visit you if your dog greets me as an old friend with slurping kisses. Don't expect me to break bread with you if your cat uses your kitchen counters as a backyard fence. [*Note:* A good younger friend of mine said that adorers of pets develop a sort of tunnel vision. They see the pet but not the peripheral effects of the pet on others; they may lose human friends because of their animal friend.]

69/M: Children should not give their parents an English Setter puppy for a fortieth wedding anniversary present.

71/W: I've always had dogs and would be lonely without one. They're expensive, however, especially when sent to boarding kennels. Solitary elders really *need* physical contact with pets.

72/M: We have had the dogs, Friend and Sandy, and several cats, Fern, Susie, Dutchess, and Bambi. Have enjoyed all of them. Makes one realize that animals have "personalities" and that caring for them can help their looks and health. It helps give elders balance and sense of humor, and even a sense of service and usefulness.

72/M: The usual wisdom holds that pets are good company. I am sure they are for many lonely old folks. But I'm not lonely, and pets are a nuisance. They have to be warehoused when you travel, fed, petted, noticed, reassured, cleaned up after, etc. I'm trying to shed all but basic responsibilities. Ixnay. No advice for others, except to suggest they don't bring their pets with them when they visit, especially yappy dogs who want you to play with them.

72/W: Although some people don't like animals, for me my cat family of strays have been a joy.

73/M: Pets do wonders for the elderly living in nursing homes. [*Note:* In a couple of nursing homes I visited, there were two or three well-trained, friendly, nonlicking dogs who were kept by the management and allowed to go about freely on certain floors and in certain lounges. These dogs were very well received!]

80/W: For me pets are essential. It used to be dogs and horses. Now it is a cat and occasional litters of kittens. (Cat now fixed so no more litters.) Pets are great company and good therapy. They're worth the bother.

Chapter 6
RELATING TO NEIGHBORS AND THE COMMUNITY

Much of what I have reported about relating to doctors, nurses, spouses, families, and friends also applies to getting along well with neighbors and being happy and useful in the community. I asked some questions specifically relating to this broader area.

One question was *Some say that the years after 65 should be a period of planned withdrawal from the affairs of the world. Others say that elders should be active for change because they have little to lose. What are your views?*

Over 85 percent of my respondents reacted with strong no's to the idea of withdrawal. Several remarked, "Ridiculous!" or "Bunkum!" Two wrote, "Hogwash!"

Here are some other, more thorough comments:

68/W: We should keep active, not withdraw. But staying in there actively doesn't have to mean rush-rush, busy-busy, what did I achieve today? As we get older, many of us have more time to attend to our inner space. We may even become happy—in a new and better way. We shouldn't be afraid to enjoy happiness, and a form of enjoyment is spreading happiness to others.

68/M: I think that the years after 65 should be a period of planned reentry, enhanced activity, and unconstrained expression of opinion regarding affairs of the world. I find I am more confident, less cocky, and more readily available for practical public work.

71/W: I think that the idea of "planned withdrawal" after 65 is ridiculous—maybe after 85—or, well, 75! Most of the 65's I know are still in their prime.

101

71/W: I certainly feel that planned withdrawal from the affairs of the world could not lead to anything but severe depression, loneliness, bitterness, and self-centeredness, all of which would be detrimental to health and well-being. Life should be lived to the fullest.

73/M: Not withdrawal but exchange. One can exchange *earning* energy for *learning*-to-serve energy. Satisfactions may be much greater.

78/W: No! Do everything you can until the last minute. It's in the "giving up" that one loses, and so does everyone else!

86/M: I'd never prescribe a blanket withdrawal of any mortal just because he has climbed beyond age 65. I don't believe in defeatism, or in dying before you die!

87/M (Charles Courtenay): Maintain your hold on life's happenings in the world of religion, politics and even economics. Keeping up our interests keeps the tides flowing and preserves life's vivid colors and patterns. We must not slip back into the backwaters and muddy flats.

Some respondents, however, do approve of various kinds of withdrawal. Their views are presented more extensively in the next chapter, "Retirement: Before and After." However, let's start here with what, to me, is a delightful claim to the right to withdraw. In his book *Going Like Sixty*, Richard Armour explains how we elders can leave a party early without making dishonest excuses. He writes:

> About nine-fifty I look at my watch and then stand up, full of authority of age.
> "It's time for us old folks to go," I say. "We have to get our rest."
> There is complete understanding. No one objects. . . . There may be those who envy us and say to themselves, "If we only had a good excuse like that."

Some of my respondents and others write:

67/W: I'm a housewife and I am "cooked out." I'd like to give it up permanently, and I'm planning how to.

67/W: Planned withdrawal is for the birds unless you have some activity, or work, to withdraw *into*. I am a painter (of pictures) and have withdrawn somewhat into that since my heart attack—socializing is fatiguing, and I can do art at my own speed.

73/W: Yes, plan some withdrawal so you can do worthwhile things that you are especially good at. Don't just flap around trying to do a bit of everything. Ask: What's needed? (write it down); what am I good at? (write it down); what do I enjoy? (write it down). Compare the lists and plan some withdrawals in order to strengthen some stick-with-its or new entries.

81/W (Agatha Christie, 1891–1976, in 1971, at the end of a long, friendly letter to a young American writer who had requested an interview): I am now 81 years of age, and I feel, having just published my 81st book, that I am entitled to enjoy the happiness of a quiet life, though still continuing, I hope, to write books. . . . Sorry if I seem disobliging, but at 81 one does know one's own mind and avoids what one does not like."*

86/M: For myself, I *think* I want to continue to be a part of the world's business, but without much in the way of detailed responsibility. All that takes planning.

My own view is that we do need to plan for the physical necessity of a reduced pace and for choosing the wonderful possibilities of relaxed pleasures as we move among our friends and neighbors and in the community. At the same time, we gain the right, if you will, to say *no* to things we don't like to do.

Are We Glum or Dominating?

My experience with some elders, plus what I had read, led me to ask this rather weighted question: *People sometimes complain that elders are either glum, silent, and retiring; or too talkative and dominating. What is your view?*

Most respondents answered, in effect, "You can't generalize" or "You stay the way you were when you were younger—but maybe get more so." Here are other comments:

* Quoted in *The New Yorker*, 26 January 1976.

70/W: As I get older, I've been aware of a tendency to shy away from initiating social contacts with youngers for fear of rejection, since some youngers want no part of elders.

71/W: The glum ones may be depressed or in pain, or simply pouting because they're ignored. The talkative ones may be living alone and so stimulated by having an audience that they can't shut up. Spouses should remind each other to beware of repetitiveness and long tales about the past. [*Note:* So should good friends.]

73/W: I've learned to keep my thoughts to myself. It may make me seem a nonentity, but it is more peaceful this way. Since I am with much younger people in the office and with younger people in the family, I try not to say much of anything.

76/W (about a 73/W): We become more free. I have a friend, and it seems that the less she has to lose, the more she has to give. She used to be afraid and embarrassed, but now she just blurts, and since her soul is good (it used to be hidden, so we didn't know), her blurts are good.

78/M: I am shy but think it is well hidden by verbal skills. If not prodded, I might become very withdrawn. Until about 60 I was considered easy to get along with; now I am often considered grumpy and contrary.

However, some of us do tend to take over a bit, to dominate, as the writers of the following comments recognize, the first one in verse:

71/M: *We have a friend of the talkative type;*
When it's said the N'th time, it all becomes tripe.
She talks and she tells with no interplay.
A little of her goes a very long way!

71/M: I'm frequently too parenthetical. One thing leads to another, and lo! I am astray and talking on and on.

72/M: Younger people are entitled to flee elder bores like a plague. Let bores bore bores.

74/W: Because we live alone, we tend to be more talkative when we get out with other people. I know that I am often rather objectionable that way.

78/W: When an elder with a good memory gets on one track, it's a long track! We take over a conversation and never know it.

Perhaps the best suggestion from all this is *Let bores bore bores.* However, there are a number of other bits of advice that will help us elders and those with whom we converse:

69/M: (1) Offer opinions, but couch them in tentative terms, like "Do you think that . . . ?" Don't come off like Sir Oracle. (2) Mix as much as possible with the young. Listen to their ideas, absorb their enthusiasm. React ("Really?" "Ha!" "Well!") and take *in.*

70/W: I find small talk and large groups (like cocktail parties) very difficult. But my courage increases. It's hard to feel love and express it, but I am learning. What works for me now at a party is just to sit down, with a place beside me, and see what happens and who comes—instead of nervously circulating. What relaxation!

72/M: Cultivate your gardens. Mind your own business, not others'. Share your delights; stow your complaints.

72/M: The best device for getting along in the community is to shut one's big mouth and open one's ears.

72/M: When talking, keep it short. Don't try to explain everything; just make a few good points.

75/W: Since all life is a great show—and the actors all need an audience—we elders can serve that purpose very well.

87/M (Charles Courtenay): Raining advice on reluctant people is a poor business, a waste of good breath, and a laceration of the feelings. The virtue of reticence is that when we do open our mouths, ears will open too. So hold yourself in, old people, even if you are likely to burst in the process.

One of my favorite stories is about Dorothy Parker (1893–1967) at a party. She got stuck in a very long, dull conversation with an elderly woman who wouldn't stop her stream of gossip. At last, Dorothy Parker pointed far across the room to a man she saw stifling a tremendous yawn, and she said, "We'd better stop, dear; I think we're being overheard." (Dorothy Parker also knew how to put people in their places. When someone held a door open for her and said loudly, "Age before beauty," she swept through the door remarking equally loudly, "Pearls before swine.")

Hearing Difficulties

I did not specifically ask any questions about hearing loss, but several of my respondents described how loss of hearing is one problem that can make them seem "glum, silent, and retiring." Perhaps the essence of it is best stated by the 1981 White House Conference on Aging:

> Hearing impairment strikes at the very essence of being human—it hinders communication with other human beings. It restricts our ability to be productive and to engage in social intercourse. It reduces our constructive use of leisure time. Hearing loss often leads to poor self-image, to isolation and to despair.

Actually, with most people, high-tone hearing loss begins in the thirties, so it can be considered normal. But some 29 percent of people over 65 are "impaired" to the extent that they could well use help. Between ages 75 and 79, the figure rises to 75 percent.

65/W: Since it became apparent that my hearing is not keen, I've been ignored and found people talking around me, over me, and through me.

72/W: When I'm sitting with a group of normal people, I feel like I'm enclosed in glass—like I'm behind a store window, looking in.*

78/M: I don't mind asking a speaker to repeat, or admitting that I don't understand. I try to do it with a smile so that I won't be relegated into the ranks of the "old geezers."

80/M: I found that being hard of hearing made people automatically assume I was in my dotage—second childhood. And people don't dote on dotards. So, about five years ago, I got tested, found I was honestly deaf, and got a hearing aid. Now I'm back again with the competent, and I very much enjoy it.

Of course, we should not assume that all elders are hard of hearing and therefore shout at them, nor talk softly near them and about them,

*Jane Porcino, *Growing Older, Getting Better.*

thinking that they won't understand. Once, toward the end of his life, Winston Churchill (1874–1965) visited the House of Commons. Two aides who were behind him, helping get him to his seat, kept murmuring remarks to each other like, "He's really getting dotty" and "They say there's not much left upstairs." Churchill turned his head and commented, "Yes, and they say he's getting hard of hearing."

Following are some comments and advice about hearing suggested by respondents. The first is particularly important.

73/W: If you have the slightest doubt about whether you're getting deaf, don't sweat it out. Also, don't rush off to a hearing-aid dealer. Many of them are ready to sell you the wrong thing for your particular condition, just to make money (and it may or may not help you). Instead, go to an ear doctor [otologist], an M.D., and have a thorough ear exam. Then get a prescription for an aid if you need one and take that to the dealer. Afterward, check back with the doctor's office to be sure that the hearing aid works right. (The medical exam is covered by Medicare.)

65/M: Don't be embarrassed by your aid. It doesn't make you old. In fact, talk about it. Often, people are interested, and to talk about it is especially welcome to other aid-wearers who are too timid to do so. It's a real social service to open up the subject.

67/M: Cup a hand behind your ear, speak very clearly yourself, and smile. Also, ask, "What did you say?" or "I missed that key word." But smile; it's your problem.

73/W: If you need it, get a doorbell and a telephone bell equipped with a flashing light.

74/W: Ma Bell will sell you louder bells and telephone receivers that amplify the sounds you can't hear.

A good organization to know about is SHHH—Self Help for Hard of Hearing People. They can give people of any age advice on all sorts of hearing problems that seem insurmountable. (Their address is 7800 Wisconsin Avenue, Bethesda, MD 20814.)

I myself have had a hearing aid since age 66. It's a great help, especially at meetings. And I have found two happy surprises. The first is that I can tune out noise and talk I don't want to hear and thus

read and write with fewer distractions. (Thomas Edison said that if
he hadn't been deaf he'd never have been able to concentrate so well
on inventions.) The other, which I first noticed in the summer, is that
if I've been outdoors with my aid turned off, when I turn it on I am
suddenly aware in a glorious new way of the marvelous noises that
crickets make. To get back something you'd lost is almost better than
having had it all along.

Some Nice Things People Do

I asked this question: *What are some especially nice things that people
have done for you or to you since you turned 65?*

Many of the answers to this question I've reported on in Chapter
5, on families and friends, but here are some others, related more to
friends and neighbors. I include not only things done to and for elders,
but also things that elders report doing for others:

65/W: We were having a snack at a local outdoor café—two other
seniors and I. My friend noticed an elderly lady with a cane who was
moving about in a seemingly confused state. My friend asked her if
she needed help, and she said she was looking for a shady spot to rest.
My friend graciously cleared a place for her at our table, which was
under an umbrella, saw her seated comfortably and asked if he could
bring her a cup of coffee. We all felt good about the episode.

69/M: A very successful and busy architect friend who, tragically,
has multiple sclerosis, found out that I needed a wooden part to repair
a folding porch chair and produced the part himself in his own
woodworking shop within two days!

69/M: One of my wife's lady friends provided me with a very
well-chosen book to keep me absorbed during the difficult part of my
present hospital stay.

70/M: We took a three-week "people-hopping" trip to Florida
and back, staying sixteen of the twenty-one nights with friends and
relatives. It was a moving experience to be greeted so warmly every
night by people, some of whom we had not seen in twenty to thirty
years.

71/M: At the time of my back operation, neighbors showed up to
mow lawn, provide transportation, food, etc., without being asked. It
was very heart-warming.

74/W: Another friend and I have a regular phone schedule. We both live alone, so we call each other every Monday, Wednesday, and Friday just to say hello.

75/M: I get calls from neighbors, when they don't see me around for a while, to ask if anything is wrong.

75/W: Gardeners are the greatest, giving away flowers and produce to us nongardeners.

78/M: Young people offer me seats on public vehicles. I accept seats from young men but not from young women. I give my seats to old women, but not to old men unless they appear worse off than me.

83/W: After my return from the hospital last April, several friends cooked and brought food to us because I was unable to cook. We enjoyed it for a week!

85/W: Some useful services are: waking people up in the morning; taking people for walks; doing shopping for people who can't get out; giving depressed people ideas that take them out of themselves and get them involved with others.

86/M: A friend invited me by her house for a meal on Christmas Day, and allowed me to eat almost more than I could. (It happens that she is Anglo-Italian and I am Bantu-Congolian!)

87/M: One friend, a former colleague, now retired, allows me to phone him at 7:00 A.M. every day just to report that I am still alive and kicking. If he gets no call, he calls me to find out whether I have just forgotten (which I very infrequently do). If there were no response, he would investigate (he has a key). This arrangement was made on behalf of my children, who were worried about my being alone.

Community Services We Appreciate

I asked, *What special services do you receive from the neighborhood and community that you especially appreciate?*

65/W: Senior Centers open opportunities for growth. It took me a long time to acknowledge this fact and take advantage of whatever was of interest to me. I used to think I was too young to mix with *them*. But at this stage in my life, *they've* grown younger.

67/M: In our community, a Mrs. Beck has organized "Beck and Call." For ten dollars an hour, she will do anything that is needed, or, if she can't do it, will find someone who can and make the arrangements. She specializes in helping older people.

69/M: I used to sweat it out trying to cook for myself. Now I use Meals on Wheels. It prepares the main meal of the day for me and delivers it. The food is good, and often I can stretch it out to cover a second meal. The cost is reasonable; in fact, they'll provide meals for nothing to those who can't afford to pay. [*Note:* Meals on Wheels is probably listed in your phone book.]

69/W: A business that makes a profit but also provides a service is Mature Outlook clothes. They have Velcro instead of buttons; bigger, deeper armholes so that I can put clothes on myself; big pockets; and all in all a bit more room for the more of me there is. Cheers for what they call the "upscale maturity market"! I don't mind being upscale, and it isn't all that expensive. Ask your local AARP office for information.

71/W: Our municipal pool invites seniors to swim free every Tuesday, and once a month the town provides a buffet lunch. Birthdays and wedding anniversaries are recognized at our Sunday church service. People who admit they're over 80 or have been married a long time are warmly applauded.

73/M and 70/W: A group of seniors called the Get Together Club meets at our church once a month for a simple lunch and program (we have shown slides for them) and occasionally goes on day trips. Transportation is provided for those who can't drive. One woman acts as treasurer and program chairman and keeps the group together. She is 81 years old!

76/W: Any person who will offer rides regularly, or even on demand, who can be counted on and doesn't charge a mint, is a saint and gets my vote for heaven—eventually.

78/W: A great service is that fat, fat catalog of *Recordings for the Blind!* Bless forever those philanthropic souls who make possible more than fifty thousand cassettes of classics or scholarly works, all free for the borrowing, with four thousand more books added yearly, and free recording of any special volume one desires—even free mailing. Manna for a fasting mind! Simply insert the tape and press the appropriate button! A neighbor reads the catalog for me and helps me select what I want.

79/M: A small group of us "sustain" a half dozen widows with neighborly help. We call it "a life-line for live-aloners."

92/W: Some years ago people began offering to help me with the groceries, etc. I was not quite aware of any change in my powers, but the offers steadily increased and it was plain that something about me had changed. I was a little shocked, and then I spread joy by being a grateful receiver of wonderful services.

There were a number of respondents who commented on *how* help is given, and how important that is. Nobody objected to Senior Citizen discounts or free or reduced-fare passes on public transportation outside of rush hours. However, several asserted the importance of maintaining their own sense of dignity and worth.

71/W: I don't want welfare; I want money, just a reasonable amount, and the freedom to spend it as *I* judge best. If some young bureaucrat has to decide whether I qualify for it, I'd almost rather starve.

76/M: When I am out alone, I can't read bus and other signs. So I have to seek aid. After six months, I learned not to ask men in my own age-group. One gets a look from them which says, "I can see, why can't you?" Women are better, but many already have their own responsibilities that they have to take care of. My advice: Look for a man or woman who could be your grandchild.

Some Annoying Acts and So-called Services

I asked, *What are some bad or annoying things that have been done or said by friends and people in the community?* Even though the majority of respondents left the answer space blank, there was a splendid array of responses:

68/W: I don't like people to offer me a supporting hand when walking on rough terrain, *unless* I ask for it!

70/W: I object to people assuming that when one lives in a Life Care Community, one will always be available, with unscheduled time, and immensely grateful for an unexpected visit. No! I have things to do. So let's telephone first and see when a visit would be enjoyable.

71/M: At 78, my skinny father was treated with excessive care by a young slip of a girl conducting him up four flights to a Pratt and Whitney executive office. At each landing she stopped and inquired, "Do you need a breather?" On the third landing, he replied by picking her up and carrying her up the final flight.

72/W: Some people think that at this stage of the game you shouldn't be doing certain things (e.g., when the trashmen saw me loading the woodchips into the cart, they shouted out loud, "Get some young folks to do that!").

79/M: What annoys me are the casual acquaintances of years gone by who show up on your doorstep just before lunch or dinnertime with no previous warning.

84/W: When acquaintances come to "cheer me up" and spend the whole time pouring out their miseries. They use me as a therapist.

86/W: Because some of us old people are deaf (not me), the general public screams at all old people. It's very tiresome.

Mellowness or Militancy?

If you had to choose between mellowness and militancy for people over 65, which would you choose? Explain. Again, a good many respondents left this one blank, but I received some provocative answers from others:

67/F: What I favor is *moderation.* It's more mellow than militant and it admits that most problems have no simple, radical solution. One of my favorite quotes is from the *New York Time*'s Flora Lewis, who wrote, "I am a rock-ribbed, hard-nosed, knee-jerk, bleeding-heart moderate."

69/M: I think a strong vigorous conviction (militancy) can be put forward sensitively and nonabrasively (mellowly?). One can be mellow and still militant. Indeed, militancy is most effective when it is expressed in this way.

71/M: I favor mellowness. I feel that age should bring increased wisdom (of course, it does not necessarily do so) and wisdom should bring us greater perspective, which rounds the sharp edges of personality.

77/M: Mellowness within the family and circle of friends is best. Militancy can be saved for outside agents who are taking advantage of one, or putting one down on the basis of age.

79/M: Mellowness. It's easy action, smooth—no sweat—no tears—no blood-letting.

Perhaps the best example of militancy is that of Maggie Kuhn and her Gray Panthers. Although one of my respondents, a 73-year-old woman, wrote, "If in doubt, be outraged; that's Maggie," a considerable number were grateful for her endeavors.

69/M: Thank God for Maggie Kuhn. She's a great struggler for improvement and a better world, without agism. I'm afraid I'm glad to have her act for me; I just haven't got the energy. All I can do is keep up my Panther membership.

86/W: Hoorah for Maggie Kuhn!! I'm with you, Maggie, even though I do enjoy a rocker.*

William Masland, 77, one of my respondents, threw out a challenge to us elders and, I think, to people of any age. (Masland is a former Pan American Airways pilot.) What he writes is a good way to close this chapter:

* I strongly suggest that you join the Gray Panthers, no matter what your age. If you want to, send $12 or more to Gray Panthers, Suite 601, 311 South Juniper St., Philadelphia, PA 19107. This will bring you their bimonthly publication, *Gray Panther Network*. If you can't afford $12, send less; if you can afford more, send more. It's tax-deductible.

Save your belligerence for matters that matter; the world is full of them, both local and planetary. Are the local schools all that they could and should be? Is local politics above reproach? Do the local law courts dispense justice, or something else? Is there any possibility of reform in the local jails? Is the natural environment both healthy and attractive? Is it possible to help save this beautiful planet from self-destruction? The world was not finished in seven days, Genesis to the contrary notwithstanding. Go get busy and improve it!

Tips & Techniques

- If you are walking arm-in-arm with a blind person, or one with dim vision, walk a bit *ahead* of the person so that he or she knows what's coming. If you're a man, it's hard to get used to this, because you're used to the "you first" form of politeness. But stay just ahead, as advance eyes. Also, don't hesitate to say, "Three pretty high steps ahead"; "a rumple in the rug here"; etc.

- If you live alone, have a friend or neighbor alternate making dinners with you, maybe three times a week. This way you "cook for two." You eat better, you get some free time, and you enjoy some company without any big deal. (You can even try "cooking for three.")

- Here's a secret: Do something you've never done before! Take a walk at 5:00 A.M. Ride to the end of the bus line and wait to see what happens. Go to the country and drive, at every turn, right, left, right, left, and see where you are in exactly twenty-seven minutes, and note it carefully. Call up someone you know and haven't spoken to for twenty-five years.

- Never say, "Now, in the good old days . . ."

- Take on an unpopular cause. After all, without the worry about having to provide for children, and with less to lose, we elderly have more freedom than the younger people do to take on causes and fight for them.

- Improve two things every day, and keep a list! Examples: (1) picked up 25 pieces of litter, (2) wrote a note to a local community worker telling her what a good job she was doing.

- This is a good one if you don't like to drive at night but still want to attend meetings, plays, concerts, and the like. Buy four tickets in advance, instead of two, and invite some "owl-eyed" friends to dinner and the show. They'll love it!

- Build orphanages next to homes for the elderly. I like the picture of elders on rockers and little kids on their laps. Or maybe even off the rocker and playing games together—a special sharing of needs and love. (More and more communities are offering young/old activities programs.)

- A Device on Advice! Old people tend to give advice. Well, O.K., it's understandable. We've seen quite a lot and, damn it, we're somewhat wise. But advice? It's poison—unless. The *unless* is if it's asked for. Then, make it too brief rather than too long!

- Sit down beside somebody else—don't worry if they think you're a sap—and ask them, "I'm looking for some good ideas about life. Tell me one." Collect the results.

- (This from Olga Knopf, author of *Successful Aging,* at age 87): "When there's wind or sleet I stand on the curb until I can get some help. I'm not ashamed to say to a young person, 'Please, will you help me across the street?' It's no disgrace and everybody *will* help."

- With the help of a staff member, two Missouri state senators gathered useful information in the large-print, telephone-book-size *Gray Pages: A Guide to Programs and Services for Older Missourians,* and made it available to senior citizens. Here is part of their introductory message:

> Dear Friends,
> No one *likes* to ask for help. Independence and privacy are highly respected values, but, so are caring and helpfulness. It is important not to let the desire for privacy interfere with sharing problems with someone who cares and wants to help.
> Sometimes, it's easier to talk confidentially with a social service person than with a friend or relative. Such professionals are trained to know what services are available and to help you get what you need. The programs are there to be used! Many of us will need to turn to them for help at some point in our lives.
> The purpose of THE GRAY PAGES is to share information which can put older adults in touch with those services and programs designed to meet their particular needs.

The Gray Pages are signed by state senators Harriett Woods and Harry Wiggins. The book is forty pages long. It was printed by the Missouri State Senate, and copies were distributed free through libraries and senior centers. Southwestern Bell paid for fifteen thousand copies. Anyone wanting a copy may obtain one by sending $1.00 for cost and postage to Janet Becker, 8655 West Kingsbury, University City, MO 63124. The contents include such items as these:

> *Energy/Utilities* (heating aid; weatherization; special telephone arrangements); *Enrichment* (senior centers; discount cards; list of places that give discounts); *Education* (community colleges, free or low-cost; elder-hostels; YMCA, YWCA, JCCA [addresses and offerings]; volunteer activities; advocacy for elders; employment opportunities); *Health Care* (Medicare; Medicaid; health insurance; medical services ombudsman; nursing homes; cost of drugs; personal care); *Helpful Telephone Numbers of relevant agencies and services* (including Elderly Hotline); *Housing* (homesharing; condominiums; housing assistance agencies; minor home repairs; home security; needed services like grass-cutting and snow-shoveling); *Legal Services* (special elderly law unit; lawyers' reference service; complaint service; guardianship service); *Nutrition* (dining centers; Meals on Wheels; Hunger Hotline; food stamps; food distribution); *Safety* (letter-carrier alert; "I'm OK Program"; crime prevention; fire alert); *Social Security* (all the relevant information in plain language, plus where to call); *Taxes* (information about deductions available to the elderly; free tax assistance service); *Transportation* (directory of special services for elderly for whom regular public transportation is difficult).

Similar collections of service facilities have been made in other communities. If none is available for your town or neighborhood, enlist a group of volunteers and make one. Funds to cover expenses may be granted, upon request, by local banks, businesses, foundations, or community-minded charities.

• Read *Helping the Elderly,* by Eugene Litwak (Guilford Publications, 200 Park Avenue South, N.Y. 10003, 1985). Its subtitle is *The Complementary Roles of Informal Networks and Formal Systems.* The book provides a clear account of the principal types of community-service activities and programs available.

Chapter 7

RETIREMENT BEFORE AND AFTER

Ernest Hemingway (1889–1961) wrote, toward the end of his life, "Retirement is the most loathesome word in the English language." Maggie Kuhn said in 1974, at age 69, "When jobs are gone, selfhood is also threatened. . . . The longer and harder we work, the more likely we are to stay alive and well."

But not everybody feels that way. One of my respondents, a 67-year-old man, wrote: "I'm not retiring *out* of a job, I'm retiring *into* life"; and a 72-year-old man was even more positive: "I enjoy retirement! The bird of time is on the wing. I'm exploring all the questions and delights I never had time for when I worked: making new friends, seeing new things, testing new ideas, checking out new films and TV specials; loving my wife more than ever; keeping in touch with more of the world than ever before. And I'd never have done it unless I'd been required to retire."

Retirement and Social Security

The concept that age 65 is the proper age to retire became somewhat established by German chancellor Otto Von Bismarck. In 1889 he created the Old Age and Survivors Pension Act, which provided a form of social-security payment upon retirement at age 65. In those days 65 was really old; not many people lived that long. In the U.S.A. today, about 12 percent of the population live to age 65 or older, and by the year 2020 that figure may be as high as 20 percent. In 1935, when the U.S. Social Security System was enacted, benefits started at the Bismarckian age of 65. That, too, was the age when employers could require employees to retire. In 1974, the mandatory retirement age was raised to 70, but that number "65" still sticks in people's minds as the number when "old age" and retirement begin.

The law today (1986) provides full social-security benefits at age 65. One may choose to retire at age 62, but that means a 20 percent reduction in lifetime benefits. However, if you earn more than $7,320 per year (as of 1985), in wages, salaries, and fees (interest and dividends on savings and investments don't count), your social-security benefits are reduced by one dollar for every two dollars earned above that amount. After age 70, your earnings may total any amount and you still get full social-security benefits. The laws and figures are likely to change, so it's wise to ask your social-security office for the latest information.

Forced Retirement

According to the 1981 NCOA study, 90 percent of Americans oppose forced retirement at any age; a person should be able to work as long as he or she wants and is able to do a good job. In my questionnaire I asked, *Do you think employed people should be required to retire at a certain age?* 52 percent answered *No;* 33 percent answered *Yes;* 15 percent answered with various expressions of "It all depends." I think that the main reason for my lower percentage of those opposing a mandatory retirement age is that so many of the respondents seem to be surprised by the pleasures and freedoms of their own retired state. The following are a few comments from those favoring required retirement:

67/M: Most of the world is larded with unproductive paper-pushers, fatly secure. How to get them out of business and government? Require retirement at a definite age, and start counseling for it at least ten years in advance.

67/W: Knowing the cut-off date allows you to plan for it—financially and mentally.

72/M: Workers should be prepared for retirement day by positive reminders and training so that the "fatal" day will not be a shock. The young should not have to support the fumblers and drowsers. If a person is indispensable, or extremely able, he or she can be rehired one year at a time.

72/M: I favor mandatory retirement at 65 or thereabouts. The best argument for this rule is that it opens the situation up for younger people and new ideas. This is a powerful stimulant to the young to keep on plugging in the knowledge that eventually the torch will pass to them.

80/W: Retirement should be required, because most bosses won't have the character to winnow out the drones unless they are backed by a rule.

82/M: I approve of the age-70 retirement cap. I know that rigorous performance reviews are much more traumatic for an elder than is a dignified retirement at a certain age. This is the position of the U.S. Chamber of Commerce, and I completely agree with it.

Rather impressive arguments! Now read the other side, against forced retirement:

68/W: Forced retirement solely on the basis of age is irrational and cruel. It is agism, just as bad and immoral as discriminating on the basis of sex, religion, or race.

70/M: The greatest crime against humanity was to establish an arbitrary retirement age. In 1935, age 65 was considered ancient— hardly anyone, if he was lucky enough to be alive at that age, was capable of working, because vital statistics of that period showed that most people did not live long beyond age 65. But times have changed, and the longevity of Americans has increased by over ten years. Many of us at 65 are at the height of our professional achievement. Society should not lose the benefits of such dependable services.

70/W: If your career is of a kind in which you can continue to be productive at your own pace, carry on.

70/W: Retirement should be required solely on the basis of competency. Competency should be judged by whatever criteria have been established for everybody else in the employment group, not by age.

75/W (Louise Bates Ames, cofounder of the Gessel Institute of Child Development): Just as we [at the institute] believe that children should start school, and be promoted, on the basis of their behavior age, not their birthday age, I have always believed that people should retire or keep working on the basis of their behavior age, not their age in years.

78/W: Perhaps the most dramatic social and economic waste is to put people out to pasture at age 65 or 70. In that forced pasture is an awful lot of talent, expertise, and high motivation to do good work.

83/W: Chronological age does not describe ability. The government should establish tests, both mental and physical, by which employers could make a fair assessment of an elder's ability to continue in his or her job. These tests should be annual. No two people age in the same way.

83/M: If we require oldsters to become nonproductive and to rely mostly on social security, it's going to be economic hell when the main Baby Boom [just post–World War II] hits Golden Pond shortly after the year 2000. Let's get good work out of everyone who can do it, and pay them for it. That's the way to have a productive nation.

My feeling is that a fixed mandatory retirement age is indeed discrimination based solely on age—agism—and therefore wrong. At any age, we should be hired for a job or kept on a job because we are competent and do it well. If we become imcompetent or lose the energy and desire to do well, we should be discharged. Mandatory retirement removes from the workplace skills and experience that are much needed for our national productivity. In addition, it perpetuates negative stereotypes about elders, both among elders themselves and among younger people. It's bad for our self-esteem.

But there is an inevitable trade-off. If there's no fixed age for retirement, then the time will come for many elders when they have to be told, on the basis of careful evaluation of performance, that they are no longer doing a good job and must quit. This is tough to take, but you either take it or you accept a fixed date instead. I think the best way out is careful retirement counseling well in advance of the time a person will stop work. (I realize that advising people who are being forced to retire that they should make careful advance preparation for it is a little like what E. B. White said about asparagus: "To plant asparagus, dig a ditch three years ago.") Large companies and organizations should arrange for this counseling process, and many have already done so. If no such counseling is available to us, we should, on our own, do some hard, objective thinking about our retirement, perhaps discuss it with friends, family, colleagues, and especially spouse. Very often, the choice will be to retire voluntarily at a certain age. According to the NCOA 1981 study of retired people aged 65 and over, 62 percent had retired by choice, while 37 percent had been forced to retire. However, of that 37 percent, two-thirds were forced because of disability or ill health, only 20 percent because of a fixed retirement age. (The remaining 13 percent gave other reasons.)

The Effects of Retirement

I asked, *If you did retire, how did it, and does it, affect you?* As you might expect, there was a wide range of reactions, just as there is a wide variety of elders. Here are some typical comments:

67/W: I have spoken to very few retirees who would "go back." The standard comment seems to be "I wouldn't go back no matter what they offered me." The runner-up comment is a shake of the head and "I wouldn't want to take that pressure again." I agree. [A common response.]

68/W: The main difficulty for me is to organize my time so things "flow"—I have so many choices as to what I might do, whereas when I was teaching, the choices were made for me.

71/M: I have become a serious backyard farmer and raise most of our vegetables. It's satisfying. My own sweat and planning and watching and digging and gathering add to the flavor of what we eat at the table. It's great.

71/M: I believe I withdrew gracefully and fully. I did not hang around the old workplace. When I drop in once or twice a year, my old colleagues seem so very glad to see me that it is heart-warming. They say my retirement contrasts with that of some others who have resisted withdrawing and keep trying to hang on, creating awkwardness for themselves and others.

75/W: I feel at this stage of life we should be able to relax and enjoy more and have less problems and worries. My husband would like to keep marching to his usual vigorous life music. We have to keep working it out.

84/W: After his retirement, my husband and I had a lot of things to work out. We argued (but love was stronger than argument), we experimented, and things did work out. (He even cooks; I earn a bit of money assisting in a school.) We'll keep on working things out till we die. It makes life interesting.

A 70-year-old woman respondent, a retired nurse and teacher of nursing, divided the retirement process into phases. First is the *honeymoon phase:* no more alarm clock; all those wonderful discounts; the Golden Age programs. Second is the *disenchantment phase:* boredom; loneliness; no fellow workers; a lot of financial, housing, and marital bothers to deal with. Third is the *reorientation phase:* learning how to deal with the challenges and problems and to develop the pleasures; adjustment. And this leads to, fourth, the *stability phase,* a new, fulfilling way of life.

A 73-year-old woman, after emphasizing that retirement should be planned for, not dreaded, said that it is a sort of rite of passage: separation, feeling confused and marginal, and then getting reincorporated into a new form of maturity. She called it a second adolescence. It's easier to deal with than the first, classic adolescence, she said, because we have a life's experience to help us, but it can seem even more urgent because we have so much less time.

Retirement and Marriage

In his book *Why Survive?* Robert Butler speaks of the "unrelenting intimacy of retirement." And one of my respondents told me a story about an old man who every day at exactly three o'clock walked slowly down the street to a park bench and sat down. He said no word to anyone but always smiled pleasantly. After an hour, he arose and walked back up the street. Another man, having observed this routine for a couple of weeks, finally got up his nerve to ask the old gentleman about it. "Well, sir," said the bench sitter, "I've been married 53 years, 266 days, 4 hours, and [looking at his watch] 59 minutes to the same woman. I figure I deserve one hour a day of solitude." With that, he looked at his watch again, smiled, and said, "It's time to go." He got up and walked back up the street.

Some of the comments quoted earlier suggest the effects of retirement on marriage, but here are two more specific responses:

79/W: When we both had retired, fourteen and sixteen years ago, we feared it might be really hard, together all the time, even though we love each other, talk things over, laugh a lot together, and have plenty of friends, not to mention four children and seven grandchildren. Well, it hasn't been hard; it's been a delight. We're as busy, and separate, and together as ever—more so.

81/M: It was tough for about six months, as I remember. But then it was great. We loved living more of life together, and when my wife died three years ago, I was so grateful we'd had those "for better and for worse *and* for lunch" years together. I even wish there had been more lunch time.

The excellent book *Love, Sex, and Aging*, by Edward M. Brecher and the editors of Consumer Report Books, documents the replies to a long and detailed questionnaire from over four thousand subscribers to Consumer's Union, aged 50 to 93. Admittedly, this is a group with better-than-average education, income, and health, and also a self-selected group in that they *chose* to return the questionnaire, as did my much smaller group. Brecher et al. write: "We found that retirement is for many husbands and wives a mere bugaboo—distressing in anticipation but enjoyable after it occurs." Of *employed* husbands, 44 percent had positive feelings toward retirement, 42 percent mixed feelings, and 14 percent negative feelings. Among the *retired* husbands, 78 percent had positive feelings, 19 percent mixed, and only 2 percent negative. The story is about the same for wives: Of those *employed,* 38 percent had positive feelings, 49 percent mixed, and 14 percent negative, while among the *retired,* 75 percent were positive, 22 percent mixed, and 3 percent negative.*

So the evidence shows that the dread of retirement is seldom realized in actual experience, a piece of good news for those facing the prospect.

* Brecher et al., pp. 62–63.

Some Advice

I asked, *What advice about retirement do you have for others?* Here is a sampling of useful, wise, and sometimes striking replies:

66/M: If you can work it, slide into a part-time job—such as real estate, writing, child care, cooking, voluntary service, phone center to the housebound, block cleanup, photography, sitting in on classes, teaching.

66/W: Build up a cluster of daydreams that you are eager to fulfill when your time becomes free. An absorbing new interest can ease the separation pain from a well-loved job.

67/W: Anticipate retirement with pleasure, and enjoy it when it arrives. And don't overdo "keeping busy." Sprinkle some idleness into your activity.

70/M: If one could really know in advance what a joy retirement is, how fulfilling it is to have time and independence (assuming reasonable income), there would not be a great hassle about dropping out of the work force. Good preparation (five to seven years ahead) for retirement is the key.

70/M: Don't let it scare you. The first six months may be a bit empty, but before long it's hard to understand where the time goes.

73/W: Decide what to answer when people ask, "What do you do?" Don't answer, "Nothing." If you're brave enough, say, "I'm retired from my regular job. What I *do* is . . ." After a while, it requires less bravery, and it encourages other older souls who are scared to say, "I've retired."

73/W: If you work beyond retirement age, ask, "Am I doing a good job?" (of yourself, your boss, your colleagues)—and *listen* to the answer. Also, recognize that the answer probably won't be frank—so *listen* and probe. Don't hang on!

74/M: It is far better to move out of the mainstream gracefully than it is to be forced out. Everyone is much happier.

75/W: Learn how to refuse jobs sweetly.

77/W: After 65 or 70, leave general administration to younger colleagues, but continue to apply your talents to more concrete goals. Don't move away from your familiar haunts and your friends unless you have to. Try to find something to give.

77/M: At some time between 60 and 70, it is wise to encourage younger people to take over the roles requiring active leadership, and for you to fall into a supporting role or roles. One feels that he still has a debt to society and is better satisfied if he can continue to contribute and, if possible, continue to earn a living or part of it. One's help in fund-raising seems to be desired longer than in most other activities.

78/W: Expand your horizons. Develop new and/or different interests. Invest in change.

86/M (a retired minister): Elders who have no responsibilities are generally unhappier. I have had to minister to many elders and found that those who felt they were needed and wanted were much more content than those who had no personal responsibilities.

Do Elders Deserve a Rest?

As one of my questions on retirement, I asked, *Do you feel at your age you "deserve a rest"? How about others?* A few people answered *Yes:*

73/M: I've worked hard, I've produced a lot, and I'm resting and having a ball, and so is my wife.

74/W: I deserve a rest from cooking and housekeeping, but I can't seem to get one. My husband can't boil water without burning it (I guess I'm not a very good teacher) and he doesn't see dirt. I deserve a rest but see no way to get it. Men: Learn housework! [*Note:* Many women expressed frustration, even anger, that husbands refuse to cook and clean. It should be laid strongly on us men to share these jobs, unless we are sure, after discussion, that our wives would rather that we stay out of their realm. And for heaven's sake, don't be one of those men who regards even a small chore as a great "favor" to his wife.]

82/W: Indeed we all deserve a rest—rest and think and sleep and enjoy!

Much more frequent, however, were replies not at all enthusiastic about rest:

69/M: I don't "deserve" a rest. And the amount of rest I seek is limited to what I can comfortably afford without getting bored.

70/W: You get all the rest you need in the grave. While alive, keep busy.

71/W: That depends on the definition of "rest." I think I deserve enough leisure to play the organ, garden, cook, and travel, with less heavy housework. But if "rest" means just sittin' and rockin', that's the road to the cemetery.

71/M: To a limited extent, this does enter my thinking. I think more of "deserving the opportunity of doing what interests me"— very selfish but very satisfying.

72/M: Those who believe they deserve a rest often die before they get comfortable.

80/M: I need more rest than I needed only ten years ago, but I do *not* need as much rest as I now get. Rest = rust = rot = rubble!

84/W: Change "There's no rest for the weary" to "With nothing but rest you become weary."

Volunteering

One of the forces that has made American society move and improve since its very beginning has been the volunteer spirit translated into action. One advantage to retirement is that it frees elders to volunteer. I asked, *Do you engage in volunteer work? Yes ___ No ___.* Seventy percent answered *Yes,* 30 percent *No.** And why do so many of my wise respondents volunteer?

65/W: Volunteer by all means. You'll be helping yourself as well as others. My beef with volunteering is that too often the irksome,

---

* This compares with only 33 percent of the NCOA 1981 sample who say they volunteer or would like to. Twenty-one percent of those over 80 volunteer.

petty, meaningless jobs are saved for you, and volunteering becomes a bore. I've done volunteering by using my clerical skills, and continue to do so.

69/M: I can only speak for myself. I keep busy. I am happier with work to do, so I volunteer. *I like to work.* The elder men I see paddling along after their wives in the supermarket depress me. When it works out best, I go to the supermarket myself while my wife does her thing.

70/W (Tish Somers, in *Gray Panther Network*): I am a full-time volunteer and have been for most of the past twenty years. I feel lucky to have that option, which is mine by choice. A volunteer can create her/his own job, take vacations at will, choose priorities, work on causes of deep concern, and select tasks for self-actualization. My volunteer occupation has a job title, *freelance agitator,* a joyous vocation. I invite my peers to enter my profession when they "retire." I guarantee no shortage of openings.

72/M: If you feel capable of doing volunteer work, you should seriously consider it, because of the tremendous need for good volunteers and the joy of fulfillment you get. We need volunteering. The government and organizations can't do everything.

78/M: Doing some volunteer work is a necessary ingredient in our form of society and government. Everyone should do some as a basic social responsibility. The degree of burden or joy is an adjustable personal matter.

78/W: Know that there are many roles for you. Experiment! People need you; you have needs. Put them together.

81/M: For me, work is essential. It is the skeleton of my life—it gives form and discipline to it. Leisure is only viable against a background of work. Against a background of idleness, it disappears. So I volunteer, and I'm needed.

83/W: Sure I volunteer, but for me it has to be something for which I have a special skill. I refuse to stuff envelopes, except in moderation.

88/W: The greatest satisfaction of old age is, if possible physically, to engage in outside activities. As I have been so involved in our museum for the last twelve years, I have realized that people of all ages become my friends. All our hostesses are volunteers, and most of them are young people, and they are so faithful and willing to help. We have about forty volunteers who act as hostesses, tend our lovely herb garden, help us refinish furniture given to us. Their enthusiasm makes me feel younger. We look up the history of the old houses and put markers on them. We have house tours and very interesting meetings. I am useful, and I love it.

Following are specific examples of what sorts of volunteer work these elders have chosen:

69/W: I've done several research projects where I have had to learn subjects from scratch and also to lecture on them. (1) How tapestries are made and used—lectured to other guides. (2) Sculpture at the art museum. (3) Victorian gardens—found authentic plant materials and supervised the planting of two styles of gardens: 1840–50 and 1860–70. (4) I researched, bought, and executed an 1860s kitchen for an historic mansion. I love to continue to learn. It never stops.

69/W: I always wanted to be an artist. So I decided to illustrate my husband's book on tropical fish. I became expert. The book was published. And I took up sculpture. I found people wanted my pieces, and so did I. We love sharing our pleasure in what I sculpt.

70/M: The synagogue to which I belong has for the past eight years put on a Jewish Festival each Memorial Day weekend. It involves about two hundred of the congregants. They prepare huge quantities of food; set up exhibits, booths of various kinds for the sale of all sorts of merchandise; organize an art show, planned entertainments, carnival activities, flower and plant shows, etc. Many of the volunteers are retirees who are delighted to be involved with a project requiring extensive planning and prolonged effort.

70/W: I help out at the nuclear-freeze office. I'm engaged in voter registration. I helped organize our block around a specific issue. This week I shall decide which of several volunteer options to tackle: a radio station crisis intervention center, reading to the blind, taking university-museum artifacts to inner-city schools, or working with immigrants at Nationalities Institute.

75/M: Becoming an amateur archaeologist.

77/M: My friend devotes long hours to working for the Salvation Army, for which she received a statewide award.

78/W: My volunteering is really a free private enterprise, with no profit but joy. It's quite specific. Whenever I read about or see somebody in the neighborhood or in a community organization who's doing an unusually fine job, I write them a letter and tell them what a great job they are doing, how much I and others appreciate it, and how much better it makes the world to live in. You should see the joyous, almost starved-for-praise answers I get. That's my volunteer job: appreciation. (Try it. It only costs a few stamps.)

79/M: Have served the local SCORE organization for fifteen years and have handled 101 cases to date. SCORE is the acronym for Service Corps of Retired Executives, a volunteer organization sponsored by the federal Small Business Administration. Our chapter has handled 1,708 cases in sixteen years.

84/W: My talents go to those who come asking to talk. You can call that volunteer work. I call it part of my profession. My lifelong job has been "giving love." I do it when I'm not withdrawn in pain and the depression that comes with pain.

86/M: A group of men in our life-care community distribute mail to patients in the medical facility. It gives us and the recipients welcome contact with many.

87/W: I can do little for groups, but I do a lot for individuals: grow flowers for friends and sick residents; get mail for housebound neighbors; take stains out of dresses for a friend with bad sight; sometimes shop for others; do mending for one with impaired vision. This week I prepared chicken for a neighbor who'd recently had a cataract operation.

88/W: Volunteering is a joy—in the Retired Senior Volunteer Program (RSVP). I spent the first winter of my forced retirement teaching a French lady who was blind how to knit! [*Note:* RSVP places volunteers in day-care centers, nursing homes, courts, libraries, schools, and many other organizations. RSVP offices are listed in the phone book.]

However, we elders aren't always ready just to leap in wherever anybody feels they need some hard work done for free. Here's some advice for those who volunteer and who use volunteers:

65/W: Volunteer as a job—faithfully and in good spirit—not for self-aggrandizement, not in a haphazard way.

65/W: I volunteered my services to a hospital and was put to work typing a revised edition of the hospital's pharmaceutical manual. It suddenly dawned on me that this hospital was a profit-making venture and that what I was doing was in no way beneficial to the patients—though it saved the organization much money in salaries. I now restrict my volunteering to nonprofit agencies.

71/M: As retirees, we should not automatically become available to fill the gaps in the social structure. Whatever we do should be freely volunteered and not required. Volunteer work should be an offering, not an obligation.

71/W: If you volunteer for a job, be sure that you treat that commitment as a professional. Be reliable and effective. It is a job, whether you get paid or not. If you use volunteers, be sure that their time and work is effectively managed and really needed.

74/M: If you can't do volunteer work cheerfully, then don't do it.

75/W: Don't go on and on about your volunteer work. It really can bore people. Also, it shames those not similarly engaged into feeling guilty.

77/M: If there are paid staff and volunteer workers in an organization, the latter usually must work under the direction of the former. This often represents a reversal of habitual roles and it takes a real effort on the part of the volunteers to keep from trying to take charge.

79/W: Volunteering needs to be specific and have a useful goal. Volunteering needs to be learned and then be offered as earnestly as a paid service. Satisfaction or joy comes from a job well done. To expect "gratitude" is an outmoded approach.

72/W: I got fired from a volunteer job at which I was a real expert (finding and arranging furniture for community organizations) because I couldn't stand the low standards of the young. Well, I learned my lesson. Now I keep my standards but promote them by example, not by complaint. I try to teach—when asked.

74/M: One trouble with good volunteers is that they get too busy and overworked. Don't let that happen to you. Learn to *declare a* *vacation,* when you vow to do nothing except laze and enjoy for a specific period—an hour, a day, a week. You can even, if you're terribly rushed, *declare a moment,* when you lie down on the grass and look at the sky, watch a bird for five minutes, or have a drink and watch *one* TV program.

79/W: Anyone who finds volunteer work a burden should cease, desist, and move on. Everyone has an interest if he or she takes time to think about it. Volunteer as an outlet for that interest and then it will be a joy—not a burden. I love plants, flowers, growing things—I volunteer at an arboretum. I love collectibles, someone else's discards, good secondhand clothes, shoes, books. So I also work in a thrift shop.

80/W: I used to volunteer a lot, but now I have resigned from almost all committees. I've seen too many people who clung too long, making the committees merely a means of social activity. Let younger people take our places unless we're sure we're very useful. If we're not sure, we should ask and expect an honest reply.

In my reading for this book, I came across reports of many useful volunteer projects in which elders were deeply involved. Here are a few:

Teaching: square dancing, pottery, painting, reading, foreign languages, English to new Americans, woodworking, greenhouse and flower care.

Assisting: in grade school classrooms, with tax questions, bookkeeping, checkbook keeping, shopping for food and other goods.

Work in nonprofit organizations: receptionist, fund-raising, clerical work, cleaning up litter, making meals, library work (shelving, checking out books, answering questions, etc.), publicity, glaucoma screening, making recordings for the blind, building outdoor trails for the blind and handicapped, repairing wheelchairs.

Organizing: Shakespeare societies, drama clubs and play-reading groups, choruses, great-books groups, various political action groups (like the League of Women Voters and the Women's International League for Peace and Freedom), Project Green Thumb (for helping to keep parks in good shape), setting up interview groups to talk with elders in institutions and at home to determine their needs; baby-sitting or infant-care services for working mothers who need them but can't afford commercial rates.

Given all these opportunities for service and activity available to people who are able to take advantage of them, you may wonder whether elders would like to have even more work. I asked, *If you were free to choose, would you like to have more work (paid or unpaid) to do than you now have?* Seventy-three percent answered *No* (they don't want more work); only 13 percent answered *Yes* (and most of them said, in effect, "Only if I were well paid, if the work could be done when I wanted to do it, and if it were interesting and didn't involve a lot of pressure"). Seventeen percent answered *It all depends* (and what it depended on, in most cases, were the same considerations as in the parentheses above).

Perhaps a good note on which to end this chapter is the comment of a 71-year-old man: "Many elders have a tendency to make volunteer work a form of martyrdom. Well, it's mighty hard to work and live with martyrs, so I'd say that if work is not given freely and with some sense of joy and satisfaction, it's probably not worth giving."

Chapter 8
WHERE TO LIVE: A TOUGH QUESTION

A century ago, even fifty years ago, elders usually didn't have to decide where they would live. It was assumed that they would continue to live at home, helped as needed by their families, until they died. Of course, there were problems and frictions, and also some wonderful love and intergenerational sharing. But not so many domestic, life-affecting choices had to be made. Today, however, with large numbers of families geographically scattered and with so many more of us elders living full, vigorous lives so much longer, there is often a multitude of decisions to make. A major one is where to live.

Today, 75 percent of us elders are living on our own, either with spouses or alone. Three-quarters of male elders live with their wives, but only 40 percent of female elders live with their husbands, because men usually marry older and die younger. That leaves a lot of widows. Also, older men are more likely to remarry, and usually they marry younger women. (Given these facts, it is fortunate that women adjust better to being widows than men do to being widowers.) Even among those aged 85 and older, 55 percent live independently in a household and 30 percent live alone. The rest live in nursing homes, life-care communities, and hospitals.

In my sample, 80 percent live in their own homes, and another 16 percent live in life-care communities (which include nursing and intensive-care facilities for those who need them), and most of the remaining 4 percent live with one of their children. Only two of my respondents live in nursing homes. (I discuss nursing homes in the next chapter.)

The Ideal Place to Live

I asked this question: *If money were no problem, where would you consider the ideal place to live at your age, state of health, and future prospects?* The great majority replied, in effect, "Right where I am, in my own home."

66/M: I like it where I am. It'll take terrible catastrophes or developments to get me to move—from my things, my friends, my habits, and my well-ingrained roots and routes.

68/W: This is home, where I am. *My* home and ideal for me. It's the home of an old folk, but it's not an old folks' home.

70/W: You say "state of health" and "future prospects." Well, I hope intensely that even if my health collapses or my prospects deteriorate, I can manage somehow to stay here. I'm going to use all my ingenuity to figure out ways.

75/M: I'm hoping that when I move from here, it'll be feet first. And I don't care who carries me.

76/W: Living in our own place may not be ideal, but it's nearer ideal than anything I can think of. Our home gives us autonomy—we're the boss. It gives us control. It expresses us: our plants, our messes, our pictures, our furniture, our gadgets, our clutter, our routines, our neighborhood, even if it's changed.

76/M: The ideal is my home. The house can accommodate a person to care for me. The only doubt comes when I think about how I could pay the person.

77/M: For us it is perfect where we are, amidst our unruly collection of books, papers, china, silverware, artifacts, photographs, furniture, and innumerable gifts and bequests that are such wonderful reminders of people and past events.

A 68-year-old man, getting down to what he considers the essentials, says, "I don't care so much where my wife and I live, but to deserve the label 'ideal,' it must have a double bed and separate studies."

Some elders didn't agree with the majority I've been quoting. Here are some other ideals:

71/M: Establish your pied-à-terre in a carefully chosen retirement community with full medical services. Then have either a summer place (Maine, Vermont, New Hampshire) or a winter place (Florida, Arizona, or the Virgin Islands) where you can be independent for three to four months. Of course, I admit this takes money.

71/M: The ideal place is on a boat. There you can follow the sun, have a treat to offer others, and evade clutter.

71/M: The factors for an ideal place for me are: being near our kids (or some of them); near some good shops; near (or in the middle of) a college or university, so we can get the education and joy we used not to have time for; and having not more drudgery work than we can or want to do.

74/W: I'd like a small place in New Hampshire or in northern Pennsylvania for summer, my own little row house right here for friends and money-saving, and a trip to Greece, Switzerland, England, and Spain every year. The last may be all fantasies, dreams to be enjoyed, but why not fantasize?!

74/W: On a farm in the country with plenty of help to do the chores. Watching crops grow, cattle graze and breed, the smell of new-mown hay, the earth after the rain, the fresh frosty morning in the fall. Simple living, which, I admit, can be expensive.

76/M: Let me have a mobile home, a big one, with a guest room, an electric organ, a telephone, a sun-deck roof, and a couple of bikes locked on behind. Then we can go where we want and stay as long as we want, or as short. I don't mean a trailer. I mean a movable *place*— you know, like Bea Lillie and the *Queen Elizabeth:* After a few days she asked a ship's officer, "When does this place get to Europe?"

Moving

Of course, we must recognize that there are some impoverished elders who would love to move from wretched environments but can't afford to. In *Why Survive?* Robert Butler writes, "The same house that has been a symbol of their independence becomes the cause of their impoverishment." But, more often (and not just for my moderately above-average sample), a house is equity, and one question that must often be faced is whether to sell it, use the proceeds to buy something smaller, and spend the leftover for the satisfactions of life.

Here are some comments on moving:

70/W: It's wise to stay within physical reach of friends and family. To be totally uprooted can be a difficult mistake and is sometimes disorienting for the elderly.

72/M: Make a required change at the appropriate time—and *in* time—and do so with ample planning and deliberation. It is a very serious decision. Then make the absolute most of it.

73/W: Don't move out of your own home just because Junior, his wife or sister, or her husband, thinks you should. Weigh remarks of family, lawyers, and others carefully before taking their advice. Don't be pushed into moving by your children.

76/W: Get plenty of advice before moving. Talk with your friends; talk with your kids; talk with everybody and add up what you've learned. Then decide for yourself, taking into account the effects on those who you need or who need you.

76/M: If you plan to go to a warmer climate and probably to live there, try it for one year—before selling your real estate. You may decide that a colder climate is more than compensated for by the deeper, warmer relationships at home. That's what happened to me.

77/W: Don't forget, it's very difficult because of moving into much smaller quarters. It's strenuous physically and emotionally.

78/W: One can't wait for readiness. It's time! It will soon be too late! If you wait too long, you will be stuck with your dependence on your family or friends.

81/W: (quoting from something she wrote at age 71): I wanted to move for the last time while I was still vigorous enough to take it rather lightly. I wanted to become a part of a new community while I was still active and aware enough to start a new life, to make a real home there before the infirmities of age forced me to curtail my activities. [*Note:* I know this person, and what she says worked. She adjusted well, with all her creative vigor, and is happy now at 81.]

86/M: Moving is somewhat traumatic! Don't leave it too late!

A friend of mine, age a mere 63, advocates what he calls "spacing down" your living arrangements once your children are grown and on their own. Pointing out that when you get older you really may be ruined by the mental and physical tasks of moving, the decisions to make, the things to get rid of, he says, "Sell your biggish house and buy a medium-size one or a condominium—'size down' your dwelling. What won't fit in the new place, give to kids, give to charity, auction off. Then you'll be more free and have dealt with a lot of the moving agony in advance!"

And several people urged fellow elders to get rid of clutter. Many years ago, the great American psychologist G. Stanley Hall (1844–1924) wrote in his book *Senescence*, published when he was 78 years old, that it was a good idea at the time of retirement to go deliberately over your house from top to bottom "getting rid of waste material."

77/W: To get ready for the physical buffeting of old age and to save your fading powers, *throw things away!* Or *give things away!* There's a lot of truth in the saying "Simplify! Simplify! Or die!"

78/W: Clutter is the problem! Why not organize a give-away party and let people who want your stuff have it so you can have some peace in exchange?—and maybe even an empty closet or two.

Getting Help to Stay Where You Are

If you decide not to move, one of the ways to stay in your own house is to get some help.

75/W: If you want to stay where you are and not be in an institution, get help. What I did was to make a sort of minicontract with my daughter and her children. We like each other; they like a little extra money; I like their company and their service: fixing, cleaning, bringing a meal. They'd probably do it for nothing (or for love), but I'd rather maintain my pride and independence and keep it businesslike.

76/M: A friend and I have a three-times-a-day telephone check, just to be sure we're O.K. If nobody answers, we have somebody younger go investigate.

76/W: I love Meals On Wheels. It's good food. I pay for it (and give a bit more), and I get at least one good solid feast a day. Sometimes I eat my wheel-meal together with a fellow Meals-On-Wheelser.

84/W: We have an "Alert Transportation Service" in our city. When I need to go somewhere, I just call and they come (sometimes at *their* convenience; I have time, but they are pressed). I found them in the phone book. [*Note:* In many communities, there is also Dial-a-Ride.]

The last person mentioned the phone book. For any help you might need, look in the blue pages section on "Guide to Human Services," subsection "Aging." If you live in a city or even small town or rural area, probably you'll find lots of agencies and services. It can be fun and useful to check them out with a friend or a member of your family. Another place to call is the AARP—the American Association of Retired Persons.

An excellent new plan that enables elders to stay in their own homes is called, somewhat ponderously, the Geographically Dispersed Continuing Care Retirement Community (GDCCRC). What it does is to provide all the services of a life-care community to people in their own homes. It is less expensive than a life-care community because no expensive "campus" is needed. The basic place of residence (for as long as possible) is the elder's (or elders') own home. The services available include: all needed medical care, for life; home-support services as needed, including Meals On Wheels and home health care; access to a central "facility" that provides "adult day care" as needed; a day hospital; a dining and recreation area for stimulation and to help develop a sense of community, as well as (probably on an at-cost basis) podiatry, dentistry, optometry, and audiological services. The population of such a GDCCRC might be about one thousand living within a ten-mile radius of the central facility. The advantages of such a service are feasible because the cost is spread over that entire population. The entry fee for such a geographically dispersed facility is only about 15 percent of a campus-type life-care community and the monthly fee only 12 to 25 percent. Elders interested in knowing what sorts of GDCCRC's are available, or may become available, in their area, may write to Donald Moon, Foulkeways, Gwynedd, PA 19436.

Living Among People of Mixed Ages

Elders have strong feelings about whether to live with people of their own age or people of all ages, including children. You'll recall from Chapter 5 that grandchildren are a great joy but that one of the nice things about them is that they go home. Well, I asked this question: *Would you rather live mainly among people about your age or among a mixed-age group? Own age __ Mixed ages __ Explain.* Eighty-two percent checked *Mixed ages;* 11 percent checked *Own age;* and 7 percent said, in one way or another, "It all depends."

Here are some comments from those who prefer mixed-age living:

65/M: See Mark Twain's *Captain Stormfield Goes to Heaven.* Heaven, he found, was heterogeneous; hell, homogeneous.

70/W: It depresses me to be isolated from the extremes. I love the turmoil of the young, the buzz of middle years, and the humor and wisdom of elders.

71/W: I think one's attitudes toward and relationships with younger people are important. Obviously, if you don't encounter them, you'll have few insights regarding them.

71/M: To know what's going on in the world, you must maintain contact with the leaders who are middle-aged and the theorists who are young-middle-aged. Also, I enjoy the energy of the young and their willingness to do what I don't want to.

72/M: "Mixed" is the word. "Own age" is narrow, confining, and *boring!* I can't understand those miserable old crabs who have "restricted" communities that exclude children and pets. Youth is in the interesting scene. Children and young people are the hope of the world. They just may not make the same damn wicked mistakes we have made. And they're so beautiful, quick, bright, enthusiastic!

75/W: Segregation by age seems terrible to me.

75/M: The trouble with living with my own age-group is that they disappear too fast. Also, most older people are chronic complainers, and who wants that!

83/W: It is more cheerful to see young faces, too—not only old ones. For this reason a university campus is a cheerful place. When I taught Russian, part of the pleasure was looking at the young faces of my students.

84/W: Young people are tiring, but it's agreeable to see young people and the very young around occasionally. But be sure to make some arrangement where they'll go away before you're worn out.

The views of those who prefer living with their own age-group are best expressed by these four comments:

67/M: It's comfortable and just stimulating enough to be in the company of people who have weathered it out.

70/W: In a same-age place, we share similar memories, build our humor on commonly held rich experience, remember some of the same jokes as a part of a common culture. In short, we feel congenial.

72/W: I like myself and I like my age-group. When I want youth, I can go out and meet with them or have them in to visit me.

81/M: Our community is a wonderful varied "rut" of common experience out of which we can leap when we wish to see the rest of the world, other people's ruts, and people of other ages.

Retirement Communities

A major issue for elders is whether to move from home to a retirement community, and if so, when? By *retirement community* I mean a place that provides independent-living apartments of various sizes; all meals in the main dining room (with one meal a day there required, in order to keep a sense of community); a medical-care facility to which you can be transferred if proper care cannot be given in your apartment; and a guaranteed connection with a good hospital.

Some retirement communities are called *life-care communities*. This means that when you move in, you buy the right to occupy your apartment for life, the right to all needed medical care (routine, acute, long-term), and you are *guaranteed* that care for life, no matter what. Life-care communities are usually quite expensive to enter, and the monthly fees are rather high, but for moderately "comfortable" people, usually the sale of their house will pay the entrance fee and guaranteed-for-life health-care needs, and other savings will pay the monthly fee, which covers everything.

Seventeen percent of my respondents live in life-care communities, a much higher percentage than for the general population. Almost everyone in such a community was glad to be there and basically satisfied. According to a nationwide study, about 15 percent of people who move to retirement communities leave after a year or less, usually because they don't like it, and 98 percent of those who stay are happy and satisfied.

I asked, *What are your feelings about retirement communities?* (Note that I did not specify *life-care communities*.) Here's a cross section of the favorable comments:

69/W: One of the great things about this place is that it gives us a secure base for our main lives. No responsibilities for my husband and me (like housecleaning, doing chores, mowing grass) except those we choose. And from our base we can travel (when we can afford it), visit our kids, have them visit us (they sleep on the floor or couch or in a nearby cheap motel). There's even a separate dining room, where we can give an effortless party if we schedule it in advance.

70/W: A good retirement community is close to Utopia. Democratic government, interesting people, stimulating daily life, and plenty of work that uses everyone's skills. Retirement communities range from superb to awful, and even good ones differ in their philosophies. "You've worked hard all your life. Now let us take care of you" would never satisfy me. But "You've worked hard all your life. You've probably got the habit. Come find where you best fit in here. There's plenty of work to be done"—that would satisfy me.

70/W: I have really *improved* in the five years since coming here. I am more independent, write on a wider range of topics, enjoy my fellow residents who have a wider range of backgrounds than most of those I knew formerly and who constantly widen my thinking and knowledge.

73/M: One of the blessings of retirement facilities is that as old friends die, new ones are made.

74/W: There, when I move, I will be free of housekeeping responsibilities. I'll have more time to explore and be creative. I can hardly wait to go from boredom/choredom to freedom to live.

75/W: The community I have joined is one that offers most kinds of human love, comfort, and fun. It's like rediscovering a supportive family life, and a reopening of the opportunities for new friendships.

75/W: They keep us so busy here (if we want) that we don't even have time to die. Some things they've got: a supervised whirlpool; a Tuesday morning travel consultant; college classes (intergenerational); an outside place to keep pets out of others' way.

78/W: Perhaps the way for us to grow old gracefully—and responsibly—is to get out of the road. We had our turn. Those of us who can should go to a retirement community and relieve others of carrying our weight. We may find this kind of retirement a fitting farewell gift to family and friends.

81/W: Many, many times in this community I have seen countenances change from bored discontentedness to eagerness when a useful, daily chore was found, suited to a person's ability and interest. Specifically, the "discovered chores" have included: simple mending/ sewing/knitting; finding and scheduling "disc jockeys" for our daily recorded music programs; exercise classes, nature walks, poetry class, and letter-writing group.

The few totally unfavorable comments about retirement communities are epitomized by these two:

69/M: Our visits with friends in such communities impress us and depress us with never-ending conversations about each one's "great deeds" of the past. Conversations in such communities are narrow and intellectually sterile. There's also too much verbal disease-sharing.

71/M: Too blah, insulated, inbred, organized, styled, and ersatz.

I also received a number of useful sound observations and pieces of advice about retirement communities that will be helpful to elders and those who care about us:

66/W: No matter how attractive the facility, and how warm the atmosphere, pulling up roots from home and transplanting them into a retirement community will require a period of adjustment that will include homesickness for a time. Allow for it. Don't be thrown by it.

69/W: In selecting a retirement community, look at the residents' faces even more carefully than you look at the apartments and public rooms. You'll know whether you're looking at faces of people among whom you want to spend the rest of your life. Forget the canes and braces. After the first week you won't notice them anymore.

70/M: The major service of retirement communities is to relieve the tension between parents and children about who will be responsible for care in the advanced years.

73/W: Retirement communities should be able to provide, for those who need them, *level* walkways to all activities (laundry, meals); individualized interior color and decorating to lessen institutional feeling in apartments. They should allow you to have your own furniture, pictures, and knickknacks.

90/W: Choose your retirement home on your own while you're mentally and physically able. Don't be "put" anywhere. Go soon enough.

Then there's a classic problem, expressed by a 69-year-old man: "I'd like to enter a retirement community when the security of assured care, the relief from responsibility, and the concern not to be a burden all outweigh the appeal of new challenges, and that is just the time when the communities don't want me." So if you want to be prepared for that eventual move, get on the waiting list now and make your (refundable) deposit.

Living With Our Families

Some elders will also consider the possibility of living with their families. To find out what my respondents thought about this option,

I asked, *Do you think elders should live mainly with their own families or elsewhere?* Seventy-one percent said, "Elsewhere"; 7 percent said, "With own family"; and 22 percent either didn't reply or said, in effect, "It all depends."

Those who favor separate living explain:

65/W: I would certainly be unhappy living in a household where teenagers turn the stereos to deafening heights, or where babies squeal. I welcome the give and take of three generations around a holiday table, but when I look forward to the peace and quiet and familiarity of my small apartment. It's mine, all mine.

70/W: Though I'm an ardent advocate of intergenerational mingling, I'm just as ardent an advocate against intergenerational living together—with family members. Each group definitely needs its own "space," especially when children are developing.

70/W: Instead of "elsewhere," I would say "independently." I could not live happily on a permanent basis with any one of our three children, much as I love them.

70/M: Older people have developed their own patterns of life. Living with family often results in serious rifts, feelings of guilt on both sides. Some elders who live with their children feel carefully sustained but somewhat excluded from family social life. They resent this and may become demanding and unreasonable.

71/W: Elderly couples feel the loss of sovereignty over a "home"— what previously was their domain. It just doesn't work very well.

74/M: It is most unfortunate to burden a young family with the care and incessant company of an aging parent. The young children in the household will not have fond memories of the aging grandparent after he/she passes on. Far better to remember occasional happy visits to or from such elders.

74/W: Those whom I know who live with their children seem to lose their own independence and complain about the treatment they get. Often the elders assume chores which they tire of doing and feel they cannot stop. It's growling or snarling, or fake saintliness.

73/W: I think it is more stimulating to try to *see* the world my children and grandchildren belong to, but I wouldn't want to *be* part of that world all day long! Too tiring!

79/W: It is far healthier not to combine two or three generations under one roof permanently. Unless the second of three generations (i.e., son or daughter) is endowed with *super* tolerance, *super* patience, *super* caring, and ability to cope with well-meaning suggestions and expressed opinions, it is asking for disaster.

86/W: From wisdom developed over four score and six years, I command you, fellow elders: Don't be a burden to your children. Let them live their own lives. It's great to *be* with them but not *live* with them.

But, of course, there's the other side of the coin:

67/M: Let's live together if feasible. This means, largely, the provision for adequate individual privacy. The practical advantages of living together are both many and mutual. Our family is an example of such. It gives us closeness. It teaches us all how to love all mankind, not easy but *so* rewarding. It is close to ideal. We have the joy of working out problems together. Another example of this is life on an Israeli kibbutz, where facilities for the very young and the elderly are close to ideal, and family closeness is the real hallmark.

71/M: It is desirable for a single elderly parent to live with (i.e., readily adjacent or proximate to) one's children *but with privacy* for both parent and the next generation. I like the intergenerational pattern of earlier centuries. (However, it must depend on the personalities involved. It is not for everyone.)

88/W: I have a small apartment (living room, bedroom, bath, and kitchenette) at one end of my daughter's home so I won't be alone, but I still have my own independence. It works well.

A good friend of mine, Harriet, now 70 years old, didn't want to fill out a questionnaire, but she did talk with me about the thirteen-year period when her mother lived with her, her husband, and three children. The children were in the prime of childhood and adolescence when their grandmother came to live with them at age 79. She stayed till age 92. Harriet recalls, "Ma made it easy for us. She helped us build a separate wing on the house for her, right there but apart, joined by a dining space, hers. She never butted in. She did her own breakfast; she and I usually ate lunch together; and supper was usually separate, but I got it for her. She had a guy to do little errands for her and to provide some transportation. So for thirteen years, it was pretty great.

"However, it wasn't ideal. She was like another child, and yet I was like a daughter, both to her and to myself. And I'll admit it's an awful job for a mother of young children. I couldn't scream and yell at them the way I should have been able to do. Why? Ma could hear. And then, as time passed, she really became lonely. Her friends disappeared, and we couldn't really be a substitute for them. So finally we agreed that she should go to a nursing home, and it was a great solution. She made new friends and had all the medical care she needed. At age 94+ she died, really in comfort where she wanted to be.

"My worry often was: Is it good for the kids? But just a year ago, I asked one of our sons, Don, whether it hadn't been pretty tough on them, and he replied at once and with certainty, 'One of the best things about growing up was having Gran here.' "

The Sandwich Generation

With more and more people living well into old age, a new phenomenon has developed: "the sandwich generation." These are the thousands of couples who are sandwiched between their own growing children, who obviously need their care, energy, guidance, and support, *and* their own parents, who very often also need their care, energy, guidance, and support. From the elders' point of view, it sometimes becomes a question of, "O.K., who takes care of those of us who *gave* care earlier?"

75/W: I need care. But I hate to need it. It's hard for a parent to be *a child of her child.*

75/W: When my kids were adolescents, it used to be "Tell us where you are going. When will you be back? Yes, you can use the car if . . . ," etc., etc. But now these same kids, mature adults, ask me, their mother, "Where are you going? When will you be back? How will I know if you're O.K.?" etc., etc. What a mix-up!

80/M: I have this gnawing doubt: Will my kids be there for me if I really need them?

80/W: My son, in a moment of frankness, told me, "People of our age have to be parents to parents, and that's all screwed up, a lot of us find." Then he said, "Of course, I don't mean you, Mom. It's just a lot of other people." But I keep thinking: He *did* mean me. And so I feel guilty, but if I show I feel guilty, he'll feel guilty too.

From what my respondents wrote, and from some studies I read, I have distilled the following suggestions for the sandwich generation and for us elders, who are the top of the sandwich:

- If you are going to live together, try if possible to provide separate spaces with a guarantee of privacy when it's wanted.

- Also agree on firmly set times to be together and times to be apart. Of course, there will be times that are unscheduled and spontaneous, but we do need those set times when we are guaranteed freedom from each other. Don't feel you must always eat together.

- If you want social gatherings with guests, let them be separate sometimes, elders with elders (maybe in the middle of the day if everybody involved is retired; that's the time of day when the rest of the family may be out of the house anyway); middle generation with middle generation (as for an evening dinner party; that's when elders may be ready for a quiet supper, a book or TV, and early to bed).

- Make up your rules for living together (space, food, times, standards, chores, styles, noise) when there is not a crisis. Sit down and work things out deliberately (it's a good idea to write them down). Then, periodically, look over and revise the arrangements.

- Be lovingly frank with each other. That keeps your relationship based on reality. Don't tell lies. Tell the truth so that it doesn't hurt.

- Let elders provide useful services if they are able to: baby-sitting, household chores, giving *asked-for* wisdom, providing the humor that perspective gives. And, elders, volunteer these things, except the wisdom (or advice).

- Admit to yourselves, but don't state to each other, any guilt you may feel. You may wish that your parent was dead, and that's a terrible thing to wish, even for a moment. But it's a normal feeling from time to time, so admit it to yourself. Or, elders, you may feel guilty for being such a bother. O.K., admit that to yourself. It's natural. But sharing guilty feelings is usually a poor thing. Go outside the family to talk about that.

• Use a part-time day-care facility. If it's a good one, it can be rewarding to all parts of any sandwich. But it must be agreed to by the elder after an experimental period. Nobody should "put" anybody anywhere or feel "put."

• Use part-time chore people, or health support people, paid for by whoever can best afford it.

• In a calm time, agree on the sharing of resources—who pays for what share of what costs? And, if possible, be sure that everybody has some discretionary funds of their own—for freedom, for gift-giving, for a lark.

• One of the needs of those who care for elders—especially elders who have grown quite helpless, and also demanding—is a mutual-support system. The care-givers often get very little reward and positive feedback from those they care for, or from others in the house. It's hard to find reasons to laugh or opportunities to weep. Some people I know of have organized small groups who meet, say, for an hour or so quite regularly each week just to share feelings and experiences.

In those ways, living together can be made more manageable. Or, if you decide, as most do, to live apart but near each other, many of these same suggestions work well. And if you think things are tough or complicated now, cast your mind forward fifty years. By 2040, according to census projections, the U.S. 85+ population will have increased from 2.2 million to 13 million, the 65+ population from 26 million to 67 million. It will have become a question of the old caring for the very old.

Chapter 9

WHEN SPECIAL CARE IS NEEDED

A difficult aspect of the "where to live" question arises when an elder, even with the best assistance, can no longer continue to live at home or with his or her family. The answer usually has to be a "nursing home." I put the words in quotes because they have become a catchall label for a variety of institutions. "Too often," a 71-year-old respondent wrote, "these institutions are seen as a prelude to death rather than as a new, useful experience." Since so much negative emotion is attached to the label, many people now prefer the terms *alternative living arrangement* or *continuing-care facility*.

A Personal Experience and a Story

One of the saddest experiences my wife and I ever had was when I was age 55 and she 49. My mother, Edie, at age 82, living in her own home, fell and broke her hip. She had always loved walking more than almost anything else, and the prospect of never walking again so discouraged her that when she was brought home from the hospital and lay helpless, under the care of nurses, she tried to take what she'd kept for years beside her bed—"my pills"—and kill herself. But she failed. Apparently she was trembling so much that she was able to get only half of them down. The nurse found her, unconscious, and in alarm called us at our home. We called the doctor, and I rushed over to Edie's house, half an hour away, and told the doctor to take her to the hospital.

In the hospital, I remember seeing her lying in a deep drugged sleep, with only a small oxygen tube under her nose. I put my ear to her chest and heard the heart beating strongly. I thought, my eyes filled with tears, "Edie believes she's dead. How sad she'll be to wake up and find that she isn't." Well, she did awaken and was moved to our house for care.

At the time, we were leading a very busy life—three children in school and college, lots of urgent projects—and it became a terrific burden, especially for my wife, to organize the care Edie needed; the shifts of nurses, the laundry, the meals, the shots, the visits, and all the necessary systems of support. It was very complicated, very costly, and seemingly unending.

So, in consultation with Edie, we decided that the only way to manage was to move her to the medical-care nursing section of Kendal, a newly opened Quaker life-care community where we all knew she would have the very best of care and encouragement. My brother and I fixed up her small private room at Kendal in advance to make it as homelike as possible, with some of her own pictures on the walls, a bit of her own furniture near the bed. Then the day came to drive her down. We all knew, without saying it, and so did Edie, that we were "putting her away."

I was teaching school and involved in some urgent meetings, so my wife had the job of driving my mother to Kendal. Edie wept silently all the long drive down, over an hour, not counting a brief stop at her own house to pick up some forgotten eyeglasses, "so that I can work on my short stories." But she knew, and we knew, that it was the beginning of the end. And, despite cheerful, frequent visits, and interesting discussions about her stories, and the marvelous care of nurses who grew to love her, within four months Edie died, a beloved nurse beside her. A little gasp and my mother was dead.

Ann Tyler, in her story "With All Flags Flying,"* describes in fiction a very true-to-life experience. First, an old man at his own home:

> Weakness was what got him in the end. He had been expecting something more definite—chest pains, a stroke, arthritis—but it was only weakness that put a finish to his living alone. A numbness in his head, an airy feeling when he walked. A wateriness in his bones that made it an effort to pick up his coffee in the morning. He waited some days for it to go away, but it never did. And meanwhile the dust piled

* Ann Tyler, *Redbook*, 1971.

up in corners; the refrigerator wheezed and creaked for want of defrosting. Weeds grew around his rose bushes.

So his children take him to a nursing home and get him installed. Here is how he feels when they leave:

The old man sat on the edge of the bed, watching the tail of Clara's car flash as sharp and hard as a jewel around the bend of the road. Then, with nobody to watch that mattered, he let his shoulders slump and eased himself out of his suitcoat, which he folded over the foot of the bed. He slid his suspenders down and let them dangle at his waist. He took off his copper-toed work boots and set them on the floor neatly side by side. And although it was only noon, he lay down full-length on top of the bedspread. Whiskery lines ran across the plaster of the ceiling high above him. There was a crackling sound in the mattress when he moved; it must be covered with something water-proof.

Some Facts

Twenty percent of us elders will spend some time in a nursing home before we die; 23 percent of those over 85 are in one now; and 20 percent of us will die in one. The average age of nursing-home residents is between 80 and 85. The ratio of female to male is 70/30.

There are numerous kinds of alternative living arrangements. Some provide only skilled nursing care, while others are more nearly boarding homes for the elderly, but most provide a gamut of services: a residence; physical and medical supervision as needed; meals (in bed or in a dining room, whichever is more appropriate); medical service; recreational activities; special physical rehabilitation activities; connection with a hospital; and safety. They provide for visits for family and friends, for transportation outside into the community, for barbers, beauticians, podiatrists, and so forth, as well as dealing with the mass of state and federal paperwork involved, which many elders cannot do without anguish and foul-ups. There's no question that nursing homes meet an essential need in our society.

As of 1986, there are some twenty-three thousand nursing homes in the U.S.A., populated by 1.4 million elderly (and a few nonelderly) persons. The main reasons for entering nursing homes are: mental incompetence; unmanageable blindness and deafness; inability to walk and get about; suicidal tendencies; misuse of home appliances and facilities so that things go to pieces; behaving in a manner that is too nasty and difficult for others to bear; inability to afford care at home or with the family. The majority of nursing-home residents are disoriented to some degree as to time, place, and people.

The other group that comes to nursing homes, temporarily, are those who have been hospitalized for a serious illness or accident, are discharged, but are not yet ready to go home and live independently. Medicare pays for the stay of such people for up to 150 days.

Twenty-five years ago, nursing homes in the United States probably deserved the negative image that many people still see in their mind's eye—"warehouses for the old," to use the Gray Panther term. But now that Medicare and Medicaid pay for much of the needed care, and facilities must meet federal standards if they are to be reimbursed, conditions have greatly improved. State licensing requirements also have helped. Furthermore, the "long-term-care industry" has taken steps to see that the nursing homes which belong to their associations do provide high standards of care.

The cost of nursing homes varies greatly. Some are luxurious and very expensive. However, the typical home or facility costs, as of 1986, $40 to $60 a day, $15,000 to $22,000 a year. Medicaid will pay most or all of these fees, but only after the resident has spent all of her or his resources, down to $1,600 for an individual, $2,000 for a couple. (And resources may not be transferred to family just before entrance. Such a transfer must be made at least two years in advance.)

A major force for the improvement of nursing homes has been the so-called advocacy groups, who help make sure that state and federal standards are met and that state and federal governments do not allow standards to be lowered. An outstanding advocacy organization is the National Citizens' Coalition for Nursing Home Reform (NCCNHR), founded in 1977.* Because of them, and the efforts of people within the industry itself (as well as those of the House Select Committee on Aging, other parts of the government, and many local organizations), standards in nursing homes have quietly and steadily improved over the past fifteen years.

Nursing-home advocates generally favor whatever arrangements

*Address: National Citizens' Coalition for Nursing Home Reform, 1825 Connecticut Avenue N.W., Washington, D.C. 20009.

are needed to assure the privacy of residents when they desire it and to provide for the possibility of private family gatherings in the home if the resident cannot go out. They also work for the establishment of "resident councils," which are elected or chosen by the residents and consult with the administration about what's good and what needs changing. Just about half of all nursing homes now have resident councils, according to the NCCNHR.

My Visits to Nursing Homes

In preparation for writing this book, I visited five nursing homes, a couple of super-posh ones in Florida and three more-average ones nearer where I live in Philadelphia (including one that, when it first opened, advertised itself on the radio as "the Ponce de León, fountain of youth nursing home, with geriatrically oriented background music"). Given the facts I've reported about homes, and the outraged reports of advocacy groups protesting the "warehousing" of the elderly, I expected to be angered and somewhat disgusted by what I saw. Well, I was indeed saddened to see so many people struggling against helplessness, and medicated against suffering, and confined to beds and wheelchairs, some groaning loudly or repeating the same sounds over and over, some giving an occasional meaningless (to me) yell or shout. But I was not angered. It's true that many sections of nursing homes are not happy scenes. But what surprised me—even amazed me—were the caring, loving, sensitive attitudes and actions of most members of the staff, including doctors, nurses, aides, food servers, and maintenance people.

When I explained to the officials of each home why I was there for my visit, they all allowed me to roam freely about the place, only asking me not to invade people's privacy by entering rooms uninvited or opening closed doors. I was given the option of a guided tour or random wandering, and usually I chose both. I think the best way to give an accurate impression of what I observed is to report a random sequence of happenings and individual impressions during one visit. (I've changed people's names.)

- There's a smell of urine, but also of bathroom cleaner, and basically the place looks clean.

- The supervisor on each floor has been told why I'm here.

- 94-year-old Molly ("I was born August 31, 1891, and that ain't yesterday") looks peaceful and happy, smiling at me and fingering her string of rosary beads.

- Mabel, who looks about 80, feeding tube in her nose, sits in her chair, groaning periodically, but she smiles at me. I talk, she obviously understands, her eyes sparkle, but she can't reply. She purses her lips and I kiss her cheek and squeeze her gently. She smiles and nods vigorously.

- Alberta—age 98, according to my guide—seems quite out of it, but when I am told that she is a descendant of Seminole Chief Osceola, she smiles and recites a long poem, pointing to herself as author.

- As I wander later, looking into rooms with open doors, I see many people in a curled-up fetal position on their beds, seeming more dead than alive. But a couple of them, hearing me talking to others, look around and wave feebly.

- With their permission, I enter the room of two elderly sisters. One, stylishly dressed, smiling and intelligent-looking, is sitting up straight in a hard-backed chair, and she looks at me encouragingly. I try to engage her in conversation, but she responds only with a bright look, a smile, and a clear "Yes!" no matter what I say. I realize eventually that she has no mind. I turn to her sister, who is sloppily dressed, slouched, looking ancient and discouraged, reading a book. I say, "How are you?" and she replies clearly, "I'm fine. Thank you. Please don't mind my sister. I have to think for both of us—but we get along. Now I've got to get back to my chapter." I learn a lesson from this: Don't judge from appearances!

- The young woman showing me around greets all the residents by name, asks how they are, touches and hugs them, and radiates encouragement. Their faces always brighten. I ask why everyone is called by first name, and she says, "That's what they ask for. We don't do it unless they want us to. It makes them feel loved." Later, I notice that a few are called, carefully, "Mr. Spencer," "Mrs. Zubin."

- A thin old woman, when I ask how she's doing, says, "Terrible! I've been here in this chair since seven-thirty this morning and they won't move me, and here it is four o'clock!" (It was 10:50.) "This place is terrible. . . ." Later I learn she was turned, cleaned, and moved, only half an hour before I saw her.

- In discussing complaints with a staff member, I am told: "You know, some residents want visits so badly from their families. But the families feel so guilty about putting their old mother (or whoever) into a home that they can hardly bear to visit. So the only way to get visits is for the resident to write an outraged letter or make an outraged phone call about how terribly they're being treated. That brings the family in, also outraged, and we have to deal with the facts and then urge more frequent visits. But sometimes it's a no-win situation and we just have to try to keep calm and get, maybe, some volunteers to encourage and arrange visits."

- A long lounge room is filled, all along the wall, with rows of wheelchairs, with people in various states of alertness sitting in them. Two TV sets are turned to different channels. I talk with some residents, touch some, and am told by a fat lady using a walker, "They love it when a handsome man comes. They don't see many of those." An older man grunts in amusement and winks at me.

- I am reminded of a report by a 77-year-old woman respondent, who wrote: "Two 90-year-old men were earnestly playing chess in a wide corridor of a retirement community. A small naked woman ran down the hallway. One of the men glanced up and said to the other man, 'Sally certainly needs to have her dress pressed.' "

- Zora, looking very cheerful in a wheelchair by her bed, when asked how she is, says, "I am getting along fine." She points to two "lover" monkeys, like Cabbage Patch dolls, sitting propped against her pillow, and says, "My friends." She picks up one and hugs it.

- I see a very complete-looking library of large-print books and a set of recordings for the blind. People are using the collection.

- I hear loud, insane-sounding, monosyllabic shouts, as if from pain. A nurse says, "We try to put the screamers together off in a wing around a corner so they don't disturb others too much. But they're people! We mustn't forget that."

- I listen, alone in a hallway, and I have the impression of a two-tier society. One tier is the loud-talking staff, socializing with each other while doing their work; the other tier is mostly-silent patients who are being served.

- I read the feeding chart on the doorway to a room. It looks like an awful lot of Jell-O, soup, and toast.

- In the dining room, people are enjoying their food, some assisted, many in wheelchairs. Mealtime is obviously a big event.

- A group of wheelchair people are in a wide corridor bowling a soccer ball at some large inflated pins. They are supervised by a young attendant. It's a game, but it doesn't look like much fun.

- The bulletin boards are covered with notices of scheduled activities: religious services and visits; happy hours; birthdays to be recognized this week; concerts; movies; discussion groups; hobby clubs; lectures.

- There are notices on each floor saying, "Today is: Wednesday, April 10, 1985," to keep forgetful people in touch with one obvious bit of reality. Also, there are plenty of large clocks around.

- On a bulletin board in the staff office, I see a set of "Rules for the X Care Facility." They are: (1) Always be positive. (2) Give encouragement, concern, and love. (3) Always use names, not room numbers. (4) Don't use first names unless requested to. (5) Give plenty of touching if it's welcome. It usually is. (6) Respect privacy; knock and wait before opening a door. (7) Expect *more*, not less!

- Occasionally I hear a loud, angry staff voice scolding a resident for being dirty, for complaining, or for being disobedient. It's too bad, I think, but staff are human, the residents can be exasperating, duties are complex, pressures great, and therefore perfection is too much to expect.

- A woman smiles warmly at the assistant administrator showing me around and introducing me to people, looks at me, grabs the administrator's hand, and says, "If she were my daughter, she couldn't be better to me!"

Attitudes of Residents

Even though a nursing home is, almost by necessity, not a joyous place to be in, it's surprising how fond of the homes most of the residents become. Recently, a home near us was threatened with closure by the state for a long list of code violations. Certainly, state rules and requirements are necessary, and certainly there are some people in the care-facility business who are unscrupulous and need watching, but when this place was threatened, residents said to reporters and others:

77/M: If I'm to spend the rest of my life somewhere, I want to spend it here.

78/W: It's awfully easy for the state to make regulations, and I believe in some rules. But we can be ruled to death by form-makers and inspectors. We residents should shout a little louder and write a few letters about the good news here. It's a home, and it provides care at amazingly low cost.

82/W: Don't close this home. I want to stay here where I love people and where I am loved. Of course people aren't perfect, and now and then a mean employee comes along, but mainly there is caring and kindness.

87/W: This is my home. I love it and the people here.

The Danger of Learned Helplessness

An 81-year-old woman wrote to me, "If we are sick, or have an accident and must quickly go to a hospital or a nursing home, they tend to infantilize us. We are disoriented and confused, and we sink into lethargy. We lost our will and our energy, but *not* our intelligence. That we keep, but we've got to be given opportunities to use it, to turn it on. I'd say that too often what we're taught is really helplessness."

Working against learned helplessness is the extraordinary capacity for mental recuperation of elders if they are returned before it is too late to a stimulating, challenging social environment. An example of this is the case of the 93-year-old mother of my jogging companion. She lives in her own apartment in Miami. She fell and injured herself badly, was taken to the hospital, treated, and then sent to a nursing home for recovery. But when her nearby family visited her, they found that she had regressed into a state of nonentity. She was incontinent, mute, hopeless. When my friend heard this, he knew it didn't sound like his spunky mother. He flew down to visit her, signed a statement that he was removing her from the nursing home against medical advice (and it was also against the advice of his mother's

Miami relatives), and brought her back to her own apartment. He arranged home care, and for her to be on her own as much as possible. Within only two or three days, she had recovered her mental and physical vigor and was her old opinionated, independent self. "Hospitals and nursing homes can kill," says my friend.

However, a contrary case is reported by author Jane Porcino about her 78-year-old mother:

> My mother's doctor called to say she could no longer safely live alone in her apartment after two minor heart attacks. And so I began the search for a health-related facility near enough to us for back-and-forth visiting. Two months later we found a home she liked and she moved in, walking with a cane and looking ten years older than her 78 years. Within a few weeks, the cane disappeared, along with many of her symptoms. The relief of being taken care of day and night was just what she needed. For the next six years she lived happily there, acting as an informal "social director" and visiting one of us on all family occasions. She was beloved by all the staff, and chose not to go to the hospital during her last illness, but to be cared for "in her own home."*

How to avoid learned helplessness? The best way, I think, is to follow the rule set forth in the best book on teaching I know, *Points Picked Up: One Hundred Hints in How to Manage a School*, written by Abbie G. Hall in 1891. Hint number 11 is: "Every thing that is explained to a pupil which he can find out for himself robs him of so much education." The point for nursing homes (and for those of us dealing with elders at home) is: "Every thing that is done for elders that they can do for themselves robs them of so much competency and possibility of recovery."

There have been two interesting, specific experiments that lend proof to this, albeit in a minor way. The first involved jigsaw puzzles. A group of elders was, unbeknownst to them, randomly divided into three subgroups: I, II, and III. Their task was to assemble a fairly easy jigsaw puzzle in the presence of a staff member. Those in group I were helped a lot with the puzzle and some of the sections even assembled for them. Those in group II were never helped, only encouraged, and now and then given some constructive advice. Those in group III proceeded entirely on their own. After this, all were given

* Jane Porcino, *Growing Older, Getting Better.*

a second puzzle to do alone, and their speed and accuracy was measured. Group I, the helped, did worst; group II, the encouraged and advised but not helped, did best; and those in group III, who were left completely alone, performed somewhere in the middle. Conclusion: Elders become more competent with encouragement and some advice but not by having things done for them.

The second experiment had to do with houseplants. New residents in a nursing home were presented with plants for their rooms. One group was told that the plant was theirs to care for and that it needed adequate light and water, which was their responsibility because people in the home were expected to share responsibilities. The other group was told that the plant was a gift, but not to worry, the staff would care for it. A number of months later the health and welfare, not of the plants but of the residents, was studied, and it was found that those elders who were expected to care for their own plants had thrived better, and more had survived, than among those who were told to let others do it.

Of course, it takes more than jigsaw puzzles and plants to avoid learned helplessness, but these little experiments seem to point the way.

Choosing a Nursing Home or Care Facility

If we elders need to choose a nursing home, or have one chosen for us by our families, here are some suggestions of questions to ask (or have asked for us) in order to help all concerned make a wise choice:

- Is the facility licensed by the state?

- Is it approved for Medicare and Medicaid?

- Will whatever insurance plan you may have be acceptable, and will the insurer pay the proper share of the costs? (Insurance policies that pay long-term costs of nursing homes are rare.)

- Does the cost include laundry and clothing care, physical therapy, occupational therapy transportation, arrangements for special diets?

- Are you allowed to help furnish your own room? What about rights to listen to radio, to watch TV, and to be protected from their invasion?

- What is the policy regarding smoking and drinking alcohol?

- What access is there to a telephone?
- How's the food? Are special diets available if needed?
- Are residents allowed to leave for visits, and under what conditions?
- Who may visit a resident and what are the hours?
- What activities are scheduled?
- Is the place well lighted and well marked so that people can find their way around easily? What about handrails and different color indications to make it easier to get about? (For example, the lounges, the TV room, the library, and the public bathrooms should be marked with large, clear signs; colored lines on the floors can lead one to certain places—a solid blue line to the dining room, a dotted yellow line to the lounge, a red-and-black line to the TV, and so forth.
- What arrangements are there with a nearby hospital? Is it a good hospital?
- What sorts of medical service are provided? May one use one's own doctor?
- What is the policy with regard to "heroic measures" to save lives? Do you agree with it? Does a patient have the right to refuse treatment requiring such things as feeding by tube through the nose? Discuss all this with your doctor as well as with the nursing-home people. "Heroic measurers" are not confined to hospitals.
- Where are personal money and possessions kept and how are they accounted for?
- May you, before you decide, visit unannounced, and visit at mealtimes, and earlyish in the morning, and once at night after bedtime? If you may, do. Share a couple of meals. If these visits are not allowed, look elsewhere.
- What is the attitude of the administrator? You will have to deal with him or her whenever a problem arises. How does he or she make you feel?
- What references are provided, and may you contact them?

One of my respondents, a 70-year-old retired geriatric nurse, sent me the following suggestions about visiting:

When you walk into the facility, make good use of all your senses. Use your nose; the sense of smell gives a great deal of information. If there are extremely disagreeable odors, walk around and try to discover if this has resulted from a minor accident or if it is a sign of very sloppy housekeeping. You might check that out again on your second or third visit. An occasional accident will always happen. But if bad odors are constant and pervasive, that's quite a different matter.

I would keep my eyes open to see if the place is reasonably clean and well kept or if it has the grubby, dingy look that suggests continuous neglect. Remember, an occasional lack of tidiness may merely be a sign of a place well lived in. That's not bad. Also, I would pay attention to other kinds of odors. Does it have a hospital-like antiseptic smell? At mealtime, do you smell the aromas of good home cooking that stimulate the residents to eat? Or does the whole place, even at mealtime, reek of Pine Sol?

Preparing for the Move

We elders will make the best adjustment to the move to a nursing home if we and those who may be helping us make the decision together and then make the actual move while keeping some facts in mind:

- The stress involved in moving and adjusting to the new environment is natural and inevitable. Most of us elders are sensitive human beings, and any major change brings stress. However, studies show that stress is usually temporary. A 78-year-old woman respondent wrote: "When I first moved to this 'place,' as I used to call it, I was angry, sad, and confused by all the things I had to get used to, including group schedules, group meals, and all the damned new geography. But then I learned my way around, I made some friends, I got to like the staff (most of them), and I found that my stress went away for the most part and I no longer called it a 'place.' It became, and still is, my home." Just knowing that there will be some stress but that it will diminish is a great help in dealing with it.

- The stress is worst for those elders who don't want to go. Therefore, it is important to do everything possible to convince ourselves, or to be convinced, that it's the best move for us. This may take time and discussion and lots of visits. O.K., so take the time, and make the visits!

• Once we are in our new home, especially at the beginning, plenty of visits to us from friends and family often help. We can invite people to share a meal or have a drink. Also, a good many social visits outside to the homes of friends and family—or enjoyable meals with friends in restaurants outside—are fun and helpful. These visits are often easier for all involved to arrange when there is the solid, reliable living-base of the institution to go back to.

A letter to Ann Landers states vigorously the case for nursing homes. I agree with it.

Dear Ann Landers: Why did you let "Barely Coping in Chicago" get off without teaching her a lesson that she needed to learn? Generally, you are a lot sharper than that.

The writer said her father was bedridden and incontinent and had to be spoon-fed. He was ill-tempered, demanding and in severe pain. She added, heroically, "I vowed that I would never put my father in a nursing home—no matter what."

There are too many martyrs like that around—people who complicate their lives and do the elderly no favors with such warped reasoning. Surely they are aware that trained professionals in nursing homes are better able to care for the elderly. . . .

The deep resentment of some of these sons and daughters is apparent. They show up every day because they feel duty-bound. They try hard to be loving, but it doesn't quite come off. The old folks feel guilty. Their discomfort surfaces in the form of hostility.

There are plenty of good nursing homes around. If a bad one is chosen, it's because someone didn't do the proper investigating. Life in a nursing home can be rewarding. There are arts and crafts, group discussions, games, music and even marriages. What does the "martyr" have to offer? Just sign me—Traveled That Road and Am Glad I Did It Right.*

* Philadelphia Inquirer, 25 August 1984.

Chapter 10

ABOUT OUR
SEXUALITY

There is a widespread notion that once people, especially women, reach their sixties, they are no longer much interested in sexual activities—too old for "that sort of thing." Is this notion true? What do we elders actually think and say and do about sexuality? In order to find out, I asked my respondents to write about their ideas on the subject. I put the matter thus: *Many people, including us elders, are much interested in and concerned about the sexual lives of people over 65. Please think about such subjects as:*

- *physical closeness*
- *sexual fantasies*
- *fondling*
- *remarriage*
- *sexual intercourse*
- *living together without marriage*
- *masturbation*
- *any related matters*

and write as fully as you can and wish to on your ideas and feelings about each of them, all under the topic of "sexuality and the elderly."

As one might expect, there was a vast range of replies, and it is impossible on the basis of them to answer with certainty how many of the respondents are "sexually active." I didn't specifically ask that question, since I felt that such a yes-or-no item would seem like an invasion of privacy and might, in many cases, discourage any replies at all. Also, as several respondents suggested, what do "sex" and "sexually active" mean? Is there not too much emphasis on sexual intercourse as the measure, whereas in reality love and the expression of sexuality take many forms?

Most respondents were quite cooperative in sharing their ideas and feelings about this rather private—but vital—subject:

67/M: Physical closeness, hand-holding on walks, kissing and fondling are very important to me. I find little change in my lifelong habits. Perhaps even greater frequency in practicing these natural bents is the fact now since my wife and I are together more of the time than we were during our "work" years. Sexual intercourse is greatly enjoyed by both of us, albeit in relative moderation.

67/W: Loving and touching are necessary for all people of all ages, at least eight hugs a day, I'd say!

68/W: Don't take love for granted—affirm it every day. Rejoice in it!

69/M: My wife and I have been married thirty-four and a half years, and I have the feeling that we achieved more happy physical adjustment during the past three or four years than ever before, a sort of new awakening to quiet, deep joy.

70/W: (a married woman whose husband can no longer have intercourse): Getting older is like falling from shelf to shelf, achieving new "lows," especially in the domain of sex. BUT!! I still love physical closeness. To cuddle up to a warm back in bed on a chilly night is great; fondling is *"in"* with me. I miss sexual intercourse. Masturbation is good sometimes, but it isn't the same thing—just a release of tensions, basically gets you nowhere. I can't *wait* to stop missing sexual intercourse!

70/M: Though I'm not sure my wife would agree, I believe that our sex life is as good as twenty to thirty years ago, in many ways more relaxed and even more experimental. There is no "proving" oneself, and no need for "prowess." Less activity, perhaps average of once a week, but weariness is often the factor, not lack of affection.

71/M: I have been unable to see any watershed whereat the normal human need for physical closeness, fondling, and intercourse becomes any less important. Our intercourse is less frequent than when we were younger, but still equally as important to us. I do not perceive difference in my sexual interests pre- and post-65. Maybe I just haven't aged enough!

71/W: I think what many elders are doing is great. If the kids can do it, why not us?

72/M: Sex, like war and the Olympics, is for the young.

73/M: The way they're talking these days, sexiness is next to godliness. After I've tried to do all the things I want to do, I'm just too weary for sex. It's not worth the bother. Is that a disgrace? After all, we can always talk and think.

73/W: For those who can do so comfortably, living together or just sleeping together on occasion should be just as open to elders as to anyone else.

74/M: Sex is so much a part of human life, and so much has been written about it, that it does not cause shock, revulsion, or even a blush anymore, thank goodness. . . . Yes, there should be fondling and intercourse and fantasies . . . without recourse to intimidation, force, or selfishness.

74/W: Sex over 65? No objection, except that too much is made of the subject. Those who have to indulge must have never been good at anything else, or had little to think about, perhaps, except bridge. Physical closeness, tenderness, and affection (expressed in many ways) are so much more rewarding and meaningful than intercourse.

77/M: I've enjoyed lots of sex in my life, and I love remembering it. But in the last few years it became such a mild pleasure that other things seemed more important, and I've stopped bothering or worrying. It's only a mild impoverishment, and life has other great riches. My late wife agreed with me.

78/M: Make the best of what you have and cherish it.

79/M: My wife and I continue a satisfactory sexual life—about once a month! We travel together, attend concerts together—but by design we go our separate ways in hobby interests. She is a wildflower expert, a rug hooker, a bird-watcher, and a superb writer of publicity and letters for local causes. I put in about half my waking hours in my workshop and on my wooded acres plus regular work on local do-good causes.

79/W: In many ways the interpretation of "sex" has been expanded with emphasis on the difference between sex as an act of temporary pleasure and sex as an act of expression of permanent love (an emotional, fulfilling, tender, compatible, and trusting relationship between two people). Sex, when it is an act of impulsive, temporary pleasure, is prevalent in today's youthful society, but for those of us who have chosen a more conservative viewpoint, sexual intercourse is a natural and beautiful expression of affection, both healthful and satisfying. Fondling is a stimulus for that, not to be ignored. Physical closeness helps to increase our awareness of a natural tendency to love and be loved. It doesn't have to be intercourse.

84/W: Genital sensations are a joy and give a sense of "I'm still alive!" Sexual activity is possible and desirable indefinitely. If one of the partners finds orgasm unavailable, O.K., use instead maximum physical closeness and touching to the extent that it is appealing to your spouse. Also, as we age, we often become anxious. Then the sorts of touching we experienced in childhood become important as security and interplay of love and being cared for. So enjoy yourself to the fullest. But *don't* demand from a reluctant or unable mate.

96/W: Sexual feelings do not entirely stop, even at 96. However, my training and character would not sanction for me what I would excuse in others. I must say that "elders" do *not* lose need for love and loving. But all this is private.

A few respondents illustrated their view about sexuality by writing lengthy, interesting accounts of their experiences throughout their lives, sometimes starting very young. They wanted to share with someone, and hoped it would be useful, everything from "a passionate kiss behind the pigpen" when the respondent was an adolescent to just what happened in the upper and lower berths of the sleeping car on the first night of the honeymoon. In some, the desire to reminisce was strong.

Others, slightly over a quarter of my respondents, felt that writing about sexuality was just not what they wanted to do and left all the sexuality spaces blank. Still others had some strong views about why they did *not* want to write about the subject or felt the whole subject to be inappropriate, repulsive, or even boring.

66/W: Is our generation liberated enough to write to you about sex? I'm not.

68/M: Sorry to be grouchy about this, but it makes me feel old-fashioned and sad that such matters have to be so talked about and strained after.

69/W: I am neither interested in nor concerned about "sex over 65." It's a media subject calculated to titillate the audience. The emphasis upon it is typical of our pimply, adolescent civilization. I'm sure we're the *only* nation in the world that would think the subject worth discussing. It's great, it's natural, so let's get on with it. Why make an *issue* of it?

69/W: I think it's disgusting that these old people go around looking for sex. When you get flabby and dry, you ought to stop trying to be young and accept your age and quit looking for sex. Memories are enough.

71/W: It's just not done to discuss these questions. Sex is private. Keep it that way.

75/W: The latest, sex for the terminally ill, strikes me as disgusting. When about to launch on the Great Adventure, who could care about screwing and masturbating?

75/W: This subject is a big bore. We've lived through the reproductive years, and silly attempts to pretend we're still handy are simply sad and pathetic.

76/M: I'm sorry, but talking or writing about any of this goes against my grain, and it's an old grain. Furthermore, put it in words and away flies Eros!

78/M: They really turn me off, these elderly sex-anxious people, grimly determined to make it. They're a bit like teenagers determined to lose their virginity. At least the teenagers have a future when they can learn better and enjoy more.

Love and Sex Are Not the Same

A major point made by several people and strongly implied by others is that love and sex, while they may be related, are not the same thing, especially for elders.

67/M: The matter of sex and the elderly, loving and touching, etc., seems ringed about with artificiality almost unique to our society. To other groups our general reactions seem to be absurd and unnatural. I feel this too. Where I come from, a gemütlich Jewish family, physical closeness, fondling, kissing, hugging (man-to-man, too) are so normal that persons with dissimilar responsiveness seem cold, unfeeling, and even deadlike.

68/W: Sex is probably necessary for most people. But it is only one facet of the marvelous spectrum of love and marriage. Physical closeness, touching come to mean more and more to me, but I imagine it's equally important for relationships of all ages. Tenderness is important and telling each other in ten thousand ways, verbal and nonverbal, that we love each other. It's so important for stability and ongoingness of a relationship.

69/M: I find myself less interested or aroused by sexual desires. There is comfort and great pleasure in being together and enjoying each other without the pressures or "hang-ups" about recapturing youth with aroused sexual desires.

70/W: I believe it is possible to live effectively without sex but not without love. When these can be combined into old age, that is ideal. Caring deeply, however that caring is expressed, is an important part of retaining personhood and remaining involved.

72/M: Loving and tenderness and touching need have little or nothing to do with sexual intercourse. Loving is necessary for human beings. Sex isn't, notably in old age.

75/W: Sex? Not for our age. But a little warmth and affection is another thing. I guess we all like that until the end. Loneliness can be frightening, so remarriage is a good idea if you know anybody you could stand having in the house all the time.

78/W: Touch, closeness, caresses, gentle massage, lying in contact or holding hands are very important substitutes for the sexual act. When we love, we do not see our mates as the young view us—wrinkled, misshapen, unattractive. We still retain, somewhere, the memory of one another as beautiful and lustful, and we see each other at our once-best. But now there is added the spiritual richness from years of patience, familiarity, and fusion of self-in-another. Our fantasies may run in any direction we choose and the touch becomes sweet to us, the warm familiar body smell a fragrance, and we slip into a peace of stillness and relaxation and safety.

80/M: Physical closeness is a basic human need. Touching is very important even to those who are about to die. That doesn't mean sex.

83/W: Loving and touching are important to me with the members of my family. This is not sex, but it is love.

84/W: Maybe a deep need for touching applies to the very old. Many of us are childlike. A caress means we are loved.

86/M: The touch of a hand can make the day—when there is that something between two people of opposite sex but with compatible hearts.

86/M: "A picture is worth a thousand words"—so is a loving touch, a kiss.

The longing to be lovingly touched is brought home poignantly by psychiatrist Olga Knopf in her *Successful Aging*:

> I know from personal experience that some of the old go for years without touching a human being other than by a handshake. This point was driven home to me by the story of a very old lady who, while sitting in a bus, made the acquaintance of a young woman who had a two- or three-year-old child on her lap. By some chance the child put her arms around the neck of the old lady. The old woman began to cry. She had all but forgotten how it felt when a little child caressed her.

I myself had a quite different experience with the longing to be touched. The 83-year-old widow of a former schoolteacher of mine was bed- and wheelchair-ridden in a retirement community. She was in her chair and, looking somewhat embarrassed, asked me if I'd scratch her back. I gladly assented. She leaned forward, and I reached under her gown and gently scratched. She made sounds of contentment and turned toward me and said, "Eric, you know, I think the back is the least embarrassing part of the human body." She paused, and then added with a twinkle, "Although it leads to a thing or two."

I've already suggested that the staff and management of some continuing-care communities tend to be a bit frightened of or puzzled by elders' expressions of sexuality. One supervisor of an old-age home said, "Yeah, we make a bed-check every night. You can't be too careful. You know, these oldies might be fooling around with each other."

And a 79-year-old woman respondent, with considerable experience in nursing homes, although she does not live in one, wrote: "In a nursing home, on the same day, a blind woman and an elderly man were admitted. After a few days the nurse found the man in the woman's bed in the morning. This event, when repeated, was reported to the administrator, who declared the man to be confused and moved him to the psychiatric ward. After considerable time, it was found out that they are husband and wife!"

What Proportion of Elders are "Sexually Active"?

As I have said, and as you may gather from the sample of replies I have quoted, it was often not possible for me to judge for sure whether or not a given respondent was sexually active. But I decided to make an educated guess about my group. I did this despite the plea of a 79-year-old woman: "*Please* don't give any activity and frequency statistics! They can be terrible put-downs. So is 'Use it or lose it.' Studies and statistics push us back to when we were in puberty and were so anxious about whether we were 'ahead' or 'behind' our friends. Let us just *be*."

As for the 26 percent of the respondents who did not reply to the sexuality questions or stated that the matter was private, it's anybody's guess whether or not they are sexually active. Five percent wrote replies that gave no hint of their own situations, even though often they had plenty to say. Of the remaining 69 percent, I judge that 70 percent are sexually active and 30 percent not. In the "active" figure I include both those who say or suggest that they masturbate ("self-pleasuring" is a phrase that some used; it's certainly a less medical-sounding term!) and those who report having recently been active and fully intending to be again "when I find the opportunity." Inaccurate as they may be, certainly these figures give the lie to the idea that most elders are not sexually active.

The percentages of sexually active elders break down by age, thus: 65–69, 83%; 70–74, 74%; 75–79, 77% (I think this indicated rise in activity is just a fluke of my small sample); 80–84, 59%; and 85+, 25%. I should make it clear that a considerable portion of the "inactives" were that way because of lack of acceptable opportunities rather than lack of desire or approval.

It's interesting to compare my figures with those reported in *Love, Sex, and Aging,* by Edward M. Brecher (himself age 74 at date of publication) and the editors of Consumer Report Books. Brecher's sample was composed of 4,296 members of the Consumer's Union organization who volunteered to answer a long questionnaire. Since CU members are likely to be better off, better educated, and healthier than the general population, and since the data is from those who volunteered to answer the sex questionnaire and therefore can be assumed to be especially interested in the subject, certainly the CU results cannot be applied to the whole U.S. population. Anyway, here are the figures on the sexually active: 60–69, 81% of women and 91% of men; 70 and over, 65% of women and 79% of men.

The "Dirty Old" Syndrome

I asked this question: *There is a widely held view that sexual activity on the part of elders is "dirty." What is your opinion about sex being "dirty" for older people?* I quote quite a few replies to this question because they are instructive, entertaining, and sometimes revealing.

66/W: Sex at any age can be "dirty" if used in an exploiting way. Conversely, sex at any age can be "clean" and good if based on love and considerateness.

70/W: Ridiculous. With the proper partner, sex is great at any age.

70/M: I think what most refer to as "dirty old men or women" has to do with the senile folks who are no longer responsible. They lose their inhibition, have personality changes. Hence, the unsocial acts of exposure, impolite and vulgar language and acts.

70/M: I thoroughly approve of the bumper sticker that reads DIRTY OLD MEN NEED LOVE TOO.

71/M: What is virility at 25 becomes lechery at 65.

71/M: If it isn't dirty for younger people, why should it be for older?

71/W: Maybe the old-fashioned syndrome stemmed from lecherous old men who had the bad taste to annoy young ladies. Contented old couples don't parade their sexuality if it embarrasses others.

71/W (about her 80-year-old spouse): All the young secretaries in my husband's office send him "dirty-old" birthday cards. *I* would be too embarrassed to buy any of them! He loves the cards, and maybe (with a laugh and at a distance) the secretaries. But I *know* he loves me totally and most.

74/W: We eat and drink as before; why not touch and love?

75/M: Sex isn't dirty for any age. The dirty part is not being able to be a participant as much as you would like.

78/M: Once, over 60, I was called a "dirty old man" by a woman of the same age. My feelings were hurt until I realized that she was a lifelong self-centered, super-sanitary single.

78/W: I cannot think that any form of sex motivated by love or even the illusion of love can be called "dirty."

80/M: Dirty old men are unhappy and frustrated old men. *I* know.

81/M: I wish I *were* a dirty old man—but I pretend to be.

84/W: I've been "pawed," but could put a stop to it comfortably, knowing that the "dirty old" man is sick in a way, and hungry for something never fulfilled. He has become immature, or has lost his sense of propriety, or is totally self-indulgent, or is becoming senile.

86/M: Age has nothing to do with it. A definition of "dirt" is "misplaced matter." Coal on the grate is not dirt. On your hands or face at dinner, it is. Sex, in God's purposes, is not dirty. Selfishly used or misused at any time, even in marriage, it is.

New Romance

Except for an occasional miraculous case, most of us, I think, believe that new romantic love doesn't develop among elders. But it does, in various ways, as these accounts show:

66/M: In another week I shall marry for the second time. Like many of our children, I have lived with this person for a year. I am marrying her because it is important to her and because the idea pleases me, too. It's fun to be puppies again. We spend more time talking about sex than doing it, which is in some ways more satisfying since it is sharing, which intercourse often isn't.

70/W: Remarriage has been a great boon for many widowed or divorced elderly persons. Once again it provides companionship, not necessarily sexual activity, and provides a social atmosphere that relieves the loneliness of being unattached. For many couples it is a real rejuvenation of the mind, the body, and the senses. It often provides the necessary impetus to join communal activities from which the single oldster might have felt excluded.

72/M: Living together first—not a bad idea. A good test—and there is no danger of pregnancy. Adjustments are probably harder to make between two older people, so a trial run is a good idea.

73/W: Remarriage is in some ways like a second chance at being young, without the learning process and the responsibilities of educating children. To be bodily close again to someone, to enjoy whatever the aging process allows is one of the greatest blessings I know and far surpasses those earlier years of deep passion without fulfillment.

77/W: In most retirement homes the women outnumber men. Sometimes the men are shy or "scared off" by all the women. And so if a man and a woman find they have enough in common on other levels to go to bed together, the rest of us should not condemn or criticize, but rejoice that at least two people have found a way to express and share an exchange of energy that will bring a new zest for life and evoke joy for others just by their new radiance.

78/M: Know that elders have sexual feelings, attractions, and desires (and temptations) just as younger people do. They can also have romantic fancies and "fall in love." They also have less time left to experience them.

79/W: I have often wondered why "we" (society) are not concerned about what goes on between a couple who grow old together. But people who first meet after they are over 65 are sharply criticized if they fall in love. Many of us have learned to accept and approve of youngsters living together, so it seems now appropriate to liberalize attitudes toward sex among elders. From my limited observation, the situation becomes a problem in old people's homes, where every move

is watched, evaluated in gossip sessions—and envied! Long live love
at an advanced age!

81/W: In recent years I have changed my reaction to seeing an
attractive much older woman artfully elicit male attention! I used to
think this seemed too forward! I can now handle my own envy! (I'm
not sure I've got what it takes to try it myself, but I understand a lot
of adolescents feel that way, too.)

87/M: Yes, sex, loving, touching are necessary, if your life's
partner is still with you. In case of loss of spouse, if you are fortunate
to find a congenial companion of the opposite sex, congratulations
and God bless you!

88/W: It is not fun to live alone. Sex is as necessary as loving and
touching to make a fully and happy life, even at 88. I have been a
widow for thirteen years. Life is hard to understand. If I were to
marry a man my own age, it would likely be some man who wanted
a nursemaid, and his interest in world affairs would be nil. An alert
gentleman age 65 to 70, whom I could enjoy, would likely be looking
for a young lady in her thirties. Therefore, there seems no way to
answer our needs, and we must live as best we can without the
greatest desires of life being answered.

On the other hand, many, perhaps most, elders seem to be content
to let the flames of romantic desire die.

65/W: Since so many elderly women are widows, and I am one of
them, I write from a widow's point of view. I very much miss physical
closeness, fondling, kissing, a man's hand in mine, a man's embrace.
I think I miss a man's presence more than actual sexual intercourse.
Yes, I've thought about remarriage and fantasized about meeting the
perfect mate. But now I question whether I want to live with anyone
(man or woman). I don't want the annoyance of someone "underfoot,"
and I question whether I really want responsibility for the well-being
of a partner. On the other hand, how deprived I sometimes feel
because I can't share pleasures and problems with someone dear. I
think of how utterly devastating it can be to be among a group of
partnered people and alone! I'm not sure I really want to share my
life intimately again, and yet—yet how good it is to be with a man!

74/W: Having learned to sublimate my sex drive in research over
the years, I have lived alone and loved it for so many years that I

would certainly be miserable trying to adapt my independent single life to someone else's life-style and habits. I would just make him miserable as well as myself.

74/W: I'm not going to marry some old geezer, even a nice one, just to "service" him sexually. I'm all in favor of deep friendship and lots of keeping company, but my desire for intercourse or capacity to fall in love are gone, and I'm glad because the past was wonderful. So, men, let's be deep friends but not lovers.

77/W: A couple of times I have gone to bed with a man to cuddle but with the distinct understanding we were not "having sex" (no penetration). These have been comfortable, happy times where we shared our deepest feeling about life, religious ideals, childhood memories—just a marvelous togetherness of human beings who craved affection and appreciation. No strings attached. No commitments— only meeting immediate human needs.

An added note: Several respondents came out in favor of what they called "sin." Here are two such replies:

72/M: I think elders should be allowed to "live in sin." Marriage is a third-party intrusion that should be needed only where children or property are concerned. But proper status is still very strong, so we submit. Also, the tax consequences are outrageous: It still costs more to be married than unmarried and living under the same roof.

81/W: I abhor the idea that people over 65 should not continue whatever sex life they like until they can't. I see no earthly reason why the elderly should not live in sin if the spirit moves them and do whatever else they want. The public is very intolerant of sex in the elderly. (Also, I hear it is good for arthritis!)

What about "Self-Pleasuring"?

Despite the opportunity given by the first question on sexuality, most of my respondents did not comment on masturbation, or simply said, in effect, that "all of the above" were O.K. if done with consideration. Two or three expressed the views of this 70-year-old man: "Masturbation is just something I've been taught (long ago) not to do or think about. I did it when I was young, but I was against it. I'm afraid the teaching *against* is much stronger than the desire *for*. Is that *old*-fashioned?"

There were more, however, who took the following point of view:

68/M: Fantasy rejuvenates, so go ahead and fantasize while stimulating yourself.

70/W: If at our age we can't get over the idea that sexually pleasing yourself, alone with your thoughts, is bad, we need a shake-up.

72/M: I'm a widower. I miss sex. I don't love (sexually) anyone. So I masturbate, and I agree with whoever it was that gave the arguments for it: "It's free, it's always available, you can't get anybody pregnant, you can't get any diseases—and you meet a better class of people." [*Note:* A woman respondent, age 75, offered the same quote.]

Rightly or wrongly, I infer from what respondents said that they would experience a sense of relief and relaxation if they felt it was O.K. to talk and think about self-pleasuring. The next eight statements may help, even though they express a variety of views:

79/W: Just because I'm happily married and have a bit of sex life doesn't mean that I don't get a bit more, a good bit, by stimulating myself. I don't even tell my husband. It might just make him feel unhappy.

69/W: I enjoy sex to some extent with manual stimulation and can reach a climax in short order. I still love the marvelous release I feel with it, and all the edgy pieces seem to be put back together again afterward.

74/W: Masturbation—you can have it. I want the real thing or nothing, and given what I find around me, I have chosen nothing. I'd rather have my good memories.

75/M: There is sex among the elderly, but it takes a little more time to get ready and even then you may not be ready. Closeness, sexual fantasies, fondling are only substitutes for the real thing. But one of the best things, because it is so easy, is self-pleasuring.

77/W (a widow): Fantasies can be great fun. One can write one's own scene and sit back or lay back and enjoy it. As long as one knows one is fantasizing, it is perfectly harmless.

78/W: Selective reminiscence, that's what I like. It can be done alone, it's free, and you can pleasurably imagine what *might* have happened—as you masturbate.

78/W: Security and happiness—being wanted—are inherent in kind, gentle, caring fondling and intercourse. Masturbation is a poor substitute, as are sexual fantasies, in my thinking.

78/W: At least, if I masturbate, I can be sure the machinery is still working. And my imagination makes it less machinelike.

Too Much Bother?

In my questionnaire, one question was: *A 70-year-old woman wrote: "Sex? It's too much bother these days, and I don't miss it. So don't shove me!" How do you react to her statement?* Only thirty or so respondents did react. Of those, a few said, in effect, "I sympathize with her"; a few more, mostly men, said, "I pity her" (one adding, "I have no desire to meet her"); still others commented that she must either be a prude or have had a bad sex life. But the largest number, men and women, agreed with her: "I feel the same way" or "Cheers for her!"

What surprised me, though, was the number of people who did not react directly to this woman's statement, but who instead used the item about her, and other items, to say that they felt there's entirely too much emphasis on sex. For example:

70/W: I have little sympathy for "cultists" who lecture the elderly on their need for intercourse, and I think what is important is that no person feel guilty about his/her sexuality, provided whatever they do is expressed with loving concern and sensitivity.

70/M (an M.D.): Probably because of the excessive publicity given over the years to first Kinsey and then Masters and Johnson [sex researchers and therapists], most older people seem to think that they would be very peculiar or even abnormal if they did not have an active sex life after 65 years of age. Hence few elders would want to admit that they did not have an active sex life and will even lie about it to "save face." I have had a few people, both young and old, tell me, as a doctor, that they were really not that much interested in sex per se and over the years had done many things to avoid it.

73/W: Loving and touching are fine, but I really don't like to "love" and "touch" (and kiss) everyone, the way some people seem to expect. I especially hate spitty kisses. I do like a cheek and a hug.

74/M (a father, happily married, with a vast zest for life): Sex: not very important in my life. I was never "very good in bed." That doesn't trouble me, and I wish it would stop troubling others.

86/M: I see no reason why "normal" sex should not be enjoyed well beyond 65. But preoccupation with ways and means of keeping it going or making it more exciting, etc., are part of the malady of our sex-oriented society, and betoken an immaturity and self-centeredness that should have been outgrown in favor of more creative contributions to meet the pressing needs about us. The *creative* energy and contribution of mature people should be channeled into our society.

The Lighter Side of Sex

As you have doubtless noticed, a number of respondents replied to questions seriously but with a pleasing twist of humor. That's a major difference between elders and the many early adolescents to whom I have given sex-education courses. Adolescents often say things about sex that would be funny to adults but are not so to the adolescents. I remember a very verbal seventh-grade boy who didn't even have any fuzz yet on his cheek, and who, as an assignment, wrote a strong defense of sex education in schools. He ended with the sentence "To this day there's a great deal I don't know about sex." When he read his paper to the class, no one laughed. It was simply a true statement.

Well, we elders can see the funny side of sex. Here are a few samples:

68/W: On a train from Boston to Philadelphia, two married women, one in her twenties, one in her seventies, happened to get into a very interesting exchange of ideas about their marriages. As they were passing through Hartford, they relaxed into a thoughtful, comfortable silence. Then the young woman asked, "Tell me, do you and your husband have mutual orgasm?" The older woman thought hard for a moment and then replied, "No, I think we have State Farm." So you see, sometimes the generations have difficulty communicating about sex!

70/M: Here's a story your readers may enjoy: To celebrate their fiftieth wedding anniversary, a couple returned to their honeymoon hotel. After retiring, the wife said, "Darling, do you remember how you stroked my hair?" And so he stroked her hair. She reminded him of the way they had cuddled, and so they did. With a sigh she said, "Won't you nibble my ear again?" With that the husband got out of bed and left the room. "Where are you going?" cried the wife. "To get my teeth!" he said.

73/M and 70/W: Several phrases which we didn't fully appreciate when we were younger include: "What was triweekly, we now try weakly"; "What we did all night now takes all night."

74/M: A couple in their late sixties were seeing a sex therapist to aid them in sexual performance. After six or seven visits at fifty dollars a visit, the therapist asked, "You seem to be doing very well—even teaching me a few tricks. Why do you keep coming in?" The man replied hesitantly, "Well, Doctor, I am not her husband. I can't go to her house. She cannot come to mine. Besides, the Holiday Inn charges sixty dollars for a room. We only pay you fifty, and Medicare reimburses."

75/W: As they say, and it's true of us: "My husband and I are still compatible. He can still come and I'm still pattable."

75/W: A young woman asked a 70-year-old woman how long sex drive lasted. The older one replied, "I don't know; ask me in twenty years and I'll try to tell you."

77/W: An elderly couple were sitting in front of the fireplace with a Christmas tree on one side of it. It was Christmas Eve. The wife said, wistfully, "I wonder whatever happened to our sexual relations." The husband paused for a while and then said, "Well, they were with us last year, weren't they?"

78/M: The late actor Pat O'Brien was on the board of directors of the National Association for Mature People, and he told a story that points out the problems of assuming too much about older people.

John, who was 65, went to the doctor for a physical examination. The doctor looked him over and said, "John, you're in great health for a man of your age. But I'm going to need a more complete medical history. How old was your father when he died?"

"Did I say he died?" asked John. "He's 85 years old, still mows his own lawn, and he's going strong."

The doctor was amazed. "That's marvelous," he said. "But what about your grandfather? How old was he when he died?"

"Did I say he died?" asked John. "He's 107, still swims twice a week, and recently got married."

The doctor was dumbfounded. "That's great," he said, "but why would a man of 107 want to get married?"

"Did I say he *wanted* to get married?" asked John.

Some "Facts" About Elders' Sexuality

Quite a few respondents expressed the hope that this book would give some objective facts about the sex lives of the elderly. Here are two typical statements:

72/M: There's so much rumor and wishful thinking and embarrassment about us elders and sex that I hope you will give us some straight facts about it. (I don't mean "where babies come from"; I *do* know that!)

75/W: I'm pretty comfortable about my sex life—I don't have much because I have no partner and am too busy on other things to find one. But what are the facts about sex and the elderly?

This is not the place for a treatise on the subject. (Read Brecher's *Love, Sex, and Aging,* to which I've already referred, if you want that.) But here are some observations with which a good many (not all) informed people would agree:

- The amount of sexual activity elders engage in usually is directly related to how strong their sex drive was when they were younger. High-sex-drive people tend to continue; low-sex-drive people tend not to.
- The generally accepted myth that people over 60 aren't or shouldn't be much interested in sex tends to affect elders themselves. They

have the impression, as do those of any age they know, that they'll lose interest and capacity. (Many doctors accept the myth and never ask elder patients about sex. Thus we elders must bring up the subject and not accept "Well, at your age . . ." responses.)

- With menopause, which usually occurs between ages 45 and 55, women can no longer become pregnant, but this does not mean a reduction of sexual desire (unless a woman is strongly convinced that it does). On the contrary, since there's no more worry about pregnancy, desire and pleasure often increase.

- Women generally do not lose their capacity to enjoy orgasm, unless they never or rarely had orgasm when they were younger. However, lack of a spouse or appealing partner may reduce the capacity for orgasm, and many women simply lose the expectation. Also, with age, it takes most women longer to reach orgasm, and sometimes their orgasms are briefer.

- Men usually take longer to develop an erection (note that I didn't use the verb *achieve*, which makes it sound like a job rather than a pleasure), and their erections are often smaller and less hard. Also, elder men ejaculate less semen than younger ones, but the ejaculation still gives great pleasure, even though it takes longer to arrive at the point of ejaculation. An advantage of this is that there's more time for sex play, and this is important for most women's pleasure and orgasm. The length of time between ejaculations—the refractory period—gets longer with age, and frequency of ejaculation decreases.

- After menopause, women's vaginal tissues tend to become thinner and more subject to irritation, since their bodies no longer produce so many tissue-strengthening hormones. Also, a woman's vagina tends to lose its capacity to lubricate itself during sexual stimulation. Thus artificial lubricants (like KY jelly) are useful and greatly increase the pleasure. Women should be sure, too, to ask their gynecologists about hormone replacement to compensate for the decline in their production after menopause. (This treatment can have medical benefits beyond the sexual, as discussed in Chapter 3.)

- One common problem related to sexuality is "performance anxiety"—men's fear that they will not be able to have an erection or ejaculate. The anxiety tends to feed on itself and hence worsen. Spouses can help alleviate anxiety by refraining from comment and by not giving up. Keep pleasantly enjoying; there's always tomorrow, or next week.

- The loss of one's sexual partner can be devastating to one's ability to enjoy sexual activity, as can be the lack of an available partner. So don't panic at the sudden lack of desire—it's not permanent if you don't want it to be. (This is especially true for women, who generally live longer than their husbands.)

- At any age, being sick—suffering from a long- or short-term disease—greatly reduces the desire and ability to have sex. Since we elders are more often sick and suffer far more diseases than younger people, our sex lives often suffer. The important thing is not to give up after your disease is cured.

- Surgery is often harmful to sexual performance and enjoyment. Part of the harm is physical, part psychological. But prostate surgery in men, and pelvic surgery in women, usually need not spoil sexual enjoyment in the long run, unless the surgeon is unaware of methods to maintain sexual capacity while treating the condition. Be sure, *if you care,* that you discuss sexuality with your surgeon and your regular doctor. It's a complex subject. You'll probably need more than one opinion.

- Medicines prescribed for common conditions, especially for high blood pressure (also insomnia and anxiety), are likely to affect sexual enjoyment, especially that of men. Keep working with your doctor until you find a combination of medicines, or diet and medicine, that is less inhibiting, especially of erection and ejaculation. [*Note:* Diabetes can cause impotence, but the medicines prescribed for it do not, contrary to what many people think.]

- Contrary to what many people believe, a heart attack does not make sexual intercourse (or masturbation) dangerous. If you can walk slowly upstairs, your heart's got what it takes to permit sexual activity. Cases, often overpublicized, of death by heart attack during sexual intercourse are very rare.

Two Closing Comments

After this burst of facts, let's return to the more general aspects of our sexuality. I found these two comments helpful:

77/M: At our age, we know there are so many pleasures in life, and sex may be one of them. If it is for us, great—relax and enjoy it.

If it's not (as in my case), well, there's lots else to be enjoyed—touching, thinking, remembering, and promoting a speck of wisdom here and there. We've got a lot more rich, varied possibilities than do rabbits, mice, guinea pigs, and hamsters.

82/W: Enjoy what you can and don't fret. Leave fretting to the young.

Tips & Techniques

This book is not a sex manual, but several respondents suggested, almost by the way, methods they used to increase sexual enjoyment, reduce sexual stress, and solve sexual problems. I present them in random order:

- Don't get stuck with the habit of having sex only at bedtime. Often that's when you're the most tired. If you're retired, one advantage of not being bound by a job schedule is that you can take advantage of good moments, like just before or after an afternoon nap.

- I've found that my husband often has an erection in the morning, when he needs to urinate, but not urgently. We lovingly agree that if he presses against me, it may be a good time for sex. Seize the moment!

- Expect the woman to reach orgasm more often and more easily than the man. And we women must be very careful not to let the man feel unsuccessful or call (or even think) him impotent if he doesn't always get erect and ejaculate.

- Forget "simultaneous orgasm"! Let each lovingly consider himself or herself and then consider the other (or vice versa). That's not selfish.

- Don't get hung up on the man-on-top "missionary" position. Use your imagination. Try some new things. This is especially important if you have arthritis or other aches and pains. As you're having sex, if something hurts, say so. How can your spouse know otherwise? *Also*, if something feels just right (like a certain kind of stroking or squeezing), say that, too. We need to learn to communicate and not just rely on body and magic.

- Keep your lubrication and your towel right beside the bed so that you can be ready when you feel like it.

- I found that I was having a very difficult time getting an erection. A friend recommended a penile prosthesis. I'd never heard of such a thing. But now I have a plastic rod implanted in my penis. This means I always have a sort of semi-erection, but it doesn't show when I'm dressed, and it doesn't interfere with urinating. It does mean, though, that I can satisfy my wife and myself very pleasingly. [*Note:* Don't consider a prosthesis until you've had a medical evaluation to make sure that medicines or some sort of illness are not the cause of failure to get an erection. Consult with a qualified sex therapist as well as with your doctor.]

- I was used to having my husband initiate most of our sexual contact. But now I've found that when I take some initiative and snuggle up close, he responds and we have a great time. Sometimes we just hold each other; sometimes we have intercourse. He now often tells me how much he likes me to "make the first move." Also, sometimes when I don't feel sexy and he does, I just make him come with my hand. I like the feeling, he loves the ejaculation.

- We've arranged a sort of code, since we really have a hard time talking directly about sex. If I touch her foot *in a certain way,* we know what it means, and the same if she touches mine.

- Think about your bed(s)! My husband and I find that we need room in bed to curl up alone (to ease certain aches and pains); we need to scratch; we need to toss around a bit. This was hard to do in our ordinary double bed. We tried closeby twin beds, but then we really missed each other's bodies. We even seemed to be growing apart. So we brought a great big king-size bed. It's almost like a house! We can be alone on our own side, or we can roll over and be close and smooch—the best of both worlds. We don't bother each other, yet we do enjoy each other. (Another solution is just to push two twin beds together as one and arrange the mattresses crossways.)

- There's a surplus of elderly women and not enough men to go round. I know some women who have decided to live together, and sleep together, and just enjoy each other sexually, with lots of touching. It doesn't matter if you call it "lesbian" or not. It's just two human beings satisfying each other—no big deal if you can get over your rigid "straight" ideas.

- If you're a widow, or a widower, take the initiative and look up friends of younger days who themselves may have become widowers or widows. It's a very promising approach, even if only for good company, but maybe it'll be for a lot more. Don't hesitate! What can you lose? And certainly your friend of youthful days won't be insulted even if he/she's not interested.

- We think of sex education as something only for the young. I know of a 72-year-old retired doctor who decided to offer a course on human sexuality to senior citizens. He reports: "What was very exciting to me was the avid interest of the participants in this course. Rarely could I speak for more than two or three minutes without a hand raised to ask a question or make a comment. They were not at all embarrassed by any of my technical remarks, my description of the genital organs, or any aspect of the sex act." So, if you're interested, why not try to organize such a course or discussion group? And it doesn't have to be a doctor giving it. Sex isn't a disease!

- I'm 78 and interested in my sex life. I needed medical advice, but for quite a period I found that doctors—and not just male ones— seemed very embarrassed to talk with me about sex. I found them uninformed or negative. "At your age," they seemed to be saying, "why talk about this?" And they seemed to have little sense of the realities of the daily lives of older women. If I didn't report a good, definite *disease*, they didn't know what to do. Well, I've changed all that with one male doctor, a geriatrician. He's really willing to help me with my problems. So, women (and probably men), make your doctors talk and listen, and if they don't seem to know anything about sex, find another! To be over 75 and want to talk about sex doesn't make you a "crock."

GEM COLLECTION

66/W: Sex is a discovery that young people make, and they think they invented it and don't want old people trying to copy them.

68/W: The now-saint, Augustine, was not unexperienced in sex. I've a feeling he prayed, "Lord, make me chaste—but not yet!"

70/M: Don't touch me unless I am free and you are free, becauseit always moves me deeply. Loving and touching are holy things to be treated tenderly and with deep consideration.

71/W: I share with you a story about a young woman who was very interested in marrying a wealthy old gentleman. In addition to her marriage proposal, she suggested that they might even have children. The old gentleman said, "But my parents won't let me." She said, "Who are your parents?" He replied, "Mother Nature and Father Time."

70+W (Maggie Kuhn on a demonstration poster): GO AHEAD AND TOUCH ME. WRINKLES AREN'T CONTAGIOUS.

74/M: *Inside* me, I am a sexy man, often filled with sexual desire. I look at a lovely young woman, and I love her so much that I project the feeling on her—she must love me, the way I feel. But I stop! I know from my mirror that I look dried-up and severe—even old. What I feel inside doesn't show. I'm not sexy to lovely ladies. So I don't touch; I just enjoy fantasies.

76/W: Do you know this verse? It's an oldie, but there's truth in it.

> *The slim young man I married*
> *Has slowly gone to pot;*
> *With wrinkled face and graying pate,*
> *Slender he is not!*
> *And when I meet a mirror*
> *I find a haggard crone;*
> *I can't believe the face I see*
> *Can really be my own.*
>
> *But when we seek our bed each night,*
> *The wrinkles melt away:*
> *Our flesh is firm, our kisses warm,*
> *Our ardent hearts are gay!*
> *The Fountain of Eternal Youth*
> *Is not so far to find:*
> *Two things you need—a double bed;*
> *A spouse who's true and kind!*

78/W: By the time you're 65 or so, they ought to abolish the idea of sin as something you shouldn't live in. I'd rather live in sin than in loneliness.

81/W: Though I'm still not aggressive about seeking sex, I'd be less than honest not to admit how basically important it was, and is becoming again for me! I guess I've always loved being an attractive, desirable female—and I shall till I leave Planet Earth!

Chapter 11

RELIGION
AND LIFE

Since elders are near the end of their lives, it's a popular fallacy that they frequently think about death and therefore turn or return to religious devotion. The fact is that most elders, both those in my small sample and those in large cross-sectional studies, are not preoccupied with death and do not in their later years experience a religious awakening. Some are and do, but most aren't and don't.

The first question I asked my respondents shows that I, too, had the same wrong idea. It read: *In some ways, elders can be said to experience, sometimes rather suddenly, a coming to terms with the meaning of life as they approach its end. Some people have even called it a "religious adolescence." What has been your experience with this?* Well, the term *religious adolescence* struck no responsive chords. In fact, the majority of my respondents reported no surge of new faith as they grow older:

67/W: I feel no more inclined toward religion at 67 than I did at 27.

70/M: My Quaker grandmother, on her eighty-third birthday, announced that she was not going to Quaker meeting anymore, because "if I haven't been saved by now, a little more won't help." She never went to meeting again, and died at 87.

71/W: I have been present at my father's death, when Mother went through the valley with him reading and reciting passage after passage from the Bible and singing his favorite hymns. Christ was in the room with us, and I knew all would be well. Father went through the curtain. We couldn't follow, but it was O.K. We were all—especially Father—in God's love and care. Remember, though, this

189

was years ago. It doesn't mean that I have recently become more religious because I'm over 65 and nearer death.

72/M: I love this world and most living things in it. I do not expect a second chance anytime or anywhere. No afterlife. No rejoining loved ones, etc. On the other hand, I fall apart when I hear the Bach Passion According to Saint Matthew or his Mass in B Minor. The Passion of Christ never fails to move me deeply. However, the church (allegedly) of Christ fills me with disgust and anger. His ideas were simple. Others made a power struggle out of them.

74/M: How can religion not be important? How can we look forward to life, thinking that the here and now is all there is? The greatest love, the greatest life's experiences may come, I should think *will* come, in that next life. Those words of Christ, "I will come again to receive you unto myself, that where I am, there you will be also," can only have meaning if the life beyond is far greater and on a loftier plane than this one. It seems to me I've always known this, not just recently.

74/M (a minister): I haven't found 70–80-year-olds any more religious than younger people. Indeed, it can happen that, as the Flash fails, people become in some instances more uncertain, more unsure.

75/W: Well, I have never been religious, so there is no change here. I definitely do not believe in a deity, the hereafter, etc. But I can assume that if anybody were of a religious temperament, and other pleasures faded, it would be indeed comforting to turn to religion. But not in my case. Too bad, I guess, but let's face facts, at least my facts.

75/M: My experience has been nothing radical or sudden; only a growing awareness of the complex interrelatedness of everything in this beautiful universe, and a growing recognition of the crime committed by us humans when we act to despoil this universe and upset its harmony. This is an ancient Chinese (particularly Taoist) concept that I have long held, but I am increasingly aware of it in recent years. As for us humans, we need a greater community of care and tenderness in this fragmented human world in which we live.

84/W: If anything, my humanist agnosticism has deepened with age.

86/M: I have been linked to my Lord and Savior Jesus Christ as a member of His "Church" since my baptism in infancy. I have never felt separated from Him. No religious adolescence for me, just a steady strengthening religion all my life.

Some respondents, however, did say that with old age came a strengthening of religious feeling or interest:

69/M: Yes, I really do experience a closer sense of abiding faith as I grow older. I find myself reflecting about life's experiences and how a Superior One has looked out for me, how He has seen me through trying times, even dangerous periods. I give considerably more thought now to His presence and prayerfully acknowledge His many blessings to our family.

70/M: I know of numerous instances where people who have been totally irreligious in their early years have turned to religion for philosophical and psychological comfort in declining years. Whether or not a belief in God is expressed verbally, many such people feel that from an ethical and moral aspect, one should make one's peace with the world.

Who knows whether God exists? I have nothing to lose by assuming yes, and I feel it appropriate not to make waves in my latter years, but to conform to what is commonly accepted as morally correct attitudes and behavior.

75/M: Most people become more religious when they become older because of the simple fact that they're unable to do much else.

And a couple of respondents found it hard to take the question seriously:

72/M: Perhaps when I die it'll be like Mencken's musing about his own demise: "If I die and find myself standing before a pearly gate and an old man in robes with a golden key to it, I'll go right up to him and say, 'My name is Henry L. Mencken, and I've made a terrible mistake!' "

75/W: I like the story about a pastor who was discussing with an elderly church member the conversion of a relative of hers who had seen the light and joined the church after a lifetime of riotous living.

"Will my converted cousin's sin be forgiven, Pastor?" the old woman asked.

"Oh, certainly, yes!" replied the pastor. "Remember, the greater the sins, the greater the saint."

The woman thought silently for a time. Then she said, "Oh, Pastor, I wish I'd known this fifty years ago."

What Do the Studies Show?

In gerontological textbooks, little or no space is given to religion, other than a few statistics about attendance at church and synagogue. In the 1974 NCOA study, 92 percent of those 65 or older said they felt religion was important in their lives (71 percent "very important," 21 percent "somewhat important"), whereas of the total population aged 18 to 64, 82 percent felt that way (49 percent "very," 33 percent "somewhat"). However, this increase in percentage is probably explained more by the general religious decline in our society than by an increase of such feeling because of growing older. In other words, many more of those who were, say, 70, had always felt religion was important, born as they were at the turn of the century, than those 18 to 64 years old, born over the period 1905–1956. There is a small increase of the religion-is-very-important percentages as people grow from old to older: 65–69, 69%; 70–79, 71%; 80+, 73%.

Both the 1974 and 1981 NCOA studies reported on frequency of attendance at church or synagogue. In 1974, 64 percent of people 65 and over said they had attended within the past month or more recently, whereas the figure was 61 percent for those aged 18 to 64. In 1981, the figures had declined to 61 and 55 percent, respectively. It is clear from comparing these figures and those in the paragraph above that many people who feel religion is important don't always show it by regular attendance at church or synagogue.

One can say, I think, that most elders are interested in religion not as a way of preparing for heaven or avoiding its opposite, but as a way of understanding life and themselves. Also, generally they don't suddenly become religious, but continue to be as they were. It has been suggested that elders may spend more time than others watching and listening to religious programs on TV and radio, but I know of no evidence to back up this theory. However, if watching or listening to these programs were considered as a substitute for attending church, the yes-I-attend figures for elders would doubtless increase, especially since with advancing years it becomes more of a struggle to get out of the house.

Life After Death

I asked what I suppose could be called a religious question about death, although a number of respondents gave quite nonreligious answers. *Do you think there is life after death? Yes __ No __. Explain your answer, including whether or not you think the question is an important one.* Some 34 percent of my respondents checked *Yes,* (there is life after death); 38 percent checked *No;* 23 percent said either that they had no idea or that perhaps there is, or that the matter is a mystery; and 5 percent left all the spaces blank. I found no correlation between the answers given and the respondents' ages.

Here are some comments from those who believe that there *is* life after death:

65/M: I moved to a new place. Since arriving here, I have been born again, baptized by submersion, and have a totally new outlook on life. After death, for the born-again, there will be eternal life— *that is a certainty.*

72/M: "Break Forth O Beauteous Heavenly Light and Usher in the Morning!" (Bach) Of course there's life after death!

72/M: I guess I agree with "Fish," a satiric poem by Rupert Brooke. It goes in part: .

> *This can't be all, wise fish aver,*
> *For how unpleasant if it were! . . .*
> *Somewhere, beyond space and time,*
> *Is wetter water, slimier slime. . . .*

83/W: The question is important. I am coming more and more to believe that there is no *individual* existence after death. (Why should all my imperfections and defects be immortalized?) On the other hand, I believe that we all return to the same source—a spiritual mass—where we all come from. We merge with it and are purified as an infinitesimal droplet, and perhaps some of this spiritual substance becomes somehow a part of some new life.

87/M: The mind of Man is God's grandest creation. It is inconceivable that the Grand Designer would use it merely as a toy, ultimately to be destroyed.

88/W: I can't explain what I think. Life after death is possible, and it is such a great comfort to believe that we will again see our loved ones who have died that I *must* believe it; and the Bible tells us there is.

Those who do not believe in life after death wrote comments like these:

67/M: You're not going to get any direction from the hand of the dead from me. I won't be there or anywhere when I'm gone, so do what makes you and my friends feel best. As for me, I won't care a whit!

68/W: Love is the only thing which endures; not you. Trust it, abandon yourself to it, show it, rejoice in it. And for God's sake— truly for God's sake—laugh at yourself sometimes.

72/M: If there were life after death, everybody would be dashing or flying around heaven, or scorching around hell, looking for their ancestors. But their ancestors would be looking for *their* ancestors, and so on, ad nauseum. It doesn't make sense. When we're dead, we're dead.

80/W: When you're dead, you're dead all over. Immortality is only what you leave behind in work or impact on others.

80/M: The only life after death I expect to have will be in the memories of those who have loved me. However, I believe it is an important question to many people because it makes them less afraid to die and gives them hope that their "self" or "soul" will survive. If belief helps, let them believe.

83/W: I do not believe in life after death, but I know many people who do, and they appear to derive much comfort from the idea. I am sure it is an important belief for them and, though the whole idea seems to me only a pleasant fairy tale, I would not try to disillusion those who are able to accept it. [*Note:* This charitable permission to others to believe was quite frequently expressed.]

84/W: A heaven or hell occupied with the infinite millions of humans who have died since man began? No! And eternal happiness would be terribly boring. And one would look "down" on the pain and struggle and mistakes and cries of descendants. No thanks!

And then, of course, there were the 23 percent who just don't know and expressed it in a variety of ways, sometimes with some advice:

65/W: Perhaps someday it will be proved that at death an invisible spark leaves our body to float in the atmosphere as energy. Maybe at conception or birth a spark enters the new living organism. Perhaps we can call this spark the divine soul. But let's not waste time worrying about something we have no control over.

69/M: When I'm dying, I hope I'll respond as a wise, humorous 82-year-old woman did when she was asked if there is life after death: "I don't know, and I can't wait to find out!"

69/M: One of my sisters says that if she finds out there's no life after death, she "won't be disappointed," and I agree with her.

71/M: I was pretty religious in my youth and middle age—church and all. Now I'm much more interested in life and action here—on earth. And when the time comes, I've no objection at all to peacefully rotting. I've always enjoyed sleeping.

71/M: I'm like Voltaire—I'm not sure there is life after death, but so many people believe in it that I intend to live so that if there is life after death I'll be in on it.

71/W: I would *like* to think there is life after death. It would make our having lived so much less wasteful. Particularly I like the idea of reincarnation. But who knows?

74/M: Just bury me under a tree so I can fertilize it—or is that illegal?

78/W: I'm pretty sure I'm not coming back to earth to haunt anyone, and beyond that I'll take it on faith!

79/W: If any experience is awaiting us, it would be a well-kept secret, and I am happy to be surprised. [*Note:* This reminds me of the story a respondent sent me about the son who said to his very old mother, "Mother, you're getting along, and who knows what may happen? I mean, shouldn't we make a few decisions about arrangements?" A pause, Mother smiling. "I mean, Mom, do you want to be buried or cremated?" The mother answered, "Well, son, I don't know. Why don't you just surprise me?"]

The Religious Life

Although, as I've reported, there is no particular distinction between the religion of elders and that of younger people, many of my respondents did express some views that I found interesting, even inspiring. They were written in response to this question: *Many people are interested in the religious ideas and religious life of elders. Think about such matters as God, worship, prayer, organized religion, ceremony, religious experience, and the meaning and purpose of life, and write about your ideas.* Here are some of the replies:

66/W: I believe in a caring God, whose nature is love; and that our life is a "school" in which we are being trained, albeit with many stops and starts, to become loving spirits. Natural disasters and manmade suffering I do not understand. However, I do believe that like the X in an algebraic equation, there *is* an answer, which at some point (not necessarily in this life) will become clear. Our job, as I see it, is to be as loving as we can here and now.

67/W: My faith and belief in eternal life, the Resurrection of Jesus Christ as the greatest event in human history—these make me feel hopeful and confident.

69/W: An accumulation of teaching, observation, history of religion become embedded in our minds as we learn from parents, friends, old and young, school experiences, and life, and we build up a vast "resource file" within our minds. The thousands of decisions we make in life put data into our inner "computer." Our genetic instincts, emotions, and abilities are all there in our minds to use. I believe that if we "set the stage" for ourselves, we can and do get insights into even the most difficult decisions and needs. Churches, prayer, nature, beauty, sermons are really the *settings* within which spiritual thoughts can emerge and affect us. The data keep coming over the years; so does a sifting process, and we grow wiser.

69/M: Theology, credal formulation, and insistence on specific religious vocabularies are unimportant to me. The human being named Jesus and his life and death are the central guideposts for living my life. I don't really care to argue about whether he is the Christ, the son of God. The question is: Does my life reflect an effort to live as Jesus lived? The proof of the pudding is in the eating, not in arguing about the brand names that go into the recipe.

69/M: For the major portion of my whole life, my religious faith and prayer have been the real supports in many serious physical and mental difficulties. It's not new, but it sustains.

70/W: I am getting more *generally* religious, and more turned off by creeds of any kind. I feel that organized religion *can* put barriers up in our search for God. Silence is meaningful. I dig it. Preaching sometimes makes me distrustful.

71/W: Since my husband died, when I was 66, I have always been most grateful that I had a deep abiding faith which supported and strengthened me to carry on. I enjoy the close friendships in the church, and the warm supportiveness and caring concerns shown me.

71/M: Religion is an inner need in man. Some attach their religious beliefs to a social or political system. Others relate it to God. We need to aspire, to find strength and force in life which is beyond us and has a uniting power, binding us to the universe and to our fellows. Each of us chooses a hypothesis upon which to base his life, and the implications of this hypothesis open up various avenues of enrichment to us. For me, the belief in God gives life a deeper meaning and satisfaction, in which I find *abiding* values.

74/W: I feel a religious connection inside of me with a force that is a source of strength, joy, love, and laughter—no matter what. Is that religious? It is helpful; it is that of God.

74/M: My first wife died from cancer. For days and weeks we both knew the end for her was near. Her staunch and steadfast faith sustained her, as it did me. I spent much time in the hospital chapel on my knees, asking God for help for her and for me. Without that I would have been devastated. Her faith and courage never once wavered during all that long ordeal. It left a deep and lasting impression upon me and our children.

82/M: Religion has inspired what is undoubtedly the world's greatest music (and also art). I have sung masses a dozen times by Bach, Mozart, Verdi, Brahms, Haydn, and others; and will keep on doing so as long as I can sing. I love the music, but I don't believe a word of the *Credo*. One does not have to believe in God in order to have a purpose in life; to be inspired by the awesome majesty of the boundless cosmos; to be thankful for the spacious firmament on high, and the beauty of the earth and the "blue ethereal sky," and the love of family and friends, the gift of life, and the wondrous subtleties of evolution.

84/W: Pray daily this prayer: "Help me to continue to grow old gracefully and be kind, loving, considerate, and compassionate. Let us all know that God's in His Heaven and all's right with the world."

88/W: I am not an overly religious person. I believe that heaven and hell are right here on Earth. Many times, in great sorrow, I have wished that I were a Catholic so that I would believe I will see my loved ones again, but this I cannot believe.

New Religious Insights

Another question I asked was *Have you, since age 65, had any new or restrengthened insights that could be called "religious"? Yes __ No __. If yes, say what they are.* Some 27 percent checked *Yes,* 51 percent checked *No,* and 22 percent left the item blank or in effect said they didn't really understand the question. What are the insights reported by that 27 percent? Here are a handful:

68/W: Yes, I have new insights all the time, but they are too numerous, gentle, and subtle to describe. No big visions or voices, but a growing sense, most of the time, of oneness, of pervasiveness of the Spirit, of "the Light which lighteth *all* people."

68/W: Of a few things I grow more sure: the importance of love and forgiveness; the tragic futility of nationalism and bigotry. I am sure that we are all one—people of this lovely planet, of the universe—part of God. Wow!

69/W: Every day I encounter with new intensity love, beauty, growing plants, growing thoughts—all the ideals "religion" is supposed to have. I don't need to go to a place of worship to find them.

72/M: I know with greater certainty that life is a collection of rules, some more binding than others, and of rewards and punishments for keeping or violating the rules. We have more influence over some outcomes than we do over others. All of the future, and what underlies most of the operations in the present, are concealed from us.

74/M: As the years advance, I worry more about my spiritual condition, although I have been a consistent, working churchman all my life. I have strong beliefs, but I also have strong doubts as to how well I have fulfilled God's expectations, or even my own expectations, of me.

79/M: Since my severe and debilitating illness, I have appreciated the nearness of the "big fellow."

84/W: As I grow older, my Christianity comes to the fore. Jesus didn't say, "Die for me"; He said, "Live for me," and that's what I'm trying to do: live for Him and spread His Kingdom everywhere I can.

Religious Words That Inspire

The words that were most commonly quoted as being the essence of religion were those of the Golden Rule. Several who quoted them apologized that they seemed a cliché. As a 76-year-old woman said, "I'm sorry, but you just can't do better than the Golden Rule, so, each day, take a new look at it; say it again; say it till you die." And, of course, the words are, reported in the gospel of Luke, King James version: "As ye would that men should do to you, do ye also to them likewise." Some quoted more modern translations, like that of the *Good News Bible:* "Do for others just what you want them to do for you."

Perhaps the second most quoted words are those in the gospel of John. An 87-year-old woman wrote, "If we believe, as I do, that there is that of God in us, then God will not completely wipe us out. Have

a little trust. Read the fourteenth chapter of John." Here are excerpts
from that chapter (in the King James version):

> In my Father's house are many mansions: If it were not so, I would
> have told you. I go to prepare a place for you. And if I go and prepare
> a place for you, I will come again, and receive you unto myself; that
> where I am, there ye may be also. . . . I am the way, the truth and the
> life: no man cometh unto the Father, but by me. . . . If ye shall ask any
> thing in my name, I will do it. If you love me, keep my commandments. . . .
> I will not leave you comfortless: I will come unto you: not as the world
> giveth, give I unto you. Let not your heart be troubled, neither let it
> be afraid. . . .

Yet another passage quoted by several is from Paul's letter to the
Romans (8:38–39):

> For I am persuaded that, neither death, nor life, nor angels, nor
> principalities, nor powers, not things present, not things to come, nor
> height, nor depth, nor any other creature, shall be able to separate us
> from the love of God, which is in Christ Jesus our Lord.

One other Bible passage, Psalm 139, verses 7–10, was also often
cited, thus:

> Whither shall I go from thy spirit? or whither shall I flee from thy
> presence? If I ascend up into heaven, thou art there: if I make my bed
> in hell, behold thou are there. If I take the wings of the morning, and
> dwell in the uttermost parts of the sea, even there shall thy hand lead
> me, and thy right hand shall hold me.

I close this chapter with two respondents' definitions of God.

67/M: My wife told me one morning when I asked her how she'd
define God, "Well, I think God is a creative, transforming harmony."
That says it for me!

73/W: Nobody has said it better than William Sloane Coffin of
Riverside Church in New York. I noted down his words: "God to me
is that creative force behind the universe who is manifested as energy,
as life, as order, as beauty, as thought, as conscience, as love." God is
love. So what else is new? Me, I don't need anything more.

Chapter 12

DYING AND DEATH

In the last chapter, we disposed of the commonly held idea that we elders spend a lot of time thinking about death. Most of us don't, and we don't talk about it much either. This is not because there is a conspiracy of silence; it is that death doesn't interest us nearly as much as life, and, furthermore, we've had more years to become accustomed to the idea that we will die.

Most elders don't fear death much either. According to a study by Vern Bengston and colleagues, reported in 1977 in the *Journal of Gerontology*, 52 percent of people between ages 45 and 49 fear death "very much" or "somewhat"; 47 percent of those between 50 and 54; 34 percent of those between 55 and 59; 30 percent of those between 65 and 69; and 24 percent of those between 70 and 74. So from age 45 to age 74 the percentage of people who fear death drops from 52 to 24 percent! (My own study of middle-class adolescents made in 1959 and redone in 1975 shows that death is among the top five worries or fears of about 75 percent of sixth- to ninth-graders, age 11 to 14!*)

The people who tend to fear death least are those who are strongly religious and those who are confirmed atheists, according to Richard Kalish's 1976 study reported in *Handbook of Aging and the Social Sciences*.

Over the centuries, until recently, it was easy to tell the moment when a person died. One's heart stopped beating or one stopped breathing, and the family could say, "He's dead." But now, with cardiopulmonary resuscitation, respirators, and other devices, breathing can be continued, even though it may only amount to ventilating

---

* *How to Live Through Junior High School,* Philadelphia: Lippincott, 1959, 1975.

a corpse; and hearts can be kept beating, or repaired or replaced. Thus people are now referring to "brain death" or "social death," the time when there is no longer any sign of interaction with the environment. Obviously, defining death has become a complex issue, a real legal tangle.

As I pointed out earlier, we do not die of "old age," we die of a disease or a combination of disease. With advancing years, we get more diseases, and finally, one or more of them get us. The most common causes of death among elders are, in descending order of frequency, heart disease, cancer, stroke, influenza, pneumonia, hardening of the arteries, diabetes, and respiratory disorders (bronchitis, emphysema, asthma).

And where do we die? Fifty years ago, most of us died at home, with our families, rather quickly, and quite inexpensively. Today, 80 percent of us die in an institution—a hospital or medical-care center—and the process is long and often vastly expensive. (It's estimated that half of people's medical expenses over a lifetime occur during their last six months.) Death, like birth, has become a medical rather than a family matter. But most of us, according to surveys, say we'd rather die at home.

The Process of Dying

I asked, *What are your feelings about the process of dying?* Some respondents answered directly about feelings; others wrote about how they hoped their own deaths would happen; and still others reported on their feelings and convictions based on their actual experiences with dying people.

66/W: I dread the process of physical and mental decline, and the pain that may be involved. I hope I'll be able to be reasonably well behaved through all that!

67/W: It is very inconvenient for people, and I expect that it will be a real nuisance for me, too.

69/W: I have no fears of death. I think you should prepare for it in a practical way—that is, your worldly goods and body—and let the Lord worry about your soul.

70/W: What is important is that untimely death and needless suffering be prevented, not that life should be sustained through "high technology." I believe that no person should be left to die alone. Everyone should be accompanied by a caring person to whom he/she matters, or a caring volunteer, as is true in hospice programs.

70/M: I consider death as natural a phenomenon as living. Though the span of life is lengthening, the inevitability of dying is as certain as always, and there should be no trauma connected with facing this. For many it is a relief, particularly as one gets very old, and infirm and bored with life.

73/M: Death and dying are a part of life. Dying is a time of celebration for the life that led to death. We should help our elderly to understand our appreciation of the life they have lived and what it meant to us.

74/W:

Dying

The wind is blowing off the shore
Out to sea.
"No more, no more," it sighs to me.

I have no sail to set me free,
My craft is small, manned by me,
My mast is broken, gone the oar.

The wind is blowing off the shore
Out to sea.
"No more, no more," it sighs to me.

No more wave-lap on the shore—
Is that a light out there I see?

75/W: The longer I'm in the world, the better I understand it; the more I understand it, the more I love it, and the worse I feel about leaving it.

75/W: Death is inevitable—so I don't waste time over it.

78/W: The things I most fear are: prolonged illness, dependency, pain, isolation, rejection, loss of dignity, being a bother, draining away all our money on misery.

78/W: My husband and I think funerals are barbaric. We will be cremated and have indicated that we would like a memorial celebration by our family and friends. We hope healthy organs can be salvaged for helping others live.

79/M: Don't fight death. It'll come by itself. Be happy and contented in your "oldster's world" and live each day as though it's your last. Be good, kind, and happy each day to its end. Next day be glad for that all over again.

81/W: Death is natural. Anything so universal as death must be a blessing.

84/W: I think of death as a transition from one state of being to another—as unknowable in detail as life must be to the child at birth.

86/M: Let me live as best I can. Let me think not of death, but of life. Let the end take care of itself. Waste not my time on the unmanageable and unattainable.

86/M: I assume death is like going to sleep. It's inevitable and inescapable. Consequently, no use to brood over it; live as well as you can and as usefully, and let the chips fall as they will.

Now here are some statements on how elders hope their own deaths will happen:

66/M: Most of the really important, deep things that have happened to me (except my marriage), the striking experiences and insights I've had, especially the interior things, I've had alone. Having had people around me at those times would have embarrassed me. They would have gotten in the way of my freedom to have a full experience. Somehow, I think that's the way I'd like to die—alone, whether it be with a groan, a gasp, a twitch, or an explosion of wonder.

69/M: I especially fear a slow and painful dying. I hope to be able to make a sudden exit when the time seems ripe for that; but I cannot be sure I will not, in the end, seek to hang on as long as possible!

70/W: As long as I don't have a lingering death, I'm sure I'll die happy! The only thing I feel strongly about is that my body be used to its fullest extent, and then that I be cremated.

71/W: My guess would be that the most potent sentences in a person's life would be (1) to hear "I love you" and (2) to say "I am dying." That's how I'd like my death to be. Keats expressed some of my feelings in his "The Terror of Death." He wrote:

> *When I have fears that I may cease to be*
> *Before my pen has glean'd my teeming brain,*
> *Before high-piled books, in charact'ry*
> *Hold like rich garners the full-ripen'd grain; . . .*
>
> *And when I feel, fair Creature of an hour!*
> *That I shall never look upon thee more,*
> *Never have relish in the fairy power*
> *Of unreflecting love—then on the shore*
> *Of the wide world I stand alone, and think*
> *Till Love and Fame to nothingness do sink.*

71/M: I want my death to be like that described in William Cullen Bryant's "Thanatopsis." He wrote:

> *So live, that when thy summons comes to join*
> *The innumerable caravan, which moves*
> *To that mysterious realm, where each shall take*
> *His chamber in the silent halls of death,*
> *Thou go not, like the quarry slave at night,*
> *Scourged to his dungeon, but, sustained and soothed*
> *By an unfaltering trust, approach thy grave*
> *Like one who wraps the drapery of his couch*
> *About him, and lies down to pleasant dreams.*

Drapery, couch, pleasant dreams—that's it!

71/M: I am trying to face up to the fact that death is not very far away. Getting there can be a horrible ordeal, and I hope that I can endure the process with reasonable grace and good spirits. I have seen examples of both kinds of dying and have great respect for those who have done it with courage and grace.

71/W: I pray I may die quickly when the time comes, without lingering on as a nuisance to everybody. I do not want any fancy life-prolonging machinery. I am scared that I might lose my wits before my body is worn out.

72/M: I don't want anyone in my family to nurse me. Therefore, I should be in a retirement home where services are. I hope the pain won't be too great.

74/M: Death should be painless, and if a person is conscious, that person should be given religious and spiritual comfort!

82/M: It's the process of dying I worry about, not death itself. Worry? No, that's not true. I'm *scared* of the process. Will it be painful, or ugly, or messy, or long, or expensive, or dull, or adventurous? However it will be, I'd like to control it. And if I can't control it, then I want somebody I trust and love to control it. I want the process to be comfortable. I want to die with somebody beside me who doesn't mind, because he (or she) loves me and knows my feelings. I wouldn't mind a cocktail and some good conversation going on. I wouldn't insist on understanding it. And I'd like, when I open my eyes, if I do that while I'm dying, to see a place and some things I love. I'd also like to think of some good "last words" to say, but I won't tell you what they might be. I just hope they'll be good and maybe even get a laugh. Yes, I'd like to die hearing someone laughing at something funny and yet profound that I said. So I guess I'll die an egoist. [*Note:* These words remind one of the words of Voltaire (1694–1778) on his deathbed. He seemed comatose, but when a draft from the window made a gas lamp flare up brightly, he said, "Aha! Already the flames!" H. G. Wells (1866–1946), on his deathbed, with friends and relatives around trying to get some "last words" from the great writer, whispered with slight impatience, "Can't you see I'm busy dying?"]

83/W: I want to die while I'm still alive, as a person, not a collection of symptoms.

85/M: When I'm dying, say, "We're here." Say, "Dad, we love you." Say, "You're doing fine." Don't be afraid of silence. Maybe let *me* set the agenda. Touch me. Look at me, eye to eye. Don't be afraid to kiss me. Help me put my arms around you. Hold me.

And here are observations of elders who have seen death and dying:

65/W: I visited a woman I didn't know, along with my clergyman husband. He left with the family to talk outside the patient's room. All I thought to do—it was a need on my part—was to hum an old country lullaby to her and stroke her hand. She seemed to relax—and then she expired. The nurse and I felt the beauty of the process. That's what I'd like—with myself humming the tune, if necessary.

68/W: I've seen a lot of people die, and I've made it a point to talk to others who have seen dying. I'd say that one of the worst mistakes we make is to assume that the dying person is unaware of the outside world. They *seem* unaware because they can't muster a response. But, except when they're asleep, I'd say that half the dying are constantly in touch, and half go in and out of touch. Only a small minority are confused or "dead to the world." Be aware of this. Keep in touch!

69/W: I sensed something unusual when my husband's mother was dying in the hospital. She was far gone and with her stroke couldn't speak. I was sitting alone with her, holding her hand. She became restless and moved quite a lot for her state of being, and then she grew very still. I felt something very strongly and wondered at what was happening. It was almost as though her "light" had gone out. Perhaps for me it had, and I told the nurse about this feeling. My mother-in-law lived through the night, and I never saw her alive again, but I felt we had shared a moment together that was very deep and important.

70/M (an M.D. who treats many elders and has seen many die): All living things are mortal. God in his wisdom has taken care of the elderly, so that when the time comes, death is not fearsome. In some cases, elderly people become senile and die, unaware that they are dying. Very often, physical illness causes unconsciousness prior to death, and again, there is no awareness of death. Very frequently, death is sudden so that there is no time to consider death. In those who live long and are still aware, many feel too tired to go on living. They feel that staying alive is an unbearable burden, and they welcome the event of death.

Nature (God) is wonderful. The proper psychological attitude is prescribed for each age of life. The infant has no awareness. The growing child cannot comprehend the notion of death. The teenager feels he is indestructible and will live forever. It is only after a few hard knocks in life, and witnessing death in others, that the person begins, first to fear the idea of death, then to accommodate it, and, finally, to accept it without rancor.

73/W: I volunteer in a hospital to work with the dying. I am convinced that when death is near, nature gives a sense of euphoria. When the moment comes, as the famous thanatologist (an expert on death) Ellie Metchnikoff says, "it is accompanied by one of the softest sensations known." Thus, I certainly disagree with Dylan Thomas's words to his dying father: "Do not go gentle into that good night, . . . Rage, rage against the dying of the light." Thank God for the ease we are given. I have seen it so often.

78/M: My feelings about dying were strongly affected by observing what I thought was going to be my own death! At age 70 I had an apparent heart attack but never fully lost consciousness. In the ambulance en route to the hospital, I was frightened, but curious about the future. The trees and foliage seemed unusually beautiful as I consciously bid them farewell. I was aware of the kindness and gentleness of the ambulance crew. I did not wish to die but knew it had to be coped with. I did not die. Since then I've read Ralph Moody's *Life After Life,** about "dead" people coming back from death. It's amazing. Read it.

79/M: During a debilitating illness, for two to three weeks, I prayed every hour, intensely. In my semicomatose state I felt the spirit leave my body. I traveled a long way to the land of my forefathers in heaven, I like to believe. And there, with me, my mother, brother, and a host of others said, "Go back and all will be well. Not yet."

79/W: I haven't seen many people die, but the few I have, and my thoughts about myself, moved me to write this poem, which describes the way death is for many.

* Available from Mockingbird Books, Box 624, St. Simon Island, GA 31522.

River

Man toils on the banks of death
Knowing he must embark
At last on that alien tide
For the deepening dark.

Urgently he calls
Across the waters of night,
Scanning the horizon,
Asking for light.

Like a singing wave thrown back
From some mysterious shore,
He hears an answering echo
Veiled and obscure.

Is it his own voice calling,
Or another's searching cry,
Bridging the silent flood
In brief reply?

81/W: Living in this retirement community, I am constantly aware of death and dying—and especially of those who linger on for years, unconscious and incontinent, or those who, having lost their memories, are lively and troublesome. This seems to me the most dreadful. But the kindness of the nurses is all but incredible!

84/W: I visited a dying old woman. We were silent. Then she said, "People come to visit me together. *They* talk, to each other. It's like being alone in New York City."

A 76-year-old man vividly described his feelings about what he has observed as a hospital volunteer, and I think many of my respondents would agree with him. He wrote: "I hate the degradation of an elaborate, prolonged death, with pain shots, intravenous tubes, nose tubes, throat tubes, tied hands, being strapped in bed, urine catheters, and pouches, suck-outs for pneumonia, with all the squirming and hiccuping and vomiting of the patient. It's all worshiping the flesh and destroying the spirit—and *at vast cost!*"

Yet dying in a hospital need not be a terrible thing; to a certain extent, your environment is what you make of it. An inspiring example is Hubert Humphrey (1911–1978)—mayor, senator, and U.S. vice president—who was admitted to the hospital in 1976 at age 65. He had incurable cancer. But he became a volunteer morale-booster. In *The Youngest Science,* Dr. Lewis Thomas describes how Humphrey behaved:

> He was somber upon admission, and knew that his chances for survival were almost nil. But the "almost" was the focus of his attention. He transformed himself, I think quite deliberately, into the ebullient, talkative Humphrey—not so much for his own sake as for what he saw around him. There were about 40 patients on his floor, and Humphrey took on the whole floor as his new duty. Between his own trips to X-ray or various other diagnostic units, he made ward rounds in his bathrobe and slippers, stopping at every bedside for brief but exhilarating conversations, then ending up in the nurses' station, bringing all the nurses and interns to their feet smiling. During his hospital stay, Humphrey's rounds became famous.
>
> One evening I saw him taking Gerald Ford along, introducing him delightedly as a brand-new friend for each of the patients. Nodding and smiling together, Ford leaning down to be close to a sick patient's faint voice, they were the best of professionals, very high class.

Visiting People Who Are Dying

A 75-year-old man wrote me some excellent advice about visiting people who are dying:

> Somewhere I read some dos and don'ts for people who visit the dying. Here's how I noted them: *Don't* be falsely cheerful. Dying people aren't comforted by insincerity. *Do* engage in small talk if it's an easy way to get the important things, obliquely. But don't just come and chatter small talk to fend off the need to share pain and grief. *Don't* bring useless gifts as a form or duty. To a rose lover, one rose will do it. *Do* speak honestly about death. It can help relieve fears and can open minds and hearts. *Don't* say "You ought . . .," especially "You ought to be thankful for life." *Do* say how much the dying person means to you. *Do* hold and touch and (if it's not unnatural in your relationship) hug and kiss. *Do* say that death, when the moment comes, is easy—sweet; nature made it that way. But *do* show your grief. Go

ahead, cry, but *don't* be so agitated that you disturb
Do speak normally and *clearly*. Hushed tones are dep
funerals). *Do* stay as long as you can, even if you are

"Places to Die Well"—The Hospice Movemen

One respondent, a 78-year-old woman, said succinctly, "It's not pleasant to die in a place that's built and staffed to keep you alive. We need places to die—die well!"

With the medicalization of death and its relocation from home to hospital, an urgent need has arisen to provide means and places for people "to die well." Despite what a number of my respondents have reported, many doctors and nurses, as well as clergymen and social workers, are deeply concerned to help people experience good deaths.

The hospice movement provides means and places that help make the experience of dying a good part of life, especially for those who cannot be aided by aggressive medical treatment and are in great pain. For centuries, hospices, often connected with churches and monasteries, provided refuge for weary travelers, the poor, the orphaned, women in labor, the dying. Sometimes they provided medical treatment, but essentially they were places of protection, fellowship, and refreshment for people in distress. In recent years, though, the term *hospice* has taken on a special meaning: a place and program that cares for those of any age who are terminally ill, and for their families. Hospices provide a caring community of people—doctors, psychologists, nurses, clergy, social workers, and volunteers. Sometimes their activities are centered in a hospice building, but often their services are offered to families at the home of the dying person. They provide care as needed, twenty-four hours a day, seven days a week, including keeping the patient comfortable, managing pain, and providing emotional support for all who are involved. Often the hospice service begins at the hospice itself, where the environment is comfortable and homelike, where privacy is assured. Also assured is a congenial sharing of experience. The reality of the impending death is accepted and talked about. The patient's own doctor provides medical service in most cases, and there is access to hospitals for more intensive medical care if that might be helpful. Quite often, once needed techniques have been learned, the patient is allowed to return home, with all needed support services provided there.

In 1977, there were about fifty hospices or hospice groups in the U.S.; in 1980, some four hundred; in 1983, twelve hundred—and the number is growing rapidly. In 1982, Medicare agreed to pay for hospice expenses if the patient was certified by medical authorities to have a life expectancy of six months or less. The cost of hospice care, including all of the nonmedical aspects, is less than that of hospital care. Two of my respondents wrote about positive hospice experiences:

67/W: An 84-year-old close friend of mine recently died at home, comfortably, painlessly, and well. She and her family learned how to manage this when she was moved from a good hospital to the expert, loving care of a hospice in a town nearby. After about a week, she came home, and the end of her life was good. I was able to help provide meals and attention and well-informed love and caring. The hospice people are loving experts with no fixed formulas.

88/W: Three months ago I was all messed up dying in a medical center, with emergency trips to the hospital. Life was hell and so was the idea of death. I couldn't write and could hardly talk. And now I'm writing this!—slowly, but I'm writing it. I'm going to die soon, but I'm in a hospice, with experts and family. I feel ready for the next adventure. I'm letting go. But I'm in touch! Please tell people.

If you are interested in knowing about hospices in the area where you live, either to use them or to help in them, ask your doctor, a local hospital, the center for aging of a university, or a chapter of the American Association of Retired Persons.

Stages in the Process of Dying

A number of my respondents referred to the work of psychiatrist Elisabeth Kübler-Ross, published in her book, *On Death and Dying*. They said they found it helpful in coming to terms with the fact of death, both the death of others and their own eventual death. Kübler-Ross interviewed over two hundred dying patients and concluded that when people know they have a terminal illness, they go through five stages: (1) *Denial* ("No, not me"); (2) *Anger* ("Why me?"); (3) *Bargaining* ("All right, me, but not until my daughter's marriage; not until I get X done. . . ."); (4) *Depression* ("Oh, God, it's hopeless"; "I feel so sad"); (5) *Acceptance* ("I'm tired; it's going to happen; I feel restful"). There is a suggestion of a further part of the acceptance stage, *Hope*—for some sort of wonderful future.

This work has been a stimulus to the hospice movement in helping the dying and their families and friends deal with death. Some have criticized the Kübler-Ross formula as being too rigid and formal, and later study shows that some dying people may move back and forth among the stages; some rush through them in a few hours, even totally skipping some of them; while still others take weeks to go through the process or never complete it at all and do "rage, rage against the dying of the light."

Does Death Look Different As We Get Older?

I asked, *Has your attitude toward dying and death changed at all since you were fifty? Yes__No__Explain.* Twenty-nine percent checked *Yes,* 62 percent checked *No,* and 9 percent didn't answer. The majority who checked *No* had no comment or said, in effect, "Why should it change? The idea isn't exactly new." A 74-year-old woman wrote, "I've had it figured out pretty well since maybe age 30. We'll die, but meanwhile let's live. Maybe if I'm told, 'You have two weeks to live,' my attitude will change, but I don't see quite how." And an 87-year-old woman wrote: "For fully forty years I have been saying that we all should be given a pill to keep in our bottom bureau drawer to take when—if—faced with intolerable pain or incurable and wretched illness."

Here are comments chosen from the few that acknowledged some change in attitude:

69/M: I give more thought to the subject now. In earlier years, personal death was thought of as a "never to come" period. Now I know it is "nearer than farther." But I do not live in fear of the end of the natural life cycle.

70/W: Two experiences—working among the Navahos and Mexicans in Arizona and watching death occur among caring friends at our retirement community—have given deeper meaning to the expression "a good death."

70/W: I am not afraid of dying people. I used to think I could not communicate with them—now I am eager to be "with" them in those last tough steps.

79/W: I have learned more about death. I find that the Kübler-Ross approach has confirmed many of my attitudes and helped verbalize feelings and thoughts on the subject.

81/M: Ironically, I think fear of death diminishes as we age. Perhaps this is because our vital powers wane. Even our cells are less clamorous and demanding.

Choosing to Die

A question that many people feel strongly about is whether or not people should be legally, or morally, permitted to choose to die. So I asked, *Do you think people should be permitted to choose to die and empowered to end their own lives? Yes __ No __ Explain.* Over two-thirds, 69 percent, checked *Yes;* 18 percent checked *No;* 6 percent said perhaps or "I don't know"; and 7 percent left the spaces blank. (The *New York Times* reported on a 1984 NYT/CBS news poll asking whether, with people who are terminally ill, doctors should stop using modern medical technology to prolong lives if the patient so requests. Seventy-seven percent of the public 18+ years old said *yes,* 15 percent *no,* and 8 percent *don't know.*)

Here are typical comments from those who support the right to die. As you will read, many do not see it as a simple question, but some do—and with vigor.

65/W: I've seen many real deaths in hospitals and nursing homes. I also look at TV and realize that steady TV watchers see about a thousand deaths a year, all fantasy! There are accidents, murders; people die in beautiful scenes or luxury appartments; it's all governed by cue cards; often there are amazing "Last Words." But what we don't see on TV, and I do see in life, are deaths of people who are lonely, ugly, smelly, pain-wracked, and hallucinating. We need to show people real, average, expensive, medical deaths. If they saw, they'd agree: Allow people to choose to die.

68/W: The abominable thing is that modern medicine prevents or protracts the process which nature might complete briefly.

69/M: The prolongation of a "vegetable" state of physical life is cruel, degrading, and senseless. I am completely opposed to unnatural, artificial means of prolonging physical life when all awareness and mental powers have ceased.

69/M: A 69-year-old friend of mine visited his father, trapped in the hospital after surgery on his larynx. He couldn't talk, but there was tragedy in his eyes. He painfully wrote on a pad, *Son, you promised me, if I ever* . . . and could go no further. He mouthed the word *promise!* That promise should be kept.

70/M: To prolong real life is virtuous; to delay dying, blasphemy.

71/M: My standing horror is that I may live uselessly in hospital for no reason, with no hope—just a burden on purse and public.

73/M: I am a strong believer in the validity of the Living Will. We must cease making our elderly ill feel guilty because of their decision to let go of life. They should be permitted to die with the same dignity they have shown in life.

74/M: I believe one should be allowed to make a graceful exodus.

78/M: "God giveth and God taketh away." O.K., God gave us life, but we have removed God's right to take it away—and that's *immoral!*

84/W: I should like a federal law that provided for death on demand—with plenty of safeguards as to assent and sound motives. I don't think people should have to endure long, drawn-out, painful dying when a quick end could be made by merciful means.

Those opposed to the right to choose wrote like this:

67/M: People live not only for themselves but for others as well. One never knows the significance of an act like suicide for others, or the importance to others of seeing a person living with suffering, gracefully, bravely. It inspires.

78/M: Most people choosing to die would be in a form of "temporary insanity," a form of suicide. It could be abused and falsified by people in power over others. I oppose it.

86/M: "Thou shalt not kill." The *way* you live speaks, as long as you live. A dead person ceases to speak.

And a few were unsure:

68/M: People should be permitted not to be kept alive—which is different from being permitted to kill themselves. Even so, when dignity is vanishing, death should be allowed, certainly not impeded. Yet hanging on, even submitted to painful, pioneer operations, may be a contribution one should try to fulfill for the benefit of others.

81/W: One member of our life-care community, when she got older and her activities were curtailed, became very irritable and difficult. Then she went into a coma. When she came out of it, suddenly she said something to the effect of "I've been wrong. I'll do better." Later that day, she died.

We have no idea what goes on in people's minds when their minds are hidden from us. Supposing she'd been allowed to die before that experience!

81/W: I checked that *Yes* quickly and then began to ask myself questions. What if there is something still to be learned that my protracted dying can teach me? What if senility itself is part of a necessary ripening process?

87/W: I favor the right to choose death, *but* with *carefully* devised safeguards. Take the person himself (if he can express a coherent opinion), next of kin, and a prearranged committee, including physician and others. They should decide. Omission of artificial feeding, respiration, kidney dialysis, etc., would be sufficient, I think. I couldn't ask any doctor to inject a lethal drug. His or her entire professional preparation and experience are against it. So how do you know?

A number of religious organizations have made careful statements of the right to die under special circumstances. Here are three:

Pope John Paul II: When inevitable death is imminent in spite of the means used, it is permitted in conscience to take the decision to refuse forms of treatment that would only secure a precarious and burdensome prolongation of life.

United Methodist Church: We assert the right of every person to die in dignity without efforts to prolong terminal illness merely because the technology is available to do so.

Central Conference of American Rabbis: The conclusion from the spirit of Jewish law is that while you may not do anything to hasten death you may, under special circumstances of suffering and helplessness, allow death to come.

One of my special expert respondents, an under-65-year-old nurse who spends much of her time working with dying people, told me convincingly of their need for "advocates"—informed people who will help the dying to assert their wishes and rights. What sorts of rights? The right to information; the right to refuse further tests, to refuse tubes and restraints; the right to be granted enlightened relief from pain; the right to provide their families secure help in dealing with their impending death. The advocate might plan to be present when doctors and specialists make their rounds, in order to help translate medical terms into plain English, spoken slowly and clearly, and to interpret what the doctors have said so that the patient can really understand and deal with it. In a sense, an advocate for the dying is a one-woman or one-man hospice to help make "the last days of living" good ones.

Suicide and Euthanasia

In 1975, the famous American theologian and former president of the Union Theological Seminary, Henry Pitt Van Dusen, age 77, and his wife Elizabeth, age 80, committed suicide together in bed by taking pills. They were both permanently very ill; they foresaw great expense and little joy in their future; they knew they would be a burden for their children and grandchildren. On the table beside their bed, they left a note explaining all this and expressing their love for each other, their friends and family, and the world. They wrote: "Nowadays it is difficult to die. We feel that this way we are taking will become more usual and acceptable as the years pass. Of course, the thought of our children and grandchildren makes us sad, but we still feel that this is the best way and the right way to go. We are both increasingly weak and unwell and who would want to die in a nursing home? We are

not afraid to die. . . ." Editor Norman Cousins commented on the
event: "They believed they had the right to die when their time had
come. It was precisely because they had placed the highest value on
life that they didn't want life to become a caricature."

In answering my question *Should people be empowered to end their
own lives?* even some of those who answered *yes* had hesitations about
outright suicide. Here are two such comments:

74/M: Everyone reaching vulnerable age should be encouraged to
execute a document demanding that heroic measures to extend life
not be used when an M.D. has certified that the condition is incurable.
But that doesn't mean that we should say to elders, "O.K., go get
some pills, or keep a gun, and kill yourself anytime you want." That
would be immoral. Depression can be brief. Death is permanent.

75/W: I don't think suicide is a very good idea. But I do think
that Living Wills are sensible—requesting that one not be kept alive
if one's life is not going to be comfortable and reasonable.

However, the majority favored the right even to suicide:

67/M: When Charlotte Perkins Gilman, an early feminist cru-
sader, killed herself, in 1935, at age 75, she left behind a note that
explained, "I have preferred chloroform to cancer." In an essay
published posthumously, she wrote, "The record of a previously
noble life is precisely what makes it sheer insult to allow death in
pitiful degradation. We may not wish to 'die with our boots on' but
we may well prefer to die with our brains on."

69/M: People should have the right to say, in effect, "Enough is
enough; let me die," and also to delegate that right to others by a
Living Will. Don't hold us on when we'd rather be off. Let us go.

72/M: A rule that would require a person to refrain from suicide
strikes me as similar to the rules forbidding migration from the
U.S.S.R.

72/M: Down with nurses and doctors (even district attorneys)
who crusade for the sanctity of life and hound and sue people who
want to make a good thing out of "the last of life" by dying well—
even dying at will.

72/M: I favor the Hemlock Society. It promotes "self-deliverance" through "rational suicide." It has over ten thousand members. It's not wild-eyed radicals. It's sensible people—like me!—who hate suffering, and who hate the $30,000 per year cost of each hospital death, and the fact that about 30 percent of the Medicare budget is spent to keep the elderly alive in their last year—*most* of it during their last month of life.

79/W: Two of my close friends, husband and wife, killed themselves at age 83. They both were costing everyone a lot of money. They had no prospect of joy in life. So they were found dead in the backseat of their car in a closed garage, together, holding hands. They'd left a note in the house, explaining and sending love. Also, they left their wills, their keys, and all their important documents. I applaud their action.

80/M (an M.D.): My brother died in a nursing home after a long, drawn-out struggle with bone cancer. During his last six weeks, he repeatedly asked me to bring in a gun and shoot him, which, of course, I could not do. Instead, I urged his doctor and nurses to keep him as comfortable as possible with the necessary sedation and pain pills and not to force-feed him. I also suggested to him that if he really wanted to move on to the next world—in which he firmly believed—he could refuse the food that was offered to him. This form of passive, voluntary euthanasia, plus large doses of sedatives and pain relievers, helped him to attain self-deliverance fairly fast.

85/W: When I was near dying a few years ago, I felt, "I'm scared! Don't take away my power to die!" I expressed it, so they promised they wouldn't vegetate me—and I lived. Knowing that I didn't have to suffer if I decided not to, energized me.

For those of us elders who believe in our right to choose to die, there are organizations to turn to:

Society for the Right to Die
250 West 57th Street
New York, NY 10019

Euthanasia Educational Council, same address

The Hemlock Society, P. O. Box 66218, Los Angeles, CA 90066

The Living Will

Perhaps the most useful and used document, available in several versions, is the Living Will Declaration. On the facing page is the text provided by the Euthanasia Council.

If you sign such a document, be sure your doctor, your close family (or best friend or two), and your lawyer know about it. Actually, many doctors, life-care communities, churches, and nursing homes provide copies of Living Wills for those who request them. Living Wills are recognized as legally binding in about half of the states in the U.S.A., and even in other states they have influence. A "miniwill" version of the Living Will is available to carry in your wallet if you so desire.

One respondent, an 87-year-old man, wrote: "I don't look forward to my death with eagerness, but I don't feel afraid of it. My wife and I both signed Living Wills a few years ago. After my wife had been in a coma for a month, the doctor in charge told me that there was no longer any chance of a recovery. I told him about the Will. He asked me to bring it to him. He read it. Then they removed the tubes and wires which had connected her to a bank of equipment that had been keeping her in a sort of vegetable 'life,' and removed her to an observation room, where she died two days later, peacefully and without pain or distress."

Do We Feel in Touch With the Dead?

One of the things that I've heard elders discuss sometimes is whether or not we can be in touch with people who have died. It seemed an interesting question to ask. *Do you, in any sense, feel in living touch with any people who have died? Yes__ No__ Explain.* Twenty-seven percent checked *Yes;* 64 percent checked *No;* and 9 percent checked neither. Few people did any explaining. Here are six comments:

65/W: I have several times dreamed about my husband and upon awakening felt his presence. In fact, one time I remember upon awakening reaching out to touch him and experiencing his physical withdrawing. I attribute the strength of this feeling to the intensity

TO MY FAMILY, MY PHYSICIAN, MY LAWYER, MY CLERGYMAN

TO ANY MEDICAL FACILITY IN WHOSE CARE I HAPPEN TO BE

TO ANY INDIVIDUAL WHO MAY BECOME RESPONSIBLE FOR MY HEALTH, WELFARE OR AFFAIRS

Death is as much a reality as birth, growth, maturity and old age—it is the one certainty of life. If the time comes when I, _____, can no longer take part in decisions for my own future, let this statement stand as an expression of my wishes, while I am still of sound mind.

If the situation should arise in which there is no reasonable expectation of my recovery from physical or mental disability, I request that I be allowed to die and not be kept alive by artificial means or "heroic measures." I do not fear death itself as much as the indignities of deterioration, dependence and hopeless pain. I, therefore, ask that medication be mercifully administered to me to alleviate suffering even though this may hasten the moment of death.

This request is made after careful consideration. I hope you who care for me will feel morally bound to follow its mandate. I recognize that this appears to place a heavy responsibility upon you, but it is with the intention of relieving you of such responsibility and of placing it upon myself in accordance with my strong convictions, that this statement is made.

Signed_____

Date_____

Witness_____

Witness_____

Copies of this request have been given to

_____

_____

_____

_____

of the dream, which I had not quite let go of even though I knew well that I was awake.

67/M: My wife died of cancer four years ago. After the years of marriage it was a terrible shock, but at the same time it was a very wonderful experience because of the way it brought us all in closer touch with the Divine in us all. She died in a truly wonderful way and our love continues to support me daily as I have remarried and am developing a new family. I am indeed in touch.

68/W: After my mother died, after so many miserable years, I had a vivid, inner seeing of her spirit, dancing upward like a fountain, sparkling and laughing merrily. I still feel this. Am I in touch?

70/M: I have great attachment to the memories of certain persons whom I loved very dearly. The fond and warm memories are really the only contact with those who have departed this earth. Memories can be very live, make vivid impressions, and last a lifetime. They are touching.

74/M: I have dreamed many times of people who have died. When I do, they do not seem dead, and we have conversations, climb mountains, fish, party, go on trips, etc. However, it always turns out to be a dream!

75/W: Well, actually the answer is yes and no. I dream of these people often and in very realistic terms. Also, my granddaughter, Sally, reminds me very much of her late mother, Emily. So, often through Sally I do see Emily.

Would We Elders Like to Talk More About Death?

At the beginning of this chapter, I suggested that, contrary to what many people believe, most of us elders do not particularly seek opportunities to talk about death. I based my opinion on replies to this question: *Which are true for you? I've got more important things to talk about than dying.__People talk with me more about death than I would like.__I'd like to talk about death, but people are too hesitant to talk about it with me.__Explain your answer, telling what your feelings are about sharing with other people thoughts about death.* Fourteen percent of my respondents left the question blank, no checks, no comments. Of the remaining 86 percent, quite a few people checked more than one space. Thus the percentages total more than 100. Sixty-four percent checked *I've got more important things;* 16 percent checked *People talk more than I'd like;* and 35 percent checked *People are too hesitant.* Another 32 percent commented but checked nothing. From these scattered percentages, we can at least conclude that about a third of the respondents would like to talk more about death than they are able to; a clear majority are more interested in other matters; and about a fifth get more death talk than they want. Here are some comments, first from those who are not interested in more talk:

71/W: Death is too inevitable to worry and talk about.

72/W: Although one's affairs should be put in order and any wishes should be made known to one's family, it seems morbid to me to plan one's funeral. Funerals are mainly for the living. Let's talk about more interesting matters.

75/M: I don't particularly care to talk about death with others, nor do I much think about it. Death of the individual is not, to me, sufficiently important to dwell on its coming.

78/M: I don't mind talking about it, but do not like to upset old people who find comfort in what I consider "magic" beliefs. I wish I could share these. For instance, my grandmother, as she died, said she saw her mother waiting to meet her. She also said the streets were made of gold. I wouldn't like to have taken that belief away from her by my logical talking.

81/M: It's obvious that billions of people have died and have thought of dying. It seems clear to me I can't add to such a mountain of thought. It's better to think of life. People who have lived well die well.

86/M: I feel that death is another unsolved venture. In sailing, that next headland has always been a lure—to sail around it and see what's beyond. I feel that way about death. Meantime, I like it here and to talk about what's here, not around the headland.

89/W: Other people don't know any more about death than I do. Why talk about it? I think it's depressing. When it comes, it comes. Think about living instead.

Those who *did* want more talk said:

65/W: My children are reluctant to talk about my eventual death. They tell me not to be morbid. I don't feel I'm being morbid or sad. I simply want to discuss a fact of life. I neither want to dwell on it nor to dismiss it as something not likely to happen.

68/W: Margaret Mead says the last, great thing we can give our children is our death. And talking and sharing enriches that gift.

77/W: What a waste of interesting subject matter not to talk about death! I'm interested in other people's ideas, and it would help comfort me about the ideas I think I hold. It's a lot to keep inside your head alone.

80/W: As a vice president of the Society for the Right to Die, I do talk about death a lot. It should not be a taboo subject.

And then there were a few interesting comments about how to talk with people who are in the process of dying:

66/W: Some of my sister's friends who cared the most for her stayed away from her during her last weeks because they couldn't bear seeing her so ill. She understood this, but still it hurt. She needed to talk. They should have come and put themselves in her place and helped her die well by listening and sharing. Listen and share, that's it—and give.

70/W: Dying seems to me to be in essence a withdrawal process. People who try to help others go through this experience have to be accepting and always ready to talk or communicate in whatever ways the dying person wishes. You must *believe* what they are telling you, and *respect* their wishes. You must help them by supporting and reinforcing whatever they communicate.

73/W: It is *very* important to allow the dying person to say whatever is on his or her mind and to listen with loving understanding, doing your best to help the dying person feel how deeply you care.

82/W: To talk with the dying, and to share deeply with them in words, looks, and touching is important not only to them but to us who are left behind. I wish now that I had spent more time with my husband while he was slipping away, instead of worrying about the funeral and obituaries and death announcements, even though I did all that out of love of him. But it meant that I was not really there during his dying, and it has made the loss greater. We did not grieve together. The busyness of the world prevented it. And how do I know what he really needed from me, needed to say to me, to hear from me?

Bereavement and Grief

In Chapter 5, I commented on the shock and disorientation that people often feel when a spouse or other loved person dies. Harriet Robey, one of my respondents, and author of *An Ordinary Marriage*, writes about this in her book. She is describing her situation at home just after he husband's funeral. She writes:

> After the last guests are gone we sit until midnight around the fire. Grief, humor, and reminiscence: children and grandchildren are welded in joint sadness and finality, yet a kind of happiness, bonded even closer together than before. It is after midnight when the last of the young leave. I stand with my hand on the doorknob until the final sound of cars fades. And then, as if struck, I see everything brilliantly and horribly. I am now alone. Of Alec and our life together nothing is left but ashes. I am only half a person; the other half of me is that urn. And I am—I shudder at the awful word—a *widow*. Forever! And so begins, in truth, my bereavement.

Bereavement: It's interesting that the word *bereave* comes from the Old English *rēafian*, "to rob," and the Latin *rumpere*, "to break." Robbed and broken is the way many people feel after a death, no matter how well they may have prepared for it.

I asked my respondents, *Have you lost a spouse or other person very close to you by death? What was the most helpful to you in coping with the experience?* Most of them had had such experiences, often well before they became elders, as with the loss of their parents. Before I tell what they found helpful—or in some cases unhelpful— in coping with dying and death, I think it will be useful to give some data from a study made in 1971 by Paula Clayton, James Halikes, and William Maurice on the effects of bereavement on 109 randomly selected widows and widowers.* More than a quarter of the subjects reported one or more of the following behaviors: crying (93%), depression (83%), difficulty sleeping (80%), forgetfulness or inability to concentrate (56%), lack of appetite (52%), general tiredness (43%), loss of interest in life (32%), and a sense of self-condemnation (27%). Furthermore, it has been found that, typically, the period of bereavement lasts about a year, although of course there is great variation.

Other studies over the past few years show that bereaved men die sooner than bereaved women. One reason, of course, is that husbands are usually older than their wives, and men in general have a shorter life expectancy than women. But another reason is that, in our society at least, women throughout their married lives tend to form more bonds of affection, caring, and sharing than do men. Most women have a sort of informal network of warm human contacts, and when their husbands die, they are supported by this network. This is good for the health! Men, on the other hand, get most of their close emotional satisfaction from their wives, who often are the only people with whom they share deeply. Therefore, when a man loses his wife, he is likely to be cut off from the emotional ties needed to maintain a healthy life. Friends at work or at the office generally have never provided a support network and are not likely to start doing so when a man becomes a widower. Fellowship at work, while important in providing a sense of purpose and accomplishment, is usually not at a deep emotional level.†

Two of my respondents expressed the essence of this research, of which, as far as I know, they were unaware:

74/M: It may be selfish to say it, but I devoutly hope that I die before my wife. When I die, she will have the wonderful fabric of friends and neighbors to hold her up—almost like rocking in a hammock. Much of her joy and satisfaction comes from these deep, wonderful, life-giving contacts. But me, I've been so busy achieving my professional goals that the friendships I've made are mostly related to those goals. I do have lots of friends outside of business, of course, but they are based on ideas and world affairs. They aren't

---

* "The Bereavement of the Widowed," *Diseases of the Nervous System,* 1971.
† For a more in-depth discussion, see "Affectional Bonding and the Impact of Bereavement," by Joan B. Stoddard and James P. Henry, in *Advances,* Institute for the Advancement of Health, Spring 1985.

emotionally deep. My wife is really my only soul-deep friend, and if she died I'd really be bereft and set adrift, in a sense.

80/W: When my husband, Hank, died, I was really thrown for a loss. I was terribly sad, for we had been married for fifty-three years, and we were wonderfully enmeshed in each other. But when he died, I was upheld in a strong way by my few wonderful deep friendships. They were life-givers and life-sharers when I needed giving and sharing. When I think about it, I'm really glad Hank died before me. I don't know where he could have gotten the support I got. I've come back to strength, and I think he might not have, even though he was a very strong person.

Following are some comments more directly related to my question about coping with bereavement.

67/M: The greatest help to me in accepting my mother's death was the memory of her spirit in dying, plus a marvelous nurse who was with us to the end, who treated dying as a perfectly natural process, like eating or being born, which one could experience in a wonderful way. The memory of this strengthened me during my period of bereavement.

68/W: Hugo [a doctor, philosopher, healer] said something like this about our cousin who recently died after a long period of triumphing over cancer. He said it just before she died. "Mary has already left. Don't cling to her. If we cling, we will be wounded when she is taken away. If we willingly release, we never lose her. Keep close to the Light, the Center. In that place there is no separation."

70/W: Let's face it. Death of a miserably sick person with no chance for recovery can be a relief for the sick person, and for the living. I felt almost joyous that Arthur was allowed to die. To my relatives and friends, I expressed relief and even joy. It seemed to comfort people who felt they ought to be grieving with me.

74/W: An understanding and empathy, and most of all, a listening ear, that's what helps accept someone's death.

82/M: My gentle, lovely first wife died of Lou Gehrig's disease, a cruelly drawn-out, deteriorating nerve disease resulting in total inability to communicate, but no loss of brain function. So, when action was taken and the inevitable end came, it was seen as a release from suffering, not so much as dying. I deeply regretted that some form of euthanasia had not been available long before. On the day of her death, I got a recording of Brahms's Requiem, which I used in a memorial service in two different places where we had lived. It was a relief to plan for this service, which included slides of her in many lovely settings in the mountains and elsewhere; and brief memorial comments by our sons and closest friend; and the Twenty-third Psalm and the thirteenth chapter of Corinthians I. I was made more free to go on living, and my family was too.

Four people were quite specific about something each of us should do now to help others prepare for *our* eventual death:

66/W: Get organized and don't leave things in a mess when you take off into the next world. I told myself this after dealing with the chaos left behind by a very elderly aunt. Straightening out messes is not a good form of bereavement activity.

71/M: It is important for you to have filled out a questionnaire about what you wish done upon your death—cremation, or giving organs or body to a teaching hospital; what type of religious service or memorial you might think appropriate; flowers or a memorial gift, etc. Your family will want to do what *you* would want, and this is the best way to let them know.

73/W: Tell your family where everything is located (will, investments, etc.)—*if* you can remember! If not, find out!

84/W: Get or keep things in order. Discard records and papers that would be of no use to inheritors; check your will and rewrite it at a happy and loving time; simplify your general possessions, giving away those that clutter. Leave life with a clean slate for your descendants.

Some respondents were quite specific about attitudes and actions that are not helpful:

69/M: One of the things I haven't learned to deal with is the competition of widows for my attention. Their motives are good (usually), but the pressure is annoying, even if a bit flattering. It doesn't help me.

71/W: I regret not having been brave enough to let my mother talk to me about death. We both knew she was dying, yet I kept up a childishly optimistic pace. It didn't help me or her, I now see. So I hope somebody (probably my youngest daughter) will not repeat my mistake, and will encourage me to talk about dying. It makes it much easier and rewarding to live with the loss afterward.

72/W: A really energy-consuming lie that some people seem to feel obliged to live out is what I'd call "idealization of the dead one." Try to avoid that. If you loved him (or her), it was because of reality, not fiction. So, please, no hushed expressions of perfection.

72/W: For God's sake don't go around looking sad and miserable because people *expect* you to. If you've got a life to live, live it. Obligatory sad-looking is a misery.

74/M: Avoid the luxury of cheap melancholy. It doesn't help anybody!

75/W: Advice is the worst thing to offer when a person has suffered loss. But faith in the person's ability to recover from the loss—*that* is essential.

77/M: It really didn't help me when my wife died to have people treat my sorrow and melancholy as if it were a weakness, or as if I were sick. "Machos don't mourn after the funeral is over"—not a useful thought for me.

78/W: There's this idea that at parties (except afternoon tea) the number of men and women must be equal. So I'm excluded even by good(?) friends who said earlier, "Don't worry, we'll all go on seeing each other just like before."

79/W: "For heaven's sake, stop weeping," says a friend. But I need to cry, and not just alone.

84/M: I think the worst thing people can say (or suggest to you) is "Don't worry, you'll get over it." You never get over it. You need help to learn to live well with it.

87/W: Religious counseling can be helpful in bereavement—but not the sort our local minister gave. He was an unfortunate fellow, my stepfamily couldn't stand him, and his first words when he called after Fred died were "It's all for the best." I felt like spitting into the phone, but I said, "That's not what I need to know."

Grief and grieving are a large part of bereavement, but opinions on the subject are far from unanimous:

67/M: I really don't like this term *grief work*. Sounds like something you ought to get paid for! We need to grieve, and some of us need help, but grief work—you can have it. I'll settle for tears and sadness and talk, and memories, and an energetic future.

69/M: Life is for the living. The death of loved ones should be left behind you at some reasonably early point.

70/W: A bereaved person has to learn to live with her grief as with a companion, and in this kind of acceptance she can then carry on more satisfactorily.

70/W: Get psychologically ready to allow family and friends to care for you when, in grief, you no longer can "do" for yourself. Think of it as being helpful to *them*, too, for I believe it is. They want to help.

77/W: One of the things we women have to get over, as we grieve, is answering when asked who we are, "I'm the wife of . . ." We're not. We *were*, but now we are ourselves, and we'd better get on with being ourselves, strengthened by our past.

78/W: Death is inevitable, and losing loved ones is a painful experience, but "grief" is often an expression of self-pity and resentment at being left alone to cope with what seems unsurmountable. Much of this can be avoided by objective and thoughtful planning.

78/M: After a loved one has died, you may need a sort of eight-week "shut-down." On the other hand, some people do wonderfully, having accepted the death and grieved in advance, by marching right out and being busy and useful again.

79/W: Don't be diverted from grief. Integrate the loss at your own speed and in your own way into your life.

82/M and 79/W: We were both helped through the grief process by our groups. For John it was a close, hardworking neighborhood association; for Isobel it was the community clothes-mending group. Groups that work and talk together are a great help.

84/W: Sometimes grief gets impacted, like a wisdom tooth or even less mentionable things. We must learn to disimpact grief! So we need someone, or someones, to ask us, "How are you feeling?" or "Are you feeling . . . ?" We don't need someone to ask, "What can I do?" but rather to say, "Come to dinner" or "Let's go for a drive."

86/M: Being a Christian, I can bring to the grieving the consolation of God's grace and the assurance of God's word.

On that note, let me point out that Christians have no monopoly on this consolation. At a memorial service, a rabbi I know said this prayer, after the words of Ben Sira, and the whole congregation, it seemed to me, felt comforted and eased:

> Fear not death; we are destined to die. We share it with all who ever lived, with all who ever will be. Bewail the dead, hide not your grief, do not restrain your mourning. But remember that continuing sorrow is worse than death. When the dead are at rest, let their memory rest, and be consoled when the soul departs.
>
> Death is better than a life of pain, and eternal rest than constant sickness.
>
> Seek not to understand what is too difficult for you, search not for what is hidden from you. Be not over-occupied with what is beyond you, for you have been shown more than you can understand.
>
> As a drop of water in the sea, as a grain of sand on the shore, are man's few days in eternity. The good things in life last for limited days, but a good name endures forever.
>
> O God, our Father, You redeem our souls from the grave, You are the Rock of our salvation. Forsake us not in time of trouble, in days of distress and desolation. Help us to endure, O Lord, for we have placed our hope in You.

A Bit of Humor, Some of It Comforting

As with most serious subjects, there is the humorous side to death, and some of my respondents suggested it directly or indirectly.

69/M: This is the way I feel: "Heaven may be my home, but I'm not homesick yet."

71/M: Back about 1950, we had a visit at our place in Maine from a 92-year-old sea captain who was reminiscing about the sailing-ship days and how he had run away to sea at age nine. Someone remarked that he looked remarkably well considering his age. His eyes misted over as he looked out over the harbor and said, "Wall, I'm a-clingin' to the riggin' just as long as I kin!"

72/W: I like the story of when John Holmes, brother of Oliver Wendell Holmes, Sr., was lying comatose in his bed, hardly breathing, seemingly dead. A nurse put her hand beneath the covers, saying to one of the watchers, "If his feet are warm, he's alive. No one ever died with his feet warm."

Suddenly a voice from the bed said distinctly, "John Rogers did." John Rogers was burned at the stake for heresy some centuries earlier.

72/M: A good game to play is making up epitaphs for each other and sharing them. One I made up for my lively wife is "Here lies Mary, my beloved wife, under the only stone she ever left unturned."

73/W: A great thing about a Quaker memorial service is that it is unprogrammed, and anyone may speak "as the spirit moves" about the person who has died. This has made possible an interesting, funny exercise that I enjoy with a younger male friend (and Friend). If we're feeling low, we say, "Well, here's what I plan to say at your memorial service." It leads to some compliments but especially to some laughter, and we both feel better.

74/M: I like the words of Mark Twain: "Let us so endeavor to live that when we die, even the undertaker will be sorry."

88/M: I had a very dear friend in her eighties who said to me, "I am very anxious to end my days on earth. I want to go and be with my mother. I can just see her up there happily running around dusting everything, or maybe playing anagrams with Saint Peter."

90/W (at the funeral of a friend, to a younger friend who had complimented her on her dress): Well, this is the dress I planned to be laid out in, but it looked so beautiful I just couldn't resist wearing it today.

I end this chapter with two humorous stories of my own, both true. The first is about an 80+-year-old alumna of a well-known school who was asked to make a three-year pledge to the endowment campaign. "Three-year pledge!" she exclaimed. "Why, I don't even buy green bananas anymore."

The other concerns the grandfather of my sister-in-law. At age 92 he bought a handsome, expensive pair of shoes. When questioned about this extravagance, he replied, "Well, they'll last me twenty years!"

GEM COLLECTION

70/W: When I die, I expect to become a whoosh of air—a zephyr in the universe.

71/M: My desire about death is to be welcomed at the right time, but I am by no means ready for it now. I have too much living I still want to do.

80/M (Bertrand Russell, 1872–1970): An individual human existence should be like a river—small at first, narrowly contained within its banks, and rushing passionately past boulders and over waterfalls. Gradually, the river grows wider, the banks recede, the waters flow more quietly, and in the end, without any visible break, they become merged in the sea and painlessly lose their individual being.

81/W: I believe that everything good I have been empowered to do is my claim to immortality—my turn in eternity is now.

82/W: I'm quoting Jean-Paul Sartre [1905–1980] since I'm in tune with his attitude: "I think of death only with tranquility, as an end. I refuse to let death hamper life. Death must enter life only to define it."

83/W: I think of death now as a part of the process of living and of the continuous rebirth of living things: plants, animals, and all the physical world as we know it.

84/W: This, to me, says it all. It's from *Four Quartets* by T. S. Eliot [1888–1965]:

Home is where one starts from. As we grow older
The world becomes stranger, the pattern more complicated . . .
There is a time for the evening under starlight,
A time for the evening under lamplight . . .
Love is most nearly itself
When here and now cease to matter.
Old men ought to be explorers
Here and there does not matter
We must be still and still move
Into another intensity
For a further union, a deeper communion
Through the dark cold and empty desolation,
The wave cry, the wind cry, the vast waters
Of the petrel and the porpoise. In my end is my beginning.

Afterword

Sexuality, religion, dying and death—what a heavy group of subjects with which to finish a book! They call for something more by way of conclusion, although one must be cautious about conclusions. An important reality I learned during my life as a schoolteacher is that no good discussion of a topic really worth considering ever concludes. And so this book cannot conclude its subject in any truly final way.

When I started writing *We Elders Speak for Ourselves*, I felt like an elder, more old than young, but not "old"—God forbid! About halfway through the writing, my editor started addressing me as a "junior elder," and I guess that's what I am, for after reading thousands of opinions from my respondents, aged 65 to 97, I have come to feel that my age, 67, is indeed young. I began saying to myself when I found a good quote from a 69-year-old man, "Well, but let's see what some *older* people say."

But, junior elder though I am, writing this book has aged me— more than the writing of any of the other thirty-odd books I've struggled with since my first one (a speller) was published in 1956. Just thinking and reading and talking about old age so much does age one. But I find that I enjoy—positively *enjoy*—being "agèd." Of course, I have observed, it depends on what kind of agèd one is.

Two Kinds of Elders

A pair of my respondents, ages 70 and 73, sent me a couple of wonderful quotes from two elders that contrast well what becoming an elder can do to you. One is from Mark Twain (1835–1910), who, toward the end of his life, wrote to his friend, editor, and fellow writer William Dean Howells (1837–1920): "I have been reading the morning paper. I do it every morning—well knowing that I shall find in it the usual depravities and basenesses and hypocrisies and cruelties that

235

make up civilization, and cause me to put in the rest of the day pleading for the damnation of the human race." Mark Twain grew bitter as he grew old.

But another way of growing old is described by Harry Emerson Fosdick (1878–1969), former pastor of Riverside Church in New York City, who, at age 65, after quoting Twain, said from his pulpit, "Once in a while one sees another kind of old man [or old woman, of course] with faith strong enough and spiritual resources deep enough so that he comes to elder years ripe in experience indeed but still unspoiled in spirit—stimulating, forward-looking, kindling new energy and hope in the younger generation, his latter life like a sunset that makes all who see it say, 'It will be a good day tomorrow.' What an asset such elders are!"

Writing this book has made me much more optimistic than I was about the wit, wisdom, happiness, and productivity of elders.

A "New Adolescence"?

I reported earlier the idea of a 73-year-old woman respondent that old age, especially at the time of retirement, can be considered to involve a sort of second adolescence, a time to grow (*adolescere*, Latin for "to grow"), to seek new ways; perhaps, to go through a rite of passage. I suggested, too, that as we come nearer to death, sometimes we take a new look at ourselves and the universe; that, too, could be considered an adolescence. But this suggestion of mine did not appeal much to most of the elders who considered it. "It's *not* adolescence," wrote an 82-year-old woman very positively, "because adolescents have no rich background of life against which to test out all those new experiences. They are often thrown by it, but we oldsters generally aren't. We're too well rooted in the earth of reality for that." Probably she's right, although I can't resist backing myself up with the words of Nobel prize winner André Gide (1869–1951): "Ordinary people have only one adolescence; geniuses several."

When I think of all the challenges and adjustments we elders face, and our responses to them, I find very appealing the idea not of the unhappily insecure sort of adolescence experienced by many teenagers but, rather, of the sort of deeply experienced adolescence that the great mathematician and scientist Sir Isaac Newton (1642–1727) wrote about when he was well over eighty:

I do not know what I may appear to the world, but to myself I seem to have been only a boy playing on the sea-shore, and diverting myself in now and then finding a smoother pebble or a prettier shell than ordinary, whilst the great ocean of truth lay all undiscovered before me.

It may be true that many of us elders are more aware than most younger people of the undiscovered ocean of truth; perhaps we're just readier to swim strongly out into it.

At the end of most sections of the questionnaire on which so much of this book is based, I wrote: *On the subject of X, suggest a few "commandments" that should be addressed to us elders or to those in the world around us.* My idea was to end each section with a neat set of commandments. But the idea didn't work out. The elders, on the whole, were reluctant to "command":

68/M: I'm willing to share my ideas, but I'm really not God-like enough to make Commandments.

73/W: Foolish youth or vain, pompous age might command. Not me.

84/W: I'll leave commanding to the Bible, to God, or maybe to the law. I do have some ideas, though. If anybody wants to take them as commands, all right, but the risk is yours.

. . . and so forth. However, as I read the replies to the questionnaires, I found a great many dos and don'ts, some of them expressed in very definite terms. In fact, when I add them all up, counting only those that can be recast as commandments, I have a stack of cards numbering over five hundred! This is interesting, because in the Hebrew scriptures (what Christians call the Old Testament), God didn't stop with the classic Ten Commandments of the decalogue. God went right on commanding from Mount Sinai until the number of commandments reached about 550.

Be that as it may, I close this chapter with two decalogues, one for those in the world around us elders, and one for us elders ourselves. To select twenty out of several hundred was difficult. I've done some minor editing for brevity and consistency of form. Also, I have omitted commandments that could apply to life in general, such as "Remember that God is Love" or "Follow the Golden Rule."

Ten Commandments for Those With Elders in Their Lives

- Remember that elders are unique individuals. Do not lump them together as a separate class.
- Never qualify a compliment by adding "for your age."
- Encourage elders, but do not say "You can" when in fact they can't.
- Enjoy elders for all the extra life they have to give—deep and often sparkling.
- Call elders in "for consultation," because those years of experience can sometimes produce wisdom.
- By love and affection, overcome the frustrations of caring for those elders who seem stubborn, difficult, mournful, empty, or boring.
- Remember that behind an age-dulled or age-prickled exterior there hides a bright, warm soul and an eager intelligence wanting to be met and recognized.
- Ask elders how they are, and listen to the answer, for sometimes they need to tell.
- Speak so that you can be heard—slowly, distinctly, but do not yell.
- Stay close to the dying, for they are venturing into new territory and need to go in touch with love.

Ten Commandments for Elders

- Keep your sense of humor and proportion and never be solemn or pompous.
- Do not give advice unless asked for it, except in rare cases, and then begin with, "I suggest . . ."
- Keep clean and neat, and if in doubt, ask if you are.
- Do not be a damper, but encourage the enthusiasm of youth, no matter how naive it may seem to you.
- Share the wit and wisdom of experience, but in moderate amounts, without stuffiness.

- Do not continue when you are interrupted, unless you are asked to; be alert to signals that you may be boring.

- Keep in touch with the young, for they will keep you open to new ideas and stimulate your enthusiasm.

- Do not concentrate on seeming slights, lest you magnify them.

- Figure out what your skills are and persist in finding ways to use them.

- Slow down if you must, but never quit—strive to laugh more and love more.

A FINAL GEM COLLECTION

66/W: Do not go gently into aging. Know what to expect as the body weakens and use every resource you can find to fight back. Reach out for new experiences, be active, *never* passive, and keep your sense of humor at all times. Then enjoy.

68/W: Remember this: If you look for beauty, you will find beauty. If you look for kindness and goodness, you will find them. If you look for ugliness and nastiness, insults and disrespect, you will find them.

68/W: Take some time each day—*consciously*—to place yourself in the "presence of the Most High."

70/M: Here is the prayer of a seventeenth-century nun that I like: Lord, thou knowest better than I know myself that I am growing older and will someday be old. Keep me from the fatal habit of thinking I must say something on every subject and on every occasion. Release me from craving to straighten out everybody's affairs. Make me thoughtful but not moody, helpful but not bossy. With my vast store of wisdom, it seems a pity not to use it all, but Thou knowest, Lord, that I want a few friends at the end.

70/M: Remember, everyone, that the seemingly unreasonable demands for attention by the elderly, often obnoxious, are really not demands as such. We are really grasping at straws so as not to lose the affection, the association of friends and family.

70/W: Accept yourself. It still leaves plenty of room for improvement.

71/M: The hardest problem is coming to grips with the fact that, at 71, the road ahead is much shorter than the one behind. So it becomes important to establish priorities about how I use both time and strength.

72/W: Accept the natural changes with good grace. Remember the good times. Bury the bad ones. Keep your mind open to new ideas. Enjoy the good things, the beautiful young people around you, the jokes, the ironies. The contemporary world seems so much more alive and interesting than the one I grew up in that I can't understand how some find it disappointing.

73/W: Work around forgetfulness *by doing it now*. If you have more than three do-it-nows, make a list!

74/W (about an 85/W): I found in my grandmother's handwriting this charming little thing: "If you are down with the blues, read the Twenty-seventh Psalm; if there's a chilly sensation about the heart, read the third chapter of Revelation; if you don't know where to look for the month's rent, read the Thirty-seventh Psalm; if you feel lonesome and unprotected, read the Ninety-first Psalm; if the stove pipe has fallen down and the cook gone off in a pet, put up the pipe, wash your hands, and read the third chapter of James; if you find yourself losing confidence in men, read the thirteenth chapter of Corinthians I; if people pelt you with hard words, read the fifteenth chapter of John; if you're getting discouraged about your work, read Psalm 126; if you're all out of sorts, read the twelfth chapter of Hebrews."

75/W: The best is yet to be, because I have time to learn and grow and share without the stress of earlier years.

76/M (Ashley Montagu, anthropologist, born 1905): Aging is not a terminal illness, but a timeless estate, a rich inheritance.

77/W: Dear friends, when you greet us, look into our eyes. See the marvelous things we elders have experienced—joy and sorrow, success and frustration, ecstasy and desolation. Ask us how it was.

77/M: Spend more time counting your blessings, less time magnifying your needs.

79/W: It's O.K. to call me "older," but not "old."

79/M (Bruce Bliven): At 79-plus, I walk with a cane so that I won't stagger into the path of a car. I go down a short flight of steps like an elephant crossing a bamboo bridge in a typhoon. I lower myself into an armchair the way they set down a Michelangelo statue with a derrick. But in my heart I'm sure I'm only pretending these expedients are necessary, that I'm just imitating someone old, and could start gamboling any minute.*

80/W: I have a valuable body: silver in my hair, gold in my teeth, and gas in my stomach.

80/W: When asked how you are, reply, "I'm in mighty good shape for the shape I'm in."

81/W: I've about decided that about the only way I can change the world or my grandchildren is to change me. I am finding that rigidity uses up more energy than I can spare. I feel impelled to relax and let live! "Easy often does it."

81/W: A very dear and admirable friend of mine said to me when I was 45: "Youth is for learning. Middle age is for doing. Old age is for enjoying."

83/W: I like the story about a jazzily dressed, alert lady of 80+ who met at the curbside a hunched-over drab lady, leaning on a cane. As they waited for a bus, the jazzy oldster said to the drab one, "I tried old age once, but it wasn't my cup of tea."

84/W: Old age is a time to drop guilt and learn to love youself, for yourself and your uniqueness. Then from you will flow love and concern and help for others.

86/M: Make a habit first thing each morning, before breakfast, of reading systematically from the Bible, or sometimes a devotional book. Then pray. Then *listen* in silence, jotting down in a notebook relevant reflections, convictions, and directions, to remember and obey all day.

*Quoted in *Modern Maturity,* December–January 1976–77, American Association of Retired Persons.

88/W: I was amazed that nothing changed at the age of 65. Not until age 86—two years ago—did I, or could I, realize I was growing old.

101/W: You know the joke about three old, hard-of-hearing women out for a ride? One said, "It's windy."
Another said, "It's not Wednesday; it's Thursday."
The third smiled pleasantly and said, "O.K., if you're thirsty, we'll stop for a drink."

Pablo Picasso (1881–1973): Age matters only when one is aging. Now that I have arrived at a great age, I might just as well be twenty.

Victor Hugo (1802–1885): When grace is joined with wrinkles, it is adorable. There is an inexpressible dawn in happy old age.

Anonymous: Old wood is the best to burn, old wine to drink, old friends to trust, old authors to read.

All of us, we elders ourselves and those who live with us, can keep in our minds and hearts the observation of John Donne (1572–1631):

> *No Spring, nor Summer*
> *Beauty hath such grace*
> *As I have seen in one*
> *Autumnal face.*

Bibliography

Armour, Richard. *Going Like Sixty*. New York: McGraw-Hill, 1974.

Atchley, Robert C. *Social Forces and Aging* (4th ed.). Belmont, Calif.: Wadsworth, 1985.

Brecher, Edward M., et al. *Love, Sex, and Aging*. Boston: Little, Brown, 1984.

Burns, George. *How to Live to Be 100 or More*. New York: Putnam, 1983.

Butler, Robert. *Why Survive?—Being Old in America*. New York: Harper & Row, 1975.

Comfort, Alex. *A Good Age*. New York: Simon & Schuster, 1976.

Courtenay, Charles. *On Growing Old Gracefully*. New York: Macmillan, 1936.

Hessel, Dieter. *Maggie Kuhn on Aging*. Philadelphia: Westminster Press, 1977.

Kanin, Garson. *It Takes a Long Time to Become Young*. New York: Doubleday, 1978.

Kimmel, Douglas. *Adulthood and Aging* (2d ed.). New York: John Wiley & Sons, 1980.

Knopf, Olga. *Successful Aging*. New York: Viking, 1975.

Kübler-Ross, Elisabeth. *On Death and Dying*. New York: Macmillan, 1969.

Porcino, Jane. *Growing Older, Getting Better: A Handbook for Women in The Second Half of Life*. Reading, Mass.: Addison-Wesley, 1983.

Robey, Harriet. *An Ordinary Marriage*. Boston: Little, Brown, 1984.

Skinner, B. F. *Enjoy Old Age*. New York: W. W. Norton, 1983.

Thomas, Lewis. *The Youngest Science*. New York: Viking, 1983.

Index

About the Author

Eric Johnson, a graduate of Germantown Friends School in Philadelphia and Harvard College, has spent most of his life, until now, as a schoolteacher of English, history, and sex education at Germantown Friends, as well as school principal, school trustee, and advisor to schools across the country. He has written some thirty books on a variety of subjects: spelling, grammar, editing, writing, adolescence, teaching school, sex education, Jesus of Nazareth, children's fiction, school governance, achievement motivation and, now, old age. From time to time, he has worked with the American Friends Service Committee (Quakers) in Portugal, Morocco, Algeria, India, France, Poland, the U.S.S.R., and Haiti. He and his wife, Gay Gilpin Johnson, have three children: a pediatrician, an architect, and a publications editor and designer. Gay Johnson works with urban community organizations and a nature program for city children. Eric Johnson's greatest pleasures, in ascending order of importance, are traveling, reading, jogging, collecting and telling humorous stories, arguing, and being married.